T0369615

Just Policing

JAKE MONAGHAN

OXFORD
UNIVERSITY PRESS

OXFORD
UNIVERSITY PRESS

Oxford University Press is a department of the University of Oxford. It furthers the University's objective of excellence in research, scholarship, and education by publishing worldwide. Oxford is a registered trade mark of Oxford University Press in the UK and certain other countries.

Published in the United States of America by Oxford University Press
198 Madison Avenue, New York, NY 10016, United States of America.

CIP data is on file at the Library of Congress

ISBN 978-0-19-761072-5

DOI: 10.1093/oso/9780197610725.001.0001

Printed by Sheridan Books, Inc., United States of America

Contents

Acknowledgments

There are many people who I need to thank for their help and support in writing this book. I should first thank Ryan Muldoon, who encouraged me as a graduate student to take up questions of political philosophy as they arise in policing. I did not plan for what were at the time side projects to become the focus of my research. Without Ryan's guidance this project would have developed very differently, and I think would have been much less interesting. Kirun Sankaran has also been a frequent source of discussion and feedback on the ideas in this book, not only during its preparation, but also before I knew my research on policing would become a book. I am indebted to Kirun for lots of great insight about institutions and incentives. The path-dependent nature of research projects means that Ryan and Kirun are surely to blame for at least some of the shortcomings of this book.

I started writing this book during my second year at the University of New Orleans. I had the great fortune of joining J. P. Messina, Danny Shahar, Crawford Crews, Eric van Holm, and Chris Surprenant at the University of New Orleans. I owe them a debt of gratitude for making it a stimulating and enriching place to do research (while it lasted). Thanks to J. P. especially for his help thinking about the structure of the book and applying proportionality to policing, and to Danny for extensive conversations about the rule of law and police discretion. Thanks to both of them for written comments, their encouragement, and regular discussion of the arguments along the way.

I am grateful to Lucy Randall at Oxford University Press for her interest in the project and for her help in the publication process.

Special thanks to everyone who read and commented on earlier drafts of *Just Policing*. Thanks to David Boonin, Bob Kelly, and Jake Wojtowicz for comments on Chapters 2 through 5. Thanks to Connor Kianpour for feedback on a complete draft. I get a lot of philosophical mileage out of Brandon del Pozo's decriminalization of diverted buprenorphine while chief of police in Burlington, Vermont. Thanks for doing that. I'm also grateful to Brandon for discussions of policing public space (some of which occurred while watching the NOPD manage Mardi Gras crowds). Thanks to the Institute for Humane Studies for running a manuscript workshop on this book, and to Brandon del Pozo, Stephen Galoob, Ben Jones, Lauren Hall, Peter Moskos, Ilia Murtazashvili, Kirun Sankaran, and David Skarbek for reading and commenting on the entire manuscript as part of the workshop. This project was made possible through the support of Grant 62405 from the John Templeton Foundation. The opinions expressed in this publication are those of the author(s) and do not necessarily reflect the views of the John Templeton Foundation.

Finally, thanks to my wife, Brooke, for her support. Philosophers are weird, but dedicating an academic monograph on policing to my wife is too weird even for me. But it wouldn't have happened without her.

1
Questions of Just Policing

Policing is a moral morass. The injustices of our world, many of them grave, seemingly require police. But police use violence to enforce laws of questionable justice, they arrest people while the trial system relies on coercive plea bargaining and many correctional facilities are unsanitary, dangerous places that hold little hope of rehabilitating offenders, they fire impact rounds and tear gas to break up disobedient demonstrations, and so on. The police are on the front lines of the criminal justice system, but they often end up as agents of injustice themselves. But it's not entirely their fault. We ask them to do it. We make their salaries depend on it. And we don't want officers simply to refuse to follow orders or to pick and choose how and when to enforce the law according to their whim. So there's a problem here, and it's a matter of life or death. What should police do, given the situation we put them in? In a society that's filled with injustice, what does justice require of the police?

This is a work of non-ideal theory. It asks what just policing looks like in a world characterized by pervasive injustice. More precisely, it is a work concerned with *realized*, rather than *idealized*, institutions. What does just policing look like in *our* world, with its actual injustices? Political philosophers have usually been concerned with fundamental questions of justice abstracted from the particularities of the world. Philosophical treatments of these questions are typically oriented toward general answers and conducted against a background of moderate to extreme idealization: What does the just society look like, assuming that people are well motivated and that our institutions work as we imagine them to? This methodological approach—ideal theory—abstracts away questions about what our institutions should look like in light of profound problems in society. And by abstracting them away, it leaves us awkwardly without the *theoretical* need for

Just Policing. Jake Monaghan, Oxford University Press. © Oxford University Press 2023.
DOI: 10.1093/oso/9780197610725.003.0001

thinking about some of those problems.[1] That typically includes the criminal justice system, about which these questions are perhaps nowhere as important.

1.1. Political Philosophy and the Police

There hasn't been much work in political philosophy on the police in the contemporary sense of that term.[2] This is in part because the institution we now call "the police" is rather new, not because political philosophy has nothing to say about *policing*.[3] Many questions of justice raised by policing are ultimately new versions of old classics.

From the beginning, political philosophy has been concerned with determining how the state should exercise power over its citizens. The question has largely been motivated by the problems large groups of humans face living in proximity to one another. Book Two of the *Republic* takes up the task of imagining the ideally just city, where ordinary human struggles to live a good life led to the conclusion that we need a guardian class to enforce the decisions of the philosopher-kings. The classic social contract theorists held that predictable human conflict, including disagreement over what makes a good life, makes an active state necessary. Hume thought that coercive political institutions are needed just because we are morally imperfect. If we were perfect, we wouldn't need them to settle our conflicts (Hume 1777). Generally, we can't be trusted to resolve our own disputes; we will naturally put our thumb on the scale for our interests, and humans are naturally

---

[1] This is not to say that all ideal theorists are unconcerned with realized institutions. Certain approaches embrace "transitional" non-ideal theory, according to which we first specify an ideal institutional arrangement and then craft a non-ideal theory that tells us how to permissibly move from where we are to the ideal. The ideal is constructed in service of transitioning away from current injustices. See Luke William Hunt's *The Retrieval of Liberalism in Policing* for this broadly Rawlsian, two-step methodological approach to just policing. My claim here is that ideal-theory-first approaches do not foreground the kinds of problems that strike me as most pressing.

[2] "Policing" once referred to urban governance in general. Today's narrow usage took over around 1800 as night watches professionalized.

[3] Though Jeremy Bentham focused on reforming corrections, he was apparently politically involved in the formation of the London Metropolitan Police (Reynolds 1998, 76–89, 163).

prone to retaliatory cycles of violence when conflicts are not resolved to mutual satisfaction. So we must relinquish them to a third party, the state, who mediates disputes and enforces the terms of their resolution.

Establishing the need for a state introduces other familiar philosophical questions about what a society should police and how it should provide that policing role. What sorts of institutional structures should the state use to enforce its decisions? What sorts of activities may the state intervene in? Who gets to make those decisions? How do we accommodate our persistent disagreements over these matters? According to the liberal democratic view, our persistent moral disagreements mean the state needs to be controlled by us together, and it needs to be neutral regarding our moral disagreements. Hence, a public executive branch that exercises police power (directed by a legislature) is required by justice and an essential element of the state. Without disputes, we may have no need for the police. But politics is born in disagreement.

On the political Right, some libertarians and anarchists have advocated for the privatization of police forces. According to this view, it would be possible to provide all of a society's security needs using private security firms that one subscribes to. Concerns about badly behaving security firms are addressed with a system of private insurance, where violent and dangerous private police officers would become uninsurable and therefore unemployable (Huemer 2013; Friedman 1989). Alternatively, like the "turnpike trusts" that paid for early policing, security services could be bundled with other services, such as when a store hires private security, a university fields their own police force, and a homeowners' association pays for private patrols (Stringham 2015, 129). Other libertarians, most famously Robert Nozick, think that policing must be provided by the (minimal) state just because a system of private security firms would be unstable and inevitably evolve into a state (1974).

The liberal and libertarian project, then, is partly one of determining the legitimate scope of political, and with it, police power. Many liberals take the legitimate scope of the criminal law and police power to be quite narrow, even if they think the state may and should do much more in noncriminal contexts than the libertarians think (e.g., Husak 2008; Feinberg 1987). Of course, this project interacts somewhat awkwardly with democratic governance which often produces illiberal results.

Alternatively, democratic theorists who reject liberal (or other) constraints on political decision-making are pushed to endorse as just and legitimate whatever kind of policing the demos selects. And those who think the role of the state is to conform others to their conception of the good and the right, whether on the Right or Left, whether utilitarians, communitarians, or (nonliberal) perfectionists, will reject many of the limits on police power set by liberals and libertarians.

Increasingly, theorists who are left-leaning, skeptical of liberalism, and optimistic about democratic authorization reject the legitimacy of public police. *Police abolitionists* tend to see U.S. policing as continuous with slavery, and police abolitionists take up the rhetorical mantle of the slavery abolitionists.[4] They tend not to be skeptical of political power in general, or of democratic procedures which purport to authorize it, in the sense that they are not proponents of a minimal state. But they are skeptical of one of the institutional mechanisms we've constructed to exercise (some of) that political power: the professional police department. While certain anarchists might reject the justice and legitimacy of the police because they reject the state that employs them, police abolitionists raise special objections to the police. The problem isn't the state, but the state's dealings with colonizers and capitalists who co-opt police power.

A quick note on terminology: the philosophical and social scientific literature on political power and policing features a variety of senses of "legitimacy." I'll rely on a normative sense of legitimacy, where legitimacy just is the permission to exercise power. On this usage, legitimacy is a weaker requirement than justice, so policing could be legitimate but not just, but not just and illegitimate. In this way, figuring out the requirements of legitimacy helps determine the requirements of justice.

The big questions that have been at the center of political philosophy all along clearly implicate the police in matters of justice. But

---

[4] Contemporary policing isn't only an outgrowth of slavery on this view. It is also continuous with schemes of social control used by capitalists and colonizers (Purnell 2021, 77–88; Vitale 2017, 34–48).

in our non-ideal world, we have to confront the fact that injustices perpetrated by police are serious enough that some theorists think that the first question to be asked about just policing is not, *What does just policing look like?*, but rather, *Would a just society have police at all?* or *Is just policing possible?*

1.2. The Problem of Policing

Some police critics hold that an ideally just world will have no criminal legal system, and thus that justice is incompatible with the police. Others hold that the actual police agencies we have are essentially unjust given their historical roots. Still others claim that the police are not only inefficacious, but that they make matters worse. Assessing these arguments will help us to focus on the various things we might want the police to do, while also foregrounding the serious injustices contemporary policing confronts us with. It will help us bring the problem of policing into full view: the injustices that motivate the police make just policing exceptionally difficult to theorize and implement.

1.2.1. Would Utopia Have Police?

According to the utopian argument against the police—one found in literature, psychology, and philosophy—the police are not part of an ideally just world because a just world would simply not have any crime or disorder. According to various ideal theories in political philosophy, if we were perfectly just, there wouldn't even be a state (Freiman 2017; Brennan 2014; Cohen 2009; cf. Kavka 1995; Hume 1777, 474). Or there may be a state, but no need for an actual enforcement role, and so the state would not have police (Rawls 1999, 211). There is now an active literature in political philosophy on whether a theory of justice can be correct if it makes demands we are unlikely to satisfy. So the relevance of these claims for what we should do now is a matter of dispute, but they might imply that justice requires us to work to abolish the police.

Others think that we can institutionalize our way out of the kinds of imperfections that lead to crime, and with it, the police role in society.

Socrates held that people act unjustly because they are ignorant, so if we had a proper system of education, we could eliminate injustice. A different but in some ways nearby vision of a just world is depicted in the popular sci-fi anarcho-syndicalist novel *The Dispossessed*. If there is no private property and everyone lives communally, how could there be any crime? "Nobody owns anything to rob. If you want things you take them from the depository. As for violence, well, I don't know, Oiie; would you murder me, ordinarily? And if you felt like it, would a law against it stop you? Coercion is the least efficient means of obtaining order," Shevek explains when asked why people don't rob and murder in a world without (much) punishment (Le Guin 1974). Instead of (only) educating people out of injustice, we can (also) engineer our economy to accomplish that goal. Of course, there is some reason to think that our psychological quirks might pose a problem for realizing these visions. As indicated by his novel *Walden Two*, B. F. Skinner apparently thought that in addition to education and the abolition of private property, we would need to organize ourselves into small-scale communes and employ a systematic program of operant conditioning to eliminate the antisocial tendencies that cause crime and other forms of injustice (Skinner 1948).

What we see in these forms of idealized, utopian thinking is that the need for social control in the hypothetical, model society under consideration varies according to how extensively we idealize. If there is no resource scarcity, or if we are moral angels, *maybe* there is no need for social control (Monaghan 2022a). But even in moderately idealized models like *The Dispossessed*'s anarcho-syndicalist society, Le Guin imagines communities occasionally relying on ostracism.

Some think that these ideal models tell us little about what to do in our world (Freiman 2017; Brennan 2014). Others, like philosopher G. A. Cohen, think we can derive principles of justice from reflections on them, even if we cannot actually live that way (2009). Rather, principles of justice can be gleaned from idealized models and then realized with other institutional arrangements. Though a camping trip realizes certain principles of justice (e.g., a certain kind of equality), we should not all move to the woods to camp. We should instead remake our institutions to be relevantly like life on a camping trip (notably absent from a camping trip are markets). The problem here is that this kind of approach, by design, is not primarily oriented toward evaluating actual institutional arrangements and policy. Utopian ideal theory leaves open crucial questions about just and legitimate social control.

So we need some institutions of social control, given our non-utopian world. Many abolitionists, though, think that a world without police is actually achievable, even if somewhat far off in the future, and that we should be making changes now that push us down the path toward those kinds of institutions. This interpretation of police abolitionism has them describing, or attempting to construct, an "end-state ideal" alongside a transitional path there. Whereas utopian ideal theorists are less concerned with achievable policy changes, the end state or transitional ideal theorist is loosely describing an actual institutional arrangement with actual policies to transition to over time.[5]

This line of abolitionist thought is important for understanding why the view is attractive for policy advocates. If the camping trip ideal is not within a generation's reach, it is not clearly a useful guide to policy change today. In reply, the abolitionist seeks not to "abandon communities to violence," but to make the police "obsolete" (Kaba et al. 2021). Abolitionists, quite plausibly, argue that social welfare spending is an effective strategy for decreasing the problems we task to the police. Instead of imagining away the need for policing, some abolitionists claim that there is a set of institutions we can create to achieve the ideal.

There is a difference, of course, between identifying an ideal and determining whether we can actually get there. And meanwhile, the institutions in our actual, approximately ideal world might look considerably different from the institutions of our ideal world. A car without a brake pedal *is* approximately a car, philosopher David Estlund points out, but does not approximate the *value* of a car with a brake pedal (Estlund 2020, 271). If institutions in our ideal look different from what we have now, we have no guarantee that they will actually realize the justice we hope they will (Gaus 2019). Our epistemic limitations mean we have to recognize the ideal as a provisionally held

---

[5] See Valentini (2012a) for a discussion of types of ideal theory.

goal rather than a detailed policy blueprint and political roadmap (Purnell 2021, 168; cf. Vitale 2017, 226).

Let's focus on the problem of violence for the moment. It helps clarify the nature of the disagreement by highlighting the difference between some of the institutions of social control that abolitionists accept and the police. All parties to the debate agree that justice requires institutions, whether public or private, for deterring violence. Abolitionists sometimes point out that police spend a small amount of their time on such crimes as part of the case for abolition: it's not like the police do all that much to solve the problem anyway. What do the abolitionist alternatives look like? Largely rejecting the "neoliberal austerity" of the last several decades in favor of social welfare programs, replacing "free trade" with "fair trade" agreements, strengthening private and public unions, "green" infrastructure investment, jobs programs, reparations, replacing capitalism with socialism, ending toxic masculinity, creating neighborhood councils with local decision-making power that aren't dominated by one group, free twenty-four-hour childcare, "green teams" that collect neighborhood food waste for composting and plant flowers and trees to "keep [residents] cool and keep down violence," and so on. If we make advancements toward "real justice," by turning to noncoercive forms of social control, then the problem of violent crime will no longer require a police force (Purnell 2021, 273–283; Vitale 2017, 53–54, 221–228).[6]

But we might wonder whether such optimism is justified. Can we eliminate the need for the police by targeting "root causes" alone? That is not obvious. Redirecting money we now spend on policing to housing support, education, healthcare, to community-based social workers, to food waste composters, and so on will treat some root causes of crime. But changing root causes works on generational timescales, and some might reasonably demand more immediate solutions (Abt 2019). And we know that there are proximate causes of crime, like a high density of certain kinds of commercial activity,

---

[6] It is worth flagging here that this view relocates social control to whatever regulations we place on commercial activity and to the enforcement of a system of wealth redistribution. There are, obviously, long-standing philosophical disagreements to be had over whether those forms of social control are permissible.

or retaliatory cycles of violence—management or prevention of which, recall, is one of the classic justifications for a state. It is also unlikely we actually know how to *solve* the problem of violence. But if we don't have the path to the ideal in clear view, we should think that justice demands incremental policy experimentation.

Further, to obviate the need for policing, these social spending programs, and other forms of organizing for real justice would need to virtually *eliminate* crime, or at least reduce it such that the remaining violence is an acceptable cost of doing business. Some will be reasonably skeptical that these reforms will create bountiful equality and thereby drastically reduce the amount of violence in society. Will changing economic policy to counter the trend toward globalism or empowering private sector unions actually enrich us? Do housing policies like rent control improve the least well-off in the housing market and empower them to participate in neighborhood councils? Or should we focus on eliminating restrictive zoning and occupational licensing instead? In other words, the problem isn't merely that we don't know *all* the changes we'd need to make to eliminate violence, but rather that there is reasonable disagreement over whether these proposals will accomplish their goals and also sufficiently reduce violence. And the actual question is not whether ideal root causes programs will work, but whether the actual programs that survive pluralistic policymaking will work. Justice might require us to retain a small homicide and violent offenders' unit.

Let's take stock. What we see here is a run-of-the-mill political dispute over how to achieve a goal everyone shares as opposed to a battle between good and evil. No one knows what the best realized institutional arrangement is, or how to pull policy levers to virtually eliminate the roots of violence (or the other needs for social control). Until we do, we'll want some social control addressing proximate causes of unwanted behavior. We have some good ideas that require experimentation, and it is likely that some of them will have grave shortcomings (like our actual police departments). And because people will have reasonable disagreements over these policy experiments, no one should expect to achieve their idea of the ideal institutional arrangement. The actual world is one of non-ideal policies and half-measures. What we need, then, is not merely to take up a non-ideal methodology in which we set out to discover principles of justice and design institutions that apply to imperfect humans in dynamic environments characterized by scarcity. What we need is a "doubly non-ideal" methodology in which we ask what our institutions should look like given human and environmental problems, as well as problems in whatever institutions we create to solve the initial problems.

1.2.2. Are Police Essentially Unjust?

If the realm of *realized* politics is the realm of non-ideal half-measures, the nature of the question changes. Independently of whether police would exist in an ideally just world, the right question is: Given our actual world, are our actual police a net-positive force for justice? We'll look at two arguments for a negative answer. The first holds that the police are essentially unjust given their institutional histories. The second holds that the balance of empirical evidence shows that police are ineffectual, and so a net injustice.

The abolitionist critique often relies on the claim that the police are essentially tools for the powerful to control the disempowered. The London Metropolitan Police was an outgrowth of Robert Peel's work managing the British occupation of Ireland; departments in the South are outgrowths of slave patrols, and departments in the Northeast are outgrowths of union-busting initiatives or an attempt to control the "dangerous classes" made up of immigrants and the indigent. The push to diversify police forces is really just refashioning the colonizer's strategy of using a member of the disempowered group to appease the oppressed and legitimize the oppressors (Purnell 2021, 87). What we see, everywhere we look, is the same: police departments being used as a tool for unjust social control. Unjust social control is in the DNA of policing, so reform and just policing are impossibilities. In fact, the criminal legal system isn't broken; this is what it's designed to do (Kaba et al. 2021, 93; Butler 2018; Alexander 2012).

The problem for this kind of view is that it relies on an overly simplified historical and political picture. Surely then, as now, police agencies were engaged in some unjust, illegitimate social control. They enforced massively unjust political decisions. But they also responded to conflicts of interest, some of which genuinely needed settling. Of course, they often settled them unjustly. But their injustices are often an unsurprising manifestation of the problem of policing; they are the result of some seizing the reigns of social control unjustly.

Here's a quick elaboration on that account. Before professional police departments existed, villages and cities had a "constable and watch" system. This system, and the "hue and cry" it relied on, was codified in England in 1285 under the Statute of Winchester. Constables made arrests, secured witnesses, served papers, and managed a watch patrol staffed by "beadles" and watchmen. Night watches (which essentially enforced a curfew), and later separate day watches, were staffed originally by volunteers. Public watches were supplemented by private watchmen paid for by merchants. Members of the watch would patrol, typically with a lantern and calling the time, and sometimes also with a wooden rattle. If they witnessed a person out a night, they would question them. If they witnessed a crime, they would raise the hue and cry, or make noise to alert others nearby, and everyone was expected to participate in apprehending the criminal (Monkkonen 1981, 32; Lane 1967, 12). This system was brought to the American colonies where settlements likely had some informal night watch from the beginning.

Boston's formal city watch system was established in 1643 (Dulaney 1996, 3; Lane 1967, 10). New York's came not too long after. Charleston, South Carolina, established a formal watch and built watch houses in 1685.[7] Legislation established a formal slave patrol throughout the colony, tasking the Charleston watch with enforcing new restrictions on slaves and creating patrols outside of Charleston in 1701 (Hadden 2001, 17, 35). There is evidence of paid watch positions in London as early as 1710, and some watches carried numbered badges as early as 1726. There were paid, hierarchical night watches in dense London parishes by 1775 (Reynolds 1998, 10–15, 57). The system lasted for around 600 years, professionalizing and growing sporadically. The first uniformed police agencies subsumed existing watch functions.

Professionalization was often motivated by a fear of property crime, especially while traveling at night (Reynolds 1998, 4–20, 57, 95–101).

---

[7] Hadden (2001, 16) notes that the watch was motivated in significant part by fear of external threats, first from Native Americans and then from the Spanish in Florida.

In London, a privately funded dock patrol was taken over by the city and renamed the Thames River Police in 1800 (Reynolds 1998, 76). In Washington, DC, the Capitol Building's watch was replaced by the Capitol Police in 1828. City watches were replaced by police forces in New Orleans in 1796, London in 1829, Boston in 1838, and New York City in 1845. Gold rush San Francisco established a police force in 1849 before it even had a watch house to detain prisoners.

In the centuries between establishing city watches and uniformed police departments, there were major changes that made the need for better policing obvious. Boston and New York City went from small towns with pastures to booming cities. Backyard wells were common, and before cities built public sewers, there were sanitation problems. The densely constructed wood buildings were fire risks. The threat of thieves pushed cities to install streetlamps requiring maintenance and lighting. They knew density heightened not only the risks of infectious disease, but it also heightened social friction. More density means more people who might bother you. It also means more claims on public space. Without public control, "volunteer" societies sometimes take up that role. Too many people walking through flower gardens and letting their animals graze in newly constructed Central Park was nearly fatal to the park (Thacher 2015). Density also meant the old informal methods of social control (like public shaming and the hue and cry) were less effective. The conservative English commitment to amateur, volunteer policing was strained by the low quality of the watchmen, and the political battle in London was resolved in favor of professionalism by 1820 (Reynolds 1998, 89, 125). In Boston, the Sheriff and the "firewards" alike increasingly struggled to force bystanders to assist with arrests and with firefighting "bucket brigades."

New cities created two new things for governments to provide *professionally*: public health and public order, and the city watches devoted much of their attention to them (Monkkonen 1981, 34–35; Lane 1967, 10–12).[8] Often, these concerns were difficult to separate, as evident in

---

[8] Fighting crime was rather low on the list of the constable and watch priorities. Professional, private "thief catchers" arose to solve crime (often facilitating the return of stolen property for a fee paid to the thief by the victim), and the military was used to calm riots, two activities the constable-watch system performed poorly.

the early history of policing urban sex work. There, people were simultaneously worried about the spread of sexually transmitted illnesses such as syphilis and the nuisance of solicitation in public in addition to the standard moralizing reasons (Thusi 2022, 29–32).

Public health, the orderly use of public spaces, and protection from property crime and violence weren't the only challenges of industrializing cities. Ethnic conflict was a problem as well. Police historian Roger Lane explains that the problem of "mob violence" induced Boston to add a "new class of permanent professional officers" to the nearly 200-year-old city watch (Lane 1967, 26). The mob violence that led to the creation of a professional, preventive police force was not made up of "unruly immigrants" or oppressed laborers. It included (among other incidents) the burning of the Charleston Convent in 1834, and later the Broad Street Riot in 1837 (a year before the professional police department was created), which was a clash between a volunteer fire company and an Irish funeral procession. The Irish, who lived along Broad Street, were attacked by a mob that grew to 15,000, or one-sixth of the city (1967, 33). There were violent conflicts between capitalists and laborers. But there were other conflicts, too.[9]

The connection between density and policing is evident in the South, too. In dense Southern cities, the need for a watch preceded the formal slave patrol, which arose typically when the slave population surpassed the white population (Hadden 2001). This explains why the watch in Charleston was multipurpose. But in rural areas, the need to control slaves and indentured servants preceded the need for a formal watch, so the slave patrols came first there. After the Civil War and Reconstruction, of course, the police forces were used to maintain racial control.

What about police departments in other cities? Empirical investigation suggests that the size of a city is a better predictor of how soon it created a uniformed department than crime rates or labor strikes (Monkkonen 1981, 54). More recent work finds that the racial composition of a city is *not* a predictor of the creation of early police departments in the Northeast, casting doubt on the view that they

---

[9] These conflicts aren't limited to early, rapidly diversifying cities. Ideologically opposed groups clashed regularly in public during the 2020 U.S. Presidential Campaign.

were primarily a response to the "dangerous classes" (Salimbene 2021). As police historian Robert Fogelson notes, the early police *were* typically antagonistic to labor unions, radicals, and minorities, and this influenced their policing (Fogelson 1977, 34). But the actual genesis and day-to-day work of policing was more complicated.

The early police departments maintained some of the personnel and many of the qualities of the watches they replaced, including their unusual-to-us list of activities. According to Fogelson:

> From the outset most Americans had only a few vague ideas about what the police should do besides maintain public order. . . . In the absence of other specialized bureaucracies, the authorities found the temptation almost irresistible to transform the police departments into catchall health, welfare, and law enforcement agencies. Hence the police cleaned streets and inspected boilers in New York, distributed supplies to the poor in Baltimore, accommodated the homeless in Philadelphia, investigated vegetable markets in St. Louis, operated emergency ambulances in Boston, and attempted to curb crime in all these cities. By the end of the century most departments engaged in a wide range of activities other than keeping the peace. (Fogelson 1977, 16–17)

If anything, Fogelson downplays the prevalence of the early police as providing welfare services. Historian Eric Monkkonen finds that such activity sometimes *dominated* their other activities:

> Almost from their inception in the middle of the nineteenth century until the beginning of the twentieth, American police departments regularly provided a social service that from our perspective seems bizarrely out of character—they provided bed and, sometimes, board for homeless poor people. . . . Often, especially in the winter or during depression years, there would be food, usually soup— nothing fancy, but something. During very bad depression years or harsh winters, *the number of overnight lodgings provided by a police department exceeded all annual arrests.* (Monkkonen 1981, 86–87, emphasis mine)

Monkkonen estimates that "between 10% and 20% of the U.S. population in the late nineteenth century came from families of which one member had experienced the hospitality of a police station" (1981, 96).

One explanation, then, of the development of professional policing looks to the unavoidable problems facing the growing city. The weakening informal social control strategies combined with new and more pronounced public health and public disorder problems demanded an evolution of the constable and watch. The "need" to guard against the threat of slave revolts in the South drew the watch system into patrolling for slaves or created slave patrols anew (the latter of which are clearly essentially unjust). But in some cases, cities created uniformed police, and expanded their departments, just because that's what most cities were doing. The innovation had become as expected as sidewalks (Monkkonen 1981, 61). The "essentially unjust" thesis has social domination at the center of the story. When we look to the history of English and U.S. police departments, though, we don't see a pure power grab by the politically empowered over the disempowered. We see the piecemeal formation of an institution for providing some important social control functions that is in some cases unjustly captured.

This historical sketch highlights the following important point. The actual policies and institutions we have are the result of a complex political process involving many agents with many perspectives and interests. The inference from the actual consequences of policy to the intentions of the policy is fallacious (Monkkonen 1981, 52). According to Monkkonen, we may just as plausibly claim that the police "were created" to house the homeless or return lost children to their parents because that is what they did. But arguing about what the intended consequences of the rise of police agencies were by determining whether the control over the working class or the provision of social services was somehow more essential to the early police agency would be to miss the point. Our political institutions manifest in different ways because an agency's behavior is never fully determined by the various intentions that went into its creation.

Importantly, though, the dispute over whether police are essentially or intrinsically unjust is not one that can be won in the arena of historical scholarship. Even granting abolitionists this position in the historical dispute, there is a hint of the genetic fallacy in the argument. Whether your city's police department is just and legitimate depends in part on what it does now. And on that question, the abolitionists and the reformists will certainly agree that much of what they do now is unjust. Yet whether justice requires *abolition*, or whether we have reason to want a police force, will depend on other facts.

The further development of policing through the reform and professionalization eras of the twentieth century can be interpreted as additional evidence of the unavoidable nature of demands for these services. While the city watches and early beat cops spent a good deal of their time on public order and public health issues, the police profession became much more focused on (violent and property) crime. Police chiefs, like influential reformer and Berkeley, California's first police chief August Vollmer, complained about vice and traffic policing because it interfered with "real policing," and ethnographies routinely find officers with similar views about "social work" aspects of policing (Brooks 2021; Brown 1988; Vollmer 1928). But people continued to complain about what we sometimes now call "quality of life" issues, and police somewhat unwillingly devoted attention to "order maintenance." The police and the policed came to have divergent views of what they should focus on (Thacher 2001). The Broken Windows hypothesis, police scholar David Thacher (2004) suggests, allowed police to attend to order maintenance issues while conceiving of their actions as fighting crime (preventing the first broken window prevents the crime wave). The point is just that people want an agency attending to these issues, and that has been a driving force throughout the history of policing that is intertwined with unjust quests for social control.

On this point, note that abolitionist alternatives raise exactly these concerns. The root and proximate causes of crime are handled separately: ending neoliberal austerity or achieving the socialist revolution targets the roots, and other forms of social control target the proximate causes. Instead of a professional police force, we might return to community patrols. Abolitionist groups are experimenting with this: an abolitionist success story comes from Brooklyn, where for five days "violence interrupter and crisis management groups" maintained a visible presence on two blocks and there were no calls to the police (Gonen and Grench 2021). But how may those community patrols police their neighborhoods? Is it ok for "the community" to, for example, engage in "positive loitering" to harass drug dealers or sex workers into dispersing?[10] Or for business owners or municipalities to turn to "hostile architecture" or civil strategies for controlling public space like hiring contractors to clear homeless encampments? When may mental health response teams coerce an individual into compliance? All abolitionist alternatives involve social control and the policing of public space. The risk of unjust policing is therefore always with us.

1.2.3. Do Police Keep Us Safe?

The claim that police are ineffectual is another motivation for abolitionism. If they don't keep us safe, then they're not worth any of their injustices. Let's turn to the social scientific disputes about police efficacy and their role in the case for police abolition.

Sociologist Alex Vitale describes the view that police exist to protect us from predators as "largely a liberal fantasy" (2017, 32). Vitale holds that policing is largely unjust, though concedes that it cannot be reduced entirely to unjust social control; police are also concerned with public safety (2017, 51). But we have empirical evidence that police do not provide public safety. Vitale relies on political scientist David Bayley, who in an influential work on policing, sharply summarizes the scholarly consensus of the 1980s and early 90s:

> The police do not prevent crime. This is one of the best kept secrets of modern life. Experts know it, the police know it, but the public does not know it. Yet, the police pretend that they are society's best defense against crime and continually argue that if they are given more resources, especially personnel, they will be able to protect communities against crime. This is a myth. (1996, 3)

---

[10] This example comes from a real case of community policing in collaboration with the Chicago Police Department, but the collaboration is incidental (Skogan and Hartnett 1997, 174). A similar case occurred in 1915 Cape Town, South Africa (Thusi 2022, 39).

Bayley cites a variety of empirical work to support this conclusion, noting in particular that there is no relationship between the number of police officers a city has and their crime rates. Additional evidence comes from specific studies of patrol, rapid response, and criminal investigation. There is no evidence, Bayley claimed, of the primary police activities reducing crime, nor is most of their time spent on that.

Though it is tempting to appeal to Bayley's findings in making the case for abolition, it is striking that he interprets these results differently:

> No one seriously proposes on the basis of these studies that police be disbanded and sent home, although that would save a great deal of money. Although criminals do not seem to notice normal changes in the number of police, they would surely notice if there were no police. It is probably also true that at some point adding police would make a difference in how much crime occurs. (1996, 4)

The problem is confusing the deterrence effect of an additional police officer with whether police deter crime at all. What Bayley claims is that the small changes in the amount of policing an area receives caused by normal policy and budgetary changes are unlikely to have an impact on crime rates. If the police chief claims a 5 percent personnel increase in the patrol division will finally solve the violent crime problem, you should be skeptical. But that does not mean that the police are ineffectual.

Additionally, policing became more proactive in the 1990s under the influence of police scholars like Herman Goldstein, George Kelling, and James Q. Wilson, and influential New York City police commissioner Bill Bratton. Rather than random patrol, proactive and pretextual stops became more common, ultimately reaching an average of over 1,200 stops per day from 2003 to 2013 in New York City (Apel 2016). Programs like Compstat enabled "hot-spots" policing, where departments deploy officers to high-crime areas. Perhaps because of some of these changes, recent results paint a different picture of the deterrent effects of police.

One study finds that the addition of one officer abates 0.1 homicides, though with the trade-off that quality-of-life arrests also increase. The result is that black Americans bear more of the burden of policing (because they are more likely to be arrested for quality-of-life misdemeanor violations), and less likely to enjoy the benefits of reduced crime (which accrue to white Americans) (Chalfin et al. 2020). Another finds that each officer added to a police force with grant money from the federal Community Oriented Policing Program prevents four violent crimes and fifteen property crimes (Mello 2019). In particular, more homicide detectives, and more investigative resources, can both increase homicide clearance rates (Braga et al. 2019). Meta-analyses find that hot-spots policing and police presence reduce crime (Dau et al. 2021; Braga et al. 2019). Finally, there are some grounds for a more optimistic assessment of foot patrol. Research conducted over a few years beginning in 2009, on foot patrol in Philadelphia, found that the strategy can reduce crime. Saturation is not required, though making the patrol beat too large does eliminate any impact (Ratcliffe and Sorg 2017). In New Orleans, the French Quarter Task Force increased the patrol presence in a tourist-dense section of the city, leading to double-digit drops in property crimes and assault (Cheng and Long 2018).

What about the effects of de-policing? A sudden 13 percent reduction in the size of the Newark, New Jersey, police department (due to layoffs from a budget shortfall) was associated with a large increase in property and violent crime when compared with crime rates of nearby Jersey City (Piza and Chillar 2020). The Capitol Hill Occupation Protest Zone in Seattle forced Seattle Police to abandon the precinct, and they stopped responding to calls for service in the occupied zone. Research finds a spike in crime during this period (Piza and Connealy 2022). Of course, these are both unusual scenarios, and we shouldn't generalize from them alone. Research on police "pull-backs" has mixed results. A reduction in arrests is not always associated with increases in crime (Cho et al. 2022). If police stopped making arrests entirely, we should probably expect to see some kinds of crime occur more frequently. But it is not as simple as "more arrests mean lower crime" or "fewer arrests mean higher crime."

To be sure, plenty of policing *is* ineffective. Critics are right when they say that policing drug use and sex work has been not only ineffective but has made matters considerably worse. They are also right that arresting as a way to eliminate informal homeless encampments is unwise, and that U.S. police are currently doing an awful job of investigating serious crimes like rape and homicide.

This is far from a full evaluation of the social scientific evidence or a full cost/benefit analysis, but that is not the goal. The point I want to establish here is not that contemporary policing in the United States is the most effective tool for providing public safety. The point is merely that we have some good evidence that policing can address some of the problems we assign to it. That certain injustices will be a cost of the crime reduction bears emphasizing and will be my main focus throughout the book. But apart from disputes about the particular social scientific research, this result shouldn't be all that surprising: we know we can shape behavior by making certain actions costlier or by raising the likelihood of incurring costs. Many abolitionists are ultimately committed to the view that some of these activities, foot and traffic patrol in particular, can deter unwanted behavior, since many are attracted to the idea of non-police alternatives like the citizen patrol and unarmed traffic enforcers.

1.2.4. Should We Reimagine Public Safety?

Some seem to think that we can bypass the problem of policing by providing all of our social control functions with other non-punitive agencies. This includes turning traffic enforcement over to unarmed civil servants, dispatching mental health professionals instead of police to many 911 calls, and replacing police patrols with volunteer (or paid but non-police) citizen patrols and violence interrupter programs. It also includes removing police officers from schools and abandoning punitive orientations to purportedly vicious activity (such as drug use, sex work, and rough sleeping).[11]

We have evidence that some of these non-police alternatives work. Chicago created a Safe Passage Program that employed community members to monitor city blocks near schools and along main routes

---

[11] Reimagining public safety typically also involves abandoning retributive punishment and eliminating incarceration in favor of "restorative" justice, but I will not take up those issues here.

students would take to and from school to protect students on their commute. Empirical investigation finds double-digit crime declines on monitored blocks (Gonzalez and Komisarow 2020; McMillen et al. 2019). Patrick Sharkey and colleagues have persuasively argued that the creation of new community-based nonprofits is an important but overlooked factor in the crime decline of the 1990s (Sharkey et al. 2017). Several cities are now following Eugene, Oregon's CAHOOTS program in dispatching mental health professionals to some calls instead of police. Eugene's program has responded to thousands of calls for service per year since the 1990s (Akinnibi 2020). The mental health teams are quite appealing in light of the history of ambulance and emergency medical service teams whose functions were originally (and poorly) performed by police in some cities. We've peeled off that function with great success and have the opportunity to do something similar again.

In the cases just described, the police alternatives are engaged in some social control activities that police are typically engaged in. They are deterring crime by patrolling, much like the city watch, and much like professional officers assigned to foot patrol. The crisis response teams are responding to those having mental health problems and de-escalating the situation in some fashion, but they are often adjudicating disputes over the use of space (after all, someone still needs to make a call for service). The violence interrupters, too, are trying to adjudicate disputes and also to break cycles of violence and retaliation. The purpose of these roles is to give its occupants the duty to protect or intervene in rights violations, perhaps to collect evidence for presentation in new, non-retributive trial systems, and to manage the social frictions that arise from our metaphysical extension into the world. These are, according to policing scholar and former police chief Brandon Del Pozo, the distinctive functions of policing (del Pozo 2022). This suggests that the temptation to identify the police as being *the* mechanism for social control is a mistake. Police sociologist Egon Bittner famously defended the view that police are not law enforcers but *a* mechanism for social control (Bittner 1967, 39). Even if we reject Bittner's conception of the police, it helps us to avoid a mistake we might make in defending abolitionism, namely assuming police alternatives aren't forms of policing.

To be clear, I am not saying these alternatives use the same *tactics* or *institutional form* that police use, or have the same goals. The differences are clear. But the alternatives are *policing*, still an expression of a claim on social control, and the reimagined public safety agencies would have genuine continuity with the foot patrols that preceded city police departments.

What would it look like to start transferring responsibilities away from the police? What proportion of current calls for service to the police can easily be turned over to an alternate agency today? The positive results we've seen unfortunately must be qualified by quantitative assessments of police calls for service. Though mental health crisis teams are increasingly popular and perhaps the paradigmatic nearterm abolitionist alternative, we have empirical work showing that only a small minority of calls are for mental health reasons. According to the Eugene Oregon Police Department, CAHOOTS diverts only 5 to 8 percent of their calls for service (Eugene Police 2020). In Philadelphia, only around 8 percent of calls to the police are medical or public health in nature (Ratcliffe 2021). An investigation of pre-COVID-19 pandemic calls for service to nine U.S. agencies (all with populations over 400,000, with a variety of geographic locations and levels of urbanization) has similar findings: no agency had mental health calls account for more than 4 percent of their call volume; 1.3 percent of calls to those nine agencies were mental health calls compared to averages of 5.8, 6.4, 10.2, and 16.2 percent for domestic, violence, property, and disorderly calls, respectively (Lum et al. 2021).[12] Ratcliffe finds that 54.7 percent of calls for service in Philadelphia are "crime" related, with 13.7 percent for quality-of-life issues (similar to Lum et al.'s category of "disorder"). Interestingly, Ratcliffe also finds that 11.6 percent of health-related calls end up resulting in a "crime disposition."

That some mental health calls end up requiring coercion explains why emergency medical technicians often call the police themselves, and why many agencies have turned to "co-response models" in which plainclothes mental health professionals ride along with uniformed officers in patrol cruisers (Morabito et al. 2018). Eugene's CAHOOTS

---

[12] Ratcliffe combines mental health and medical calls for service, and this likely explains the lower proportions found by Lum and coauthors.

program will dispatch civil responders alone in some cases; in 2 percent of those cases the mental health responder will call for police backup. CAHOOTS responders called for police backup in a third of the cases where they were dispatched to a trespassing call. The Eugene Police Department emphasizes that the bulk of CAHOOTS responses would not normally involve calls to the police (Eugene residents are aware of CAHOOTS and will make calls knowing they can get a nonpolice response). This shows that it is easy to overestimate the diversion rates of these models. It also shows that there remains a large appetite for a response team available at all hours that helps solve many of the problems we originally turned to city watches for.

Beyond the practical need for an agency available 24/7 to respond to calls for service, another fact about our world suggests that something importantly like today's police departments will always be a part of realized societies. There is only so much room for specialization. We can continue to hand off police functions to specialized alternatives as we have with emergency medical services and public health agencies before that. But the unavoidable vagueness and complexity in the world suggest that there is a real limit to specialization (both for statutes and agencies). When we hit that limit, we'll have to turn over the "residual category" to a more generalist agency (Thacher 2022; 2014, 123).

This suggests that in the near term, before a substantial amount of policing can be rendered obsolete through expansive economic and social reforms, there will remain a need for agencies that look much like the police: on call around the clock, with limited legal powers of coercion, and perhaps even some "tactical hardening" defensive equipment or the ability to call upon it.[13] The upshot is that while our world will require some kind of policing, it need not look like the big, generalist, multifunctional agencies we have now. It probably shouldn't. There is more room for specialization and for interagency collaboration even if there is a limit to how specialized our agencies of social control can be.

---

[13] After several years and a lot of turnover, Boston's co-response model had a staff of four mental health professionals as of 2018 (Morabito et al. 2018). The difficulties in starting up a co-response model help explain why our police departments do so much today: when you've only got one generalist 24/7 response team, it is no surprise that people call them and that they respond in some way.

1.3. Substantive Questions of Just Policing

The question I've focused on so far is the abolitionist's: Should we have professional police departments? I've tried to show that the question helps us see why we need policing of some kind while keeping in clear view that it is costly in ways that make reasonable people want to abolish the whole enterprise. But I want to suggest that the question distracts us from substantive normative questions about social control faced by reformists and abolitionists alike.

The problems that generate a need for social control also entail that institutions of social control can be sources of great injustice. In other words, the imperfections of our world include fallible responses to the initial problems. We needed to craft institutions of social control, but we didn't do a great job. Even before we think about the police, the criminal code has deep problems of justice, criminalizing too much and unfairly. One need not be overly cynical or pessimistic to take the criminal code as it exists now to be a scathing indictment of (realized) democratic decision-making.

Our fixes won't be perfect. Everyone will be unhappy in some way with near-term reform. We are unlikely even to see the elimination of police unions in the near term, despite widespread desire to do so.

This raises questions about just policing, most of which apply in some form to institutions of social control generally. Police famously enjoy much discretion in their work, but is police discretion a necessary evil or a key part of just policing? Given that resources are limited, how should police wield their discretionary power and set priorities? What is it that ultimately justifies street-level police power?

A wide body of scholarship finds that policing and the criminal legal system have harmful side effects, to put things mildly. How do we evaluate these effects of policing? How should police react to the fact that some kinds of policing are harmful and even criminogenic?

Police (or community patrols) are called upon to maintain order or keep the peace. How should they deal with conflicts over the use of space? How do we determine what kind of order we should be maintaining? This is a real challenge: we have every reason to expect many of these disagreements are persistent because they are rooted in diverse perspectives.[14]

How do, or should, police agencies secure democratic authorization? From the criminal code, participatory democracy mechanisms, or something else? In light of the pathologies of realized democratic law-making, should police be controlled by majoritarian decision-making in the first place? Finally, we know that people can misuse or abuse their political roles, and likewise that institutional roles and expectations shape behavior. So how should political power be allocated across policing agencies?

1.4. Looking Ahead

The view I'll defend instructs police to take up a constrained but strategic justice-seeking role in society. This stands in contrast to two broad views. The first is a kind of vigilante or "thin blue line" view of policing according to which justice requires freeing the sheepdogs to defend us from the wolves. On this view, community organizations, prosecutors (progressive or otherwise), and the courts are mainly an impediment to the police securing justice. We might associate this view with a pre-professional-era beat cop who thinks the best way to protect his beat is to dole out punishment on the street or to give suspects the "third degree." The second kind of view, in contrast, is a serious view. It is a form of *legalism* that flows naturally from high-level theories of political obligation. The police, on this view, should ideally be passive conduits through which legislative and executive decision-making—themselves conduits of our political decisions and preferences—flow.

In the next chapter I'll explain some of the realized injustices in U.S. policing and use them to situate and inform the theory of just policing I defend. Chapter 3 argues that police discretion is an important tool for justice rather than an unavoidable evil to which we must resign ourselves. Chapter 4 lays out a general framework for evaluating policing at the agent and agency level. In Chapter 5 I argue that a

---

[14] I follow Ryan Muldoon (2016) in using "perspectives" to refer to worldviews including evaluative standards and ontological commitments.

principle of proportionality helps police take the negative side effects of policing into account. I take up issues of order maintenance in diverse societies in Chapter 6, where I appeal to a diversity-preserving principle of liberal neutrality for guidance. Chapter 7 offers a critical assessment of community policing initiatives and addresses concerns about the tension between democratic principles and just policing. Finally, in Chapter 8 I explain how these principles of just policing inform the question of the just institutional form of policing agencies.

2

Policing in a Complex and Coupled Criminal Legal System

Policing reaches deeply into life. Police agencies, through their power of arrest, influence what occurs in later states of the criminal legal system. What happens after an arrest determines, in a sense, what an officer has done to a suspect. If the trial system is prone to error or overly harsh punishment, this risks rendering the arrest unjust. But police do more than make arrests. They stop and search people, they write tickets and summonses, they make people disperse, and they use (sometimes lethal) force. Their impact extends beyond the criminal legal system to shape other parts of society. We must, then, pay special attention to the fact that the police operate in a world characterized by deep and pervasive injustice. Legislatures pass unjust laws, the trial system doles out too much punishment, and background injustices make it more likely that certain groups get caught up in the criminal legal system, compounding existing injustice.

The pathologies of policing therefore depend on pathologies in other parts of society. The police are not cogs in a machine, and a theory of just policing should not assume so. So, if we want to be sophisticated in our thinking about just policing, we must pay attention to these interactions, and we must acknowledge that the tangled web of political and social institutions makes the problems difficult to anticipate or control. The task of this chapter is to defend this claim by highlighting some of the problems that emerge from such interactions.

Just Policing. Jake Monaghan, Oxford University Press. © Oxford University Press 2023.
DOI: 10.1093/oso/9780197610725.003.0002

2.1. Catastrophic Failure in Complex and Coupled Systems

Sociologist Charles Perrow, in the 1980s, famously wrote on the challenges of living with high-risk technologies like nuclear reactors and weapons, chemical plants, and the like (Perrow 1984). He explained that paradoxically, the safety systems we build into these high-risk technologies can exacerbate their risks by making systems more *complex* and more tightly *coupled*. When the systems fail, it can be catastrophic. Because these systems are already complex and coupled, and because making them more so increases the risk of a catastrophic accident, Perrow called these system accidents "normal" in the sense that they are not anomalies, but rather to be expected. Some of today's injustices might be caused by mustache-twirling villains, but many of them are normal accidents.

2.1.1. System Accidents

To get an intuitive sense of how a system accident occurs, imagine the following case.[1] You need to get to work on time because your boss is a jerk. Showing up even a couple of minutes late could result in your termination. Normally, you drive. But today your car won't start. Fortunately, you live near a bus route. You check your public transit agency's app, and you discover that there is no bus service today. The drivers are on strike. You have another backup plan: although it's more expensive, you can use a ridesharing service. Bad luck strikes again: because everyone who normally takes the bus has the same backup plan, there are no Lyfts or Ubers available in time. You arrive late and are promptly fired.

In this toy example, you are met with a kind of catastrophe. The reason is not because of any one failure. In fact, the failures are not all that serious in isolation. The system accident emerged from the interaction of minor "subsystem" failures. First, the environment in which

---

[1] This case is a modified version of the case Perrow begins with (1984).

your method of transit operates caused subsystem failures (e.g., the low pay for bus drivers caused the strike, breaking the bus component of your safety mechanism). Second, some aspects of the system are just independent bad luck: the car not starting was completely unrelated to the bus drivers striking. But third, some aspects are *coupled*: the factors which caused a stop in bus service also, though indirectly, caused the ridesharing services to fail you (no bus service means the rideshare services are overloaded). Ideally, your safety mechanism or subsystem would have been decoupled. You should have purchased a bicycle.

2.1.2. Coupled Systems

Consider another example, this time of an actual disaster.[2] The hospital "system" is designed to heal patients. That requires lots of machinery hooked up to electricity, including ventilators, but also nonmedical equipment like air conditioning and elevators. Backup generators are a safety mechanism. But they only run for so long. So an additional safety mechanism is the ability to evacuate if things go badly, which includes loading docks and helipads. All of these subsystems interact.

In a bad storm, wind and floodwaters will knock out power, requiring the generator. Enough flood water will break the generator or the electrical system that connects it to the hospital and submerge the loading docks. Power outages and the elevator shaft flooding will render the elevators inoperable. That will make it impossible to evacuate patients through the loading docks and difficult and time-consuming to get patients to the helipad for evacuation. During that time, seriously ill patients will be difficult to care for and are at risk of dying during transit, raising difficult triage questions.

The relationship between these systems illustrates coupling. Failure in one can causes failure in another, or they can share a common cause of failure, and more coupling means more opportunity for failure

---

[2] This case is from Sheri Fink's *Five Days at Memorial*, which covers the flooding and subsequent possible intentional killing of patients at Memorial Hospital after Hurricane Katrina hit New Orleans in 2005.

to spill over. The criminal legal system, we'll see, is characterized by coupling.

2.1.3. Complex Systems

Complex systems are highly coupled systems with many parts. Complexity can make systems interact in unpredictable ways. The systems responsible for weather are so complex that sophisticated modeling software and trained meteorologists are unable to accurately predict weather patterns more than a few days out. Because of extensive coupling, small changes in the system interact to produce large changes over a relatively short amount of time.

Climate change is a paradigmatic large-scale example. Burning fossil fuels releases carbon dioxide, a greenhouse gas. Greenhouse gasses trap heat in the atmosphere, in turn raising temperatures. This causes polar ice to melt, releasing H_2O and decreasing the amount of sunlight reflected into space. H_2O is also a greenhouse gas. Less reflection (a lower albedo) means more absorbed heat. Both, in turn, increase temperatures, increasing the rate of ice melt. As temperatures rise, oceans carry less carbon dioxide, further increasing the amount of greenhouse gas in the atmosphere. And so on.[3] Each part of this system interacts, and the complexity and coupling can generate a variety of feedback loops that are self-reinforcing.

2.2. Coupling and Criminal Justice

Systems created by humans, whether physical technology like nuclear reactors, or social technology like criminal legal systems and democracies, are characterized by varying levels of complexity and coupling. The complex and coupled nature of social systems has been a crucial element of the case against "rational planning," whether of

---

[3] Though, to be clear, not all feedback loops are amplifying. Increasing carbon dioxide also increases the growth of plants, which pulls more carbon dioxide out of the atmosphere.

cities, economies, or utopian political systems more broadly (Gaus 2019; Scott 1998; Hayek 1945). My goal is not to appeal to system accidents to argue against central or rational planning. Rather, it is to contextualize the questions of just policing. To that end, in this section I'll detail several real system accidents involving the police.

2.2.1. Mandatory Arrest Policies

Consider laws that require police officers to make arrests when they respond to calls for service about domestic abuse. These are well-motivated policy responses to serious problems. The first problem was police officers not taking domestic violence seriously enough and too often declining to invoke their authority to make an arrest. The second problem concerns the dynamics of abusive relationships. People in an abusive relationship often call the cops to intervene in what might turn into, or has turned into, a violent dispute. But they also typically care about their abusive partner and don't want to see them arrested, charged, and detained. So they ask police officers not to make an arrest, or the officers don't believe they can make an arrest because the offense is a misdemeanor they didn't witness.[4] Once the dispute has been temporarily calmed, officers leave. Outsiders understand that the dynamics of the relationship are unhealthy, that a system that typically fails to do anything about domestic violence will not deter it, and that officers will end up spending an inordinate amount of time responding to calls for service at the same households and for the same reasons. Some jurisdictions have responded with policies that eliminate police discretion by requiring police to arrest the abuser.

The results have been mixed. Though the policy is intended to deter abusive behavior, it does not eliminate abusive relationships. Mandatory arrest policies appear to cause an increase in domestic violence arrests, though this effect is partially explained by an increase in "dual arrests" where both partners are arrested, probably because police arrive after the altercation and have no evidence of who was the

---

[4] See Brooks (2021, 195) for an ethnographic account of the mandatory arrest policy in action.

aggressor (Hirschel et al. 2007; Rajan and McCloskey 2007). Despite, or perhaps because of, increasing arrest rates, the policy makes some domestic violence victims more reluctant to call the police. Survey-based research of women receiving care in domestic violence shelters finds that those who do not support mandatory arrest policies are more likely to stop reporting incidents of domestic violence (Novisky and Peralta 2015).

To the extent that these policies deter victims of domestic violence from reporting it, they come with extreme risk. If people avoid calling the police to prevent a mandatory arrest, domestic violence incidents could continue to escalate and become more severe. Some research has found that while increasing arrest rates reduces intimate partner violence for some groups, it increases violence for others (Sherman 1992). More recently, one study found that mandatory arrest policies were followed by an increase in intimate partner homicides, consistent with a decreased domestic violence reporting hypothesis (Iyengar 2009). This result has failed a replication attempt, so the effects of mandatory arrest policies may not be as catastrophic as increasing homicides (Chin and Cunningham 2019). The jury is still out on the effects of these mandatory arrest policies, but an increase in dual arrests and a reduction in domestic violence reporting for those who would otherwise like police assistance hardly look like a win. It is also important to emphasize the distributional consequences: the policy appears to deter calling for service for some subset of the population, so the failure of the policy may disproportionately burden some groups.

In this example, the system originally included the abuser, the 911 caller, and the police. A "failure" in the system that is the relationship occurs, and the police respond. The police appear (in virtue of the discretion they exercise) to be an insufficient safety measure to the policymakers, so policymakers intervene. They add to the system a new safety measure and a new attempt at control, the mandatory arrest policy. But that new safety measure interacts with the original one (the officer responding to the call) in a way that exacerbates the system accident. When the new measure fails (to deter domestic violence), it causes the original safety measure to fail as well, rendering the accident even worse for some.

The costs associated with being arrested surely play a role in people not wanting their abusive partner arrested. It turns out also to play a role in the police not wanting to make an arrest in certain cases, such as when the policy forces bad arrests. In addition to dual-arrest cases, there are many cases where the policy wrongly calls for arrest, such as when a normal dispute between a teenager and a parent gets a little out of hand and a neighbor calls the cops. Law professor and reserve police officer Rosa Brooks details a case like this where it was not clear that the incident even counted as domestic violence, but it was clear (to her) that the minor shoving match that caused the 911 call did not justify an arrest. The next section will explain why it is unfortunate that her partner interpreted the event as domestic violence, triggering the mandatory arrest policy.

2.2.2. The Unjust Misdemeanor System

Our next example of a criminal legal system accident, the unjust misdemeanor system, is larger in scale and illustrates the severity of problems caused by iterated failure across coupled systems. It also highlights the police role as gatekeepers or filters at the "entrance" of the criminal legal system where they have significant influence over who bears the costs of the system. The process begins with an arrest for driving on a suspended license, disorderly conduct, loitering, shop-lifting, sleeping in one's car, drug possession, among many others. In most cases, the statutes permitting the arrest are rather vague (e.g., When is a shove an assault?), and the only evidence is often the officer's testimony. The decision to make a misdemeanor arrest puts arrestees into a system rife with procedural problems and a high risk of dispro-portionate punishment. The problems are so bad that many victims of violence do not call the cops and resist urges by prosecutors to press charges.[5]

After an arrest, prosecutors screen cases to determine whether they will file charges. Rather than use the screening process to weed out

---

[5] See Purnell (2021, 140) for a discussion of this phenomenon.

arrests on insufficient evidence, or to determine which charges that could be filed most accurately reflect the circumstances, prosecutors often charge as much as they can to increase their leverage during plea bargaining. Rather than eyeing the police report critically, it is common for prosecutors simply to charge whatever is in the report (Natapoff 2012, 1337). If there were never a wrongful arrest, this would be of little concern. But realized criminal justice systems are always imperfect.

After screening, those who will be prosecuted are often detained pretrial. Because the United States, unlike almost every other country in the world, relies on cash bail, it often takes money to be released while one awaits their trial. The rules typically differ between jurisdictions, but only some defendants will be released on their own recognizance. Others are released on unsecured bonds, meaning they only pay if they fail to appear for their hearing. Everyone else must pay around 10 percent of their bail as a deposit to encourage them to show up for their trial. If the bail amount is high, or if defendants are indigent, they will often be detained while they wait for their trial simply because they cannot afford their bail. Pretrial detention can cause defendants to lose their jobs, to be evicted from their house, or even to lose custody of their children.

Most people imagine that the next step in the process is the trial. But only the extreme minority—1 or 2 percent—of misdemeanor cases go to trial (Natapoff 2018, 67). The sheer volume of them means that almost everyone involved in the process is motivated to speed things up, and securing guilty pleas is an effective way to do that. Prosecutors aim to secure plea deals (Butler 2017, 220). Even if a defendant is innocent, defense attorneys think that accepting a plea deal is usually the best choice (Forman 2017, 122).

There are at least two reasons someone, even if innocent, would plead guilty. First, in the misdemeanor system, by the time someone has their trial, there is a good chance that they will have already served the amount of time they would have received as a sentence if convicted. Accepting a plea deal that counts pretrial detention as one's punishment lets one go home rather than fighting a trial that they are unlikely to win.

Second, the failures of the realized adversarial legal system make going to trial risky. The idea behind the adversarial system is that two opposing sides doing their best to win the case before a neutral arbiter is likely to produce the most accurate outcomes.[6] Procedural rules for achieving justice are ineffective if defendants lack competent legal counsel. For those unable to pay for their own legal defense, they must rely on chronically underfunded public defenders, and this puts them at a serious procedural disadvantage (Roberts 2012). This introduces an asymmetry in the quality of legal representation. Additionally, many scholars think there is a "trial penalty" in which defendants who exercise their right to trial receive longer sentences than they would if they accepted a plea deal, making it rational to take the deal.[7]

Ideally, we could take solace in the fact that jails are not terrible places. In reality, we can't. Homicide and suicide together account for almost 10 percent of jail deaths (BJS 2015). Assault and insufficient medical care are common as well. At the time of writing, COVID-19 is rapidly spreading through jails and prisons, with inmates in crowded conditions and limited or no access to various safety measures (Burki 2020; Equal Justice Initiative 2020).

Finally, once the misdemeanor process is over, people often continue to be punished. Those who cannot pay their fines or fees end up with late fees and criminal debt. Criminal debt can land one in civil contempt of court and time in jail. Criminal debt also shows up on credit reports, making it harder to obtain credit and market housing. A misdemeanor record can also result in the loss of one's job and difficulty finding a new one. Misdemeanants can lose out on public benefits, like housing, SNAP vouchers, scholarships, and cash transfers. Misdemeanor convictions, in other words, exacerbate poverty (Natapoff 2018).

The misdemeanor system lays bare the risks of complexity and coupling. Errors are inevitable, and we see them at virtually every stage. Although perhaps not severe in isolation, they are compounded by

---

[6] One complication I'm ignoring here is that procedural rules sacrifice accuracy for lenience. Punishing the innocent is worse than letting the guilty go free. We modify burdens of proof and evidentiary standards, not to make the system as accurate as possible, but to reduce the likelihood of false findings of guilt.

[7] There is some scholarly dispute on this point. See Abrams (2013) and Kim (2015).

later errors in the system. Because the system is so tightly coupled, the failures are hardly isolated. They produce a strikingly unjust misdemeanor system.

For our purposes, one of the upshots is that given complexity and coupling, police officers can't overlook adjacent components of the criminal legal and broader social systems. The decision to make an arrest on even a misdemeanor charge is a significant one. The compounding failures described here explain why bad (even if mandatory) arrests aren't minor problems, as we might have hoped. Making an arrest puts people into a coercive system that, because it flouts many of the normative requirements for a criminal justice system, is not itself genuinely a criminal justice system (Natapoff 2018, 193). That's the sort of thing that must be done with caution.

2.3. Complexity and Criminal Justice

The effects of policing extend beyond the criminal legal system, of course. We'll start with the example of drug prohibition, in part because it has been so influential on U.S. policing. Prohibition has provoked a huge amount of attention and a voluminous literature, almost all of it critical. My goal here is not to retread terrain that is probably familiar to most readers. The point is to cast the issue in terms of system accidents to draw our attention to problems of realized criminal legal systems. After discussing the more direct effects of policing in an age of drug prohibition, we'll very briefly see the more diffused effects on major aspects of society (persons, families, economies, and politics).

2.3.1. Prohibition and Black Markets

The effects of drug prohibition emphasize the problems of complexity and feedback loops. Consider the interaction between three subsystems: ordinary police patrol, narcotics policing, and the legislation that prohibits narcotics. The enforcement of these laws can be extremely difficult, producing surprising consequences. In "open air" drug markets of the 1980s and 90s, sellers rarely had drugs on their person, instead hiding a cache nearby to supply customers. They would also separate the transfer of drugs and money so that no one person completes the full transaction to limit liability (Moskos 2008, 66). That means that when an officer approaches, it might be obvious that they are selling, but difficult or impossible to legally justify an arrest on drug charges. This situation encourages officers to make *instrumental* stops or arrests—instrumental in investigating or punishing another violation—on a different charge.

This is common practice. The charge will vary depending on the jurisdiction, but arrests for misdemeanor loitering or disorderly conduct, tools ostensibly for ensuring the orderly use of public space, are often the tools of choice (Moskos 2008, 55). Inevitably some of those arrests will be in error. This couples a fourth subsystem, the misdemeanor trial process. In a well-functioning criminal system, this might mean it is a low-cost enforcement strategy. But as we saw above, entering the misdemeanor system can be seriously harmful and carry with it serious (de facto) punishment even if the charge isn't prosecuted. Further congesting the misdemeanor system exacerbates problems. And, of course, this game of cat and mouse will draw police attention away from the other issues typical patrol officers might be focusing on.

Relatedly, the difficulty of enforcing prohibition encourages officers to rely on instrumental stops to pursue "filtering strategies." The problem of filtering is pronounced in traffic enforcement, where officers regularly employ pretextual traffic stops. The Drug Enforcement Administration (DEA) works with local police agencies to repurpose traffic laws as a filtering device. By stopping large numbers of cars on traffic violations, officers can more closely examine motorists and their vehicles. U.S. police rely on permissive Fourth Amendment jurisprudence regarding vehicles to conduct warrantless searches and seizures (Seo 2019). By definition, these strategies will cause large numbers of innocent people (with respect to the target of enforcement) to be stopped or arrested (typically on misdemeanor charges).

In this way, drug prohibition interacts with another policing subsystem—this time traffic regulation—to change it by taking the focus away from maintaining orderly and safe roads and toward stopping and searching large numbers of people who might possess illegal drugs. This naturally changes officer priorities. Because the traffic stops are intended to interdict drug traffickers, rather than enforce traffic laws, any bias in who officers think are likely to possess drugs will surface in traffic stops (Seo 2019, 215, 256).[8]

Drug prohibition, by creating black markets, is criminogenic. Markets create opportunities, and some people will take them. For a dramatic example, consider children in the drug market (Moskos 2008, 69). The relatively low probability of being arrested caused lawmakers to make penalties harsher to make drug dealing too risky. One way to adapt to the risk is to involve minors in the transaction: if the one who hands off the drugs is a minor, the risk is lower. Minors face reduced penalties. When they are arrested, however, they enter the criminal system, and exposure to the criminal system tends to close off opportunities.

Black markets also cause violence (Resignato 2002). Unfortunately, it is common for proponents of drug prohibition to attribute the violence directly to the drugs and ignore the police and legislatures' causal role. The mechanism is nevertheless widely known at this point. In well-functioning markets, the police (or regulators) and the court system can be relied on to settle disputes. Businesses can trademark product names, patent innovative designs, file lawsuits for damages or injunctions when these are infringed, open a location and call the police if someone trespasses on the property, and so on. In black markets, the police and the courts can settle none of these disputes nor protect any of these rights. Disputes over territory and market share can be deadly.[9]

---

[8] This contributes to the well-known problem of "driving while black" (Pierson et al. 2020; Baumgartner et al. 2018).

[9] A dramatic contrast to this is the "Oxy Express," part of the opioid epidemic of the 2000s. Because physicians were overprescribing opioids, many recreational users could get them in gray market "pill mills," pain management clinics established to sell prescription opioids. Because laws were favorable to pill mills in Florida, many opened there. People bought prescription opioids there and drove them out of Florida, which ended up supplying a large portion of the recreational oxycontin on the East Coast. The clinics were technically legal (at the time), so there was no territorial violence we typically associate with recreational drug markets. In fact, journalists documented the orderly lines that snaked out of the pill mills containing people waiting to get in, quite unlike the images of open-air drug markets and "crack houses" (Beall 2018).

Prohibition also increases the potency of drugs sold on the black market and health problems associated with their use (Beletsky and Davis 2017; Boettke et al. 2012). Because police are trying to incarcerate drug traffickers, traffickers are motivated to find ways to increase the potency of the drugs they sell, not only to increase profits but also to make transportation easier. Decreasing the number of trips needed and making the product harder to find reduces their risk. Alcohol prohibition increased consumption of liquor. The war on drugs increases consumption of more potent forms of narcotics.[10]

In addition to increasing overdoses, prohibition makes the consumption of drugs more dangerous in other ways. Because the recreational use of drugs is illegal, paraphernalia like syringes or pipes are difficult to access legally and can be used as evidence of crime. This means that their supply is limited. But again, prohibition doesn't eliminate the consumption of these drugs. Instead, it typically leads to the reuse and sharing of syringes or pipes, spreading HIV and Hepatitis C. These dangers increase because of prohibition.

Drug prohibition also risks undermining the effectiveness of policing (beyond changing the nature of policing as described above) in at least two ways. First, it contributes to mass incarceration, which has the effect of displacing reliance on informal social control, in turn overburdening police forces and creating "counter-deterrent" effects (Fagan and Meares 2008).[11] Second, it undermines perceptions of police legitimacy. Social scientists working on policing have recently argued that perceived legitimacy—determined in part by personal evaluations of policing—is crucial for securing compliance with the law and cooperation with law enforcement (Tyler 2004).

What we see, then, is a kind of policing that interacts with several other subsystems, both in and out of the criminal legal system. Drug prohibition in the United States creates and influences the nature of criminality. It encourages instrumental (or pretextual) enforcement of other laws, congesting the misdemeanor system. It changes

---

[10] Cracking down on recreational use of prescription overdoses probably cost thousands of lives per year by causing people to substitute heroin and fentanyl (Goodnough et al. 2019; Evans et al. 2018).

[11] The role of drug prohibition in causing mass incarceration is often exaggerated. Nevertheless, it has at least some non-negligible role in incarceration rates.

seemingly independent aspects of policing, such as order maintenance and traffic enforcement. It makes drugs and drug consumption
more dangerous. And it devastates trust and perceived legitimacy in
policing. Yet it does not come close to eliminating drug use. This is a
result of complexity: failures in one area lead to others, which in turn
feed back into the system. This system accident is nothing short of a
catastrophe. Unfortunately, the mountain of evidence we have that it
has failed and will continue to do so has been slow to yield legislative
change.

2.3.2. Persons

The cases discussed above lay out many of the obvious effects on
individuals associated with entering the criminal justice system.
Of course, the costs are much wider and more diffused than these
cases show.

To whom those costs accrue depend in no small part on decisions
about how to deploy police resources and the choice of police
strategies. Resource scarcity means such decisions are unavoidable.
The decision about where to set up a "pretext regime" that searches
for illegal drugs, for example, will determine who enters the criminal legal system. Targeting one group with a pretext regime entails
not targeting others. When police focus on certain communities and
neighborhoods, particularly considering the housing segregation in
the United States, it is unavoidable that there will be racially unequal
funnels into the system.

These effects extend beyond the costs of pretrial detention and incarceration. The instrumental, filtering strategies employed by the
police shape the kinds of lives people can live in other ways, too.
According to legal scholar James Forman:

> In the ghetto, you are not presumed innocent until proven otherwise.
> Rather, you are presumed guilty, or at least suspicious, and you must
> spend an extraordinary amount of energy—through careful atten-
> tion to dress, behavior, and speech—to mark yourself as innocent.
> All with no guarantee that these efforts will work. (2017, 155)

In his *Chokehold: Policing Black Men*, Paul Butler, former federal prosecutor and law professor, relays tips from police officers and defense attorneys on how not to get stopped by the police if you are a black man. Things that make a black man look suspicious include driving in a black SUV, being with a white woman, being in a group with other black men and laughing too loudly, wearing sagging pants, and wearing a hoodie. According to Butler, the "cops don't only enforce the criminal law; they also enforce the politics of respectability. Many will rebel. The black teenagers with their pants hanging down their behinds know that it makes the police look at them extra hard" (2018, 203).

The same goes for cars. In addition to wearing dreadlocks or gold jewelry, one's car can be taken as evidence of criminality because it fits the profile of the drug dealer created by the DEA in Operation Pipeline (Seo 2019, 215, 256). Cars are a symbol of freedom and status for most Americans, as well as a means of self-expression. But when you know that Grateful Dead or religious bumper stickers are interpreted by police as evidence of possible drug trafficking in a pretextual stop regime (at the instruction of a how-to manual for *criminal patrol*), you might think twice about using your symbol of freedom to freely express yourself (Remsberg 1995, 55).

The effects of interactions with police, especially when there is a presumption of guilt, go well beyond costs to free expression. For just one example, empirical investigation of men in New York City, during the stop-and-frisk era, shows that the strategy carried serious mental health costs. Greater trauma and anxiety symptoms were correlated with more frequent stops by the police (Geller et al. 2014).

2.3.3. Families

The structure of families, in particular the distribution of labor, rights, and responsibilities within them, shapes the kinds of lives people can live. If governments are going to enact legislation or tax policies that favor those living in families, then who has the right to marry whom is tremendously important. If social norms place most domestic labor on women, then their economic opportunities and quality of life at home will suffer. Whether women have control over their pregnancies further influences the amount of freedom in their lives. Family life matters, and the costs of decisions about how to police accrue to families as well.

The challenges of policing domestic violence discussed above are easy examples of policing influencing some private aspects of family life. Underpolicing can make it difficult for families to spend their time together in public, as can overpolicing. If a neighborhood has high crime rates, people might withdraw into their homes and forgo the use of neighborhood parks (either because of the threat of crime or the threat of aggressive police). Sociologist Sudhir Venkatesh details the relationship between off-book entrepreneurs—"hustlers"—and families in a majority-black Chicago neighborhood and the difficult role police have in mediating these competing uses of public space:

> Hustlers create a variety of problems in Maquis Park, and there are approximately one dozen police officers who work to navigate relationships between West Street hustlers and other members of the community. Some work solely with a small set of store owners and managers by helping them create a safe business climate. [...] Other officers help Parks Department personnel deal with hustlers who sleep in recreational areas or use park areas for economic purposes. They may forcibly remove individuals or ask that they congregate in areas away from children. This is not easy, because hustlers gravitate to playgrounds, baseball fields, and basketball courts to find customers. (2006, 200)

This is difficult precisely because the balance between underpolicing and overpolicing is hard to achieve. Underpolicing means families lose access to public spaces like playgrounds. Overpolicing means hustlers lose income, and their customers (most of whom live in the neighborhood) lose the opportunity for affordable automotive repair, childcare, prepared food, and so on.

Other police decisions have a more direct and more profound affect. Because police are the filter on the system, decisions about policing affect who is saddled with fines, fees, pretrial detention, or incarceration. Spouses and children share in these costs. Children with incarcerated parents tend to have worse mental health and behavioral problems (Geller et al. 2009). Given racial inequities in incarceration and the violence caused by drug prohibition, black children are less likely to have fathers playing an active role in their life (Western and Wildeman 2009, 233). Decisions about how to police shape not just the kind of family life, but also the kinds of families, available to people.

2.3.4. Economies

Economic systems have been one of the most thoroughly discussed issues in political philosophy. Clearly, the material resources one has play a consequential role in one's life, and the economic system one lives in impacts one's material resources. Here, too, we see the reach of policing and criminal justice.

Policing affects one's economic opportunities through its influence on education. Whether one's school employs a police officer for security will play a role in determining how it handles student misbehavior, in turn helping to determine whether one graduates (Weisburst 2019). Felony records reduce one's chances of admission to higher education (Stewart and Uggen 2019). They also make it harder to get hired (Agan and Starr 2018). Insofar as decisions about policing influence who has a felony record, they impact economic opportunities.

Policing also affects the number of jobs there are in an area. Commercial investment in a neighborhood's formal economy is partly determined by the amount of foot traffic and its crime rate. To the extent that policing fails to reduce (or even causes) crime, it affects the quantity and quality of economic opportunities available (Rosenthal and Ross 2010).

As mentioned in the section on drug prohibition, prohibition creates economic opportunities. And the nature of the informal economy depends largely on policing decisions; policing influences whether someone can turn to vending instead of property crime to get by (Venkatesh 2006; Duneier 1999, 85, 141). The capacity for policing to create economic opportunities operates in tandem with the diminished economic opportunities caused by arrest, making the illicit market opportunities even more attractive by comparison. Some policing decisions have the effect of pushing people into the off-book, even illegal economy, generating a feedback loop.

2.3.5. Politics

In some ways, it is strange to say policing influences politics, because policing is just part of politics. But policing influences our political decision-making processes. Legislation determines which laws police have to enforce, and the executive partially determines whether and how those laws will be enforced. Decisions about policing, in turn, transform who participates in these political processes in the first place and how the processes play out.

The most direct way this occurs is through felony disenfranchisement. In most states, felons are not permitted to vote. Those incarcerated are unable to vote; in many states, anyone with a felony *record* is disenfranchised. The rules vary by state, but it is common for former felons to have to navigate a complex legal process to restore their franchise. Empirical research suggests that the practice has been instrumental in changing the results of presidential and congressional elections (Uggen and Manza 2002).

The effect on the political system is not restricted to formal disenfranchisement. Political scientists have found that the further one enters the criminal legal system, from arrest to indictment to conviction, the less likely one is to participate in politics by exercising their franchise (Weaver and Lerman 2010). Even those who are not disenfranchised are less likely to vote. It is true that in some cases, bad policing motivates people to speak out or protest. Unfortunately, this does not always translate into political change.

Of course, as discussed above, negative interactions with the police are also likely to reduce one's cooperation with the police. Recipients of bad policing are less likely to cooperate with the police. They're less likely to avail themselves of the political services, like policing, that should be available to everyone. And it's not just policing services. People in contact with the criminal legal system are likely to engage in "system avoidance," or in other words to avoid institutions that keep formal records (Brayne 2014). Because medical, financial, educational, and other systems are "surveilling," they are commonly avoided.

Finally, the police are often powerful political voices. Police unions protect special legal privileges for police officers, make it difficult to fire even bad and unprofessional officers, and engage in political campaigning. Members of the police profession are usually recognized as experts by mayors and city council members and included in discussions about how to respond to citizen concerns about crime and other issues. The police chief is a high-profile political figure in most cities and can shape public opinion.

These institutions are coupled in such a way that feedback loops are everywhere. The relationship between the police, the criminal legal system, and the broader political systems create a significant feedback loop. That our police and criminal law institutions are deeply flawed is obvious to anyone who pays attention. Political solutions are required. But bad democratic decisions (like the one to wage a war on drugs or to engage in pretextual filtering police strategies) determine who enters the criminal legal system. Those who enter the legal system reduce their political participation, voluntarily and involuntarily. This means many of those who are most familiar with these problems, and most motivated to change them, are less capable of doing so. The political mechanisms for fixing those bad policies are therefore undermined.

2.4. Just Policing in an Unjust System

We've now set up the problem: we have a need for various kinds of social control (as we saw in the introduction), but our institutional attempts at social control are necessarily fraught, and we should expect them to produce injustices of their own. The injustices, however, are only sometimes of the villainous or conspiratorial variety. Some are the result of honest disagreements over what justice requires and how to get there. But others are a result of small problems in one area of society interacting with others and amplifying existing injustices. Policing institutions are coupled with key social arrangements basically everywhere, such that pathologies in other social arrangements can affect the justice of police practices and vice versa. The manifestation of our institutions is not the product of people simply implementing political decisions handed down from the legislature. Unintended consequences, misaligned incentives, and feedback loops are the rule rather than the exception.

The complex, coupled nature of the systems of which policing is a part generates special problems for the just policing. When there are serious failures in the criminal legal system that interact with life outside it, the police cannot simply make arrests and turn people over to the prosecutors on the assumption that the system will likely produce justice. Merely "following orders," even if possible, is not justice.

As a result, approaches to political theorizing that treat policing as little more than "the mechanism through which justice is enforced" will inevitably fail to provide useful insight into the real challenges of building toward a just social order. In politics as in many domains, we often cannot effectively evaluate a rule apart from its implementation. These two points are incompatible with what I take to be the common view of the ethics of policing.

On this view, good policing amounts to diligently enforcing the criminal code, avoiding excessive uses of force, avoiding corruption, and treating people with respect and decency. But, according to this view, even if the criminal code includes unjust or harmful laws, or if the trial system will handle cases inappropriately, they are nevertheless required to enforce them. Objections to lawful police activity ought to be objections to legislators. An appreciation for the complexity and coupling of the systems the police operate in helps to show that good policing can't be quite that simple. At least not when we're thinking about realized institutions.

The complexity of the system cautions us against trying to solve the problem, at least exclusively, with new rules operating as safety mechanisms and by eliminating rules that permit objectionable policing. Adding safety mechanisms are likely to increase complexity and coupling, exacerbating system accidents. That is not to say we should ignore rules. Surely, we would make significant improvements by *removing* many laws. But the ills of contemporary policing are not purely the result of overcriminalization. Police do not need an expansive criminal code to abuse or badly exercise their power, so getting the criminal code right is no guaranteed route to justice.

The problem with certain laws is their mode of enforcement, and eliminating those laws is not always an attractive option. What we need is an account of how police should exercise their power, and the realized problems of policing suggest the account can't be "diligent, impartial enforcement of the law" because that is likely, in at least some cases, to make things worse. The problems canvassed in this chapter suggest that we want a thoughtful approach that is sensitive to the huge range of relevant considerations, rather than a mechanistic or overly rationalistic approach. Thoughtful, discretionary policing, I'll argue, is a tool for reducing the problems associated with complexity and coupling in social systems.

3

The Problem of Police Legitimacy

The search for police legitimacy is made difficult by the fact that the problems that give rise to policing—conflicts of interest in public space, moral disagreements, injustices and predation, and so on—also produce imperfect and unjust social control, as well as persistent disagreements about these matters. It is also complicated by policing's competing goals. One of the earliest scholarly uses of the narrow sense of "policing" attributes to the London police the distinctive tasks of *prevention* and *detection* (which are separate from the magistrate's task of punishment; Colquhoun 1806, 8). The tension between these goals is evident in decisions about equipping patrol officers: Should they stand out or blend in? Standing out with uniforms, badges, or lights serves a deterrence function. But blending in enables detection. The Los Angeles Police Department (LAPD) introduced the famous "protect and serve" motto to U.S. policing. If "protection" is associated with the law enforcement function of policing, then we have a similar tension: the service functions of policing sometimes can come at the expense of the enforcement functions. Even within broad categories of policing, deterrence and detection, or enforcement and service, there are a host of competing goals: various calls for service to respond to, different statutes to enforce, conflicting problems to target proactively.

The first issue invokes the possibility of disobedience or departure from official decisions. If diligently enforcing the law can produce catastrophic injustices, perhaps justice requires disregarding certain laws or department policies. The second issue entails that some amount of professional judgment will be necessary in policing. Officers will have to decide how to satisfy their competing goals and priorities. Both issues point in the same direction: we might have good reasons for police discretion, and it is unavoidable anyway. That's the position I'll defend: police discretion, in particular *discretionary non-enforcement*—opting not to enforce unjust or unjustly punished

Just Policing. Jake Monaghan, Oxford University Press. © Oxford University Press 2023.
DOI: 10.1093/oso/9780197610725.003.0003

laws—is an important tool for producing just policing. The sense of discretion I'm using here includes both *interpretive* discretion, or the judgment of whether a law has been violated, and also *priority* discretion, or the judgment of which violations justify invoking police power.[1] Discretion of both kinds can make for a more just criminal legal system, in part by reducing its coupling. But this poses a theoretical problem for constructing an account of legitimate and just policing.

Criminal justice scholars typically think that the solution is to rework the criminal law and the trial and penal systems to prevent such failures. Police should continue to make arrests, and other parts of the system should address these concerns (e.g., with lenience at sentencing). Police discretion, on this view, departs from the requirements of legitimacy and justice. Even if discretion produces good results, it is an impermissible use of power. Full enforcement may be practically impossible, but many theorists endorse a *resignation theory* of discretion where it is a problem to be accepted begrudgingly. I think this view is widely shared by non-scholars as well. This follows from a *legalistic* view of policing I began to describe in the last chapter.[2]

This chapter begins by detailing legalism. I then raise several objections to the view, including that it is inappropriately ideal theoretic, that it fails to explain how police power is just and legitimate in the first place, and that the political commitments that would induce one to accept legalism actually better support the kind of discretionary policing I'll go on to defend. The essential claim is that the criminal code provides tools rather than marching orders for the police. Although police discretion is unavoidable, this is not a fact we must resign ourselves to. A positive theory of strategic, just policing, which is largely a theory of just police discretion, follows in the later chapters.

---

[1] In this respect, the problem of police discretion is broader than the oft-discussed problem of judicial discretion. While both roles require interpretation, judges aren't faced with quite the same need to prioritize their efforts.

[2] This term is used in a variety of ways. I think there is considerable overlap in how the term is used by police scholars, but I will use the term in a technical sense.

3.1. The Legalistic View of Just and
Legitimate Policing

Because few philosophers have written on policing, there is not a developed landscape of views one might adopt or critique. But common commitments in political philosophy can be assembled into a view. The task of this section is to develop the composite view I'll call legalism. The components fit naturally together, and many philosophers appear committed to something like it. Further, it seems to me that the legalist view is represented in (and offers a justification for) some mainstream thinking about the police, both by the police and others. The core of the view is that police legitimacy comes from the law.

3.1.1. Legalism in the Field

Ethnographic research suggests a strong current of legalism flows through the police profession. This is evident in attitudes toward police discretion and the source of legitimacy. The *Peelian Principles*—claims apocryphally attributed to Robert Peel—have had an undeniable influence on the field. Those principles include the following:

> To seek and preserve public favor, not by catering to public opinion, but by constantly demonstrating absolutely impartial service to the law, in complete independence of policy, and without regard to the justice or injustice of the substance of individual laws.

What matters is that police enforce the law impartially, rather than use their power in a way that satisfies the perceived desires of the public. Laws on the books must be enforced even if the policed don't like them, and even if they are unjust. Justifications of police power come from the law, not from public perceptions of legitimacy or justice. Nearly 150 years after the founding of the London Metropolitan Police, it was sued for having a policy of not enforcing gambling laws. The judge in the case, Lord Denning, apparently finds Peelian legalism compelling: "I hold it to be the duty . . . of every Chief Constable to enforce the law of the land . . . he is not the servant of anyone save of the law itself. . . . He is answerable to the law and to the law alone" (Reynolds 1998, 32).

This sentiment has endured. The dominant model of policing in the twentieth century sought legitimacy in the criminal code. According to George Kelling and Mark Moore, "a generation of police officers was raised with the idea that they merely enforced the law" (1988, 5–6). This idea, says Herman Goldstein, means that police claim to be "committed to a policy of full enforcement," and that "the mere suggestion that a police administrator exercises discretion in fulfilling his job may be taken as an affront—an attack upon the objective and sacrosanct nature of his job—that of enforcing the law without fear or favor" (Goldstein 1963, 141–143).

Of course, the police downplay their discretion in part to avoid taking responsibility for what happens after an arrest, not because they imagine that policing is possible without it. James Q. Wilson's classic ethnography cataloguing various approaches to policing finds that the legalistic approach generates high rates of arrests and citations. This tends to result in accusations of harassment. Doubling down on legalism, officers blame the legislature: the officers "don't make the law" (Wilson 1978, 172–181).

Legalism is certainly not universally endorsed by practitioners, but it is well represented in the field. Research on police operational styles shows that officers vary regarding how aggressive and how selective they must be in acting upon violations they witness. More aggressive officers think they must be more proactive and take the initiative in finding violations, and more selective officers think they must devote more attention to felonies and less attention to misdemeanors (Brown 1988, 223). Using these metrics, the legalist favors aggressive but not selective officers.[3]

---

[3] Brown takes "aggressive" officers to be more comfortable with illegal tactics. I don't mean to import that component of "aggression" into my own analysis.

3.1.2. Legalism in the Academy

The commitment to legalism by practitioners may reflect nothing more than a contingent development of occupational culture or a desire to shirk responsibility ("blame the politicians, not us!"). Whatever their actual source, these commitments follow naturally from both broadly democratic and constitutional approaches to political legitimacy and justice.

Such an assessment will benefit from an analogy to the philosophical literature on just war theory. Critics persuasively argue that the military/police analogy has had an overwhelmingly negative effect (Coyne and Hall 2018; Balko 2013). Still, it is a useful model for thinking about normative aspects of police power, not least because militaries occasionally take on policing missions. There are three major positions regarding the morality of war: pacifism, just war theory, and realism. Pacifists hold that war is never justified, and realists hold that war is not subjected to moral principles. In contrast, just war theorists hold that (only) some war is justified (Lazar 2020). We can draw a similar taxonomy for policing: a certain kind of abolitionism might be analogous to pacifism. Something like the "thin blue line" attitude that looks at the police as the only thing preventing societal collapse might be analogous to realism in holding that police are only prudentially, but not morally, bound by restrictions on their power. The middle ground is a view that holds (some) policing to be justified, subject to important moral restrictions (about which we naturally disagree).

Policing and warring raise some of the same questions about these restrictions. In both cases, injustices raise questions about rule departure and discretion. There are questions of just tactics and just goals, and they come apart. These questions are made more pressing by the fallibility of our realized decision-making systems that bring substantive and procedural principles of justice into conflict. But, because we need to divide labor to accomplish large goals, the agents (officers, soldiers) typically need to simply follow orders.

With respect to rule departure, political philosophy in the wake of World War II takes as axiomatic that the "Nuremberg defense" fails. "I was just following orders" is never a justification for engaging in seriously unjust behavior. Soldiers may not torture prisoners of war just because they have been commanded to do so. Analogously, in our context, it would imply that police likewise may not commit an atrocity simply because their commanding officer orders them to. It was impermissible for proto-police officers to arrest enslaved people without passes to return them to their captor. At the extreme end, then, no sensible theory of justice can be absolute in its rejection of discretion. But this anti-Nuremberg principle doesn't extend to "ordinary" injustices. It does not, therefore, commit one to a broad acceptance of police discretion even if it rejects the legitimacy of grave injustices. What's important for present purposes, then, are milder forms of injustice.

This detour highlights a key feature of legalism. Most think that political agents are typically required to follow orders and enforce political decisions even if they're not *perfectly* just. Within academic political philosophy, typically only anarchists and libertarians endorse the view that the police ought to refuse to enforce unjust laws (e.g., Huemer 2013, 161). This is rooted in skepticism about the view that realized political entities have legitimacy. Those who aren't legitimacy skeptics are naturally much less likely to endorse discretionary nonenforcement. The mainstream view is thus *proceduralist*, holding that appropriate procedures rather than substantive values justify their outcomes, and *fallibilist*, meaning political procedures legitimize their results even if they're (mildly) unjust.

There are several defenses of this position in just war theory, including an appeal to epistemic considerations (the political process knows better than the agent), to patriotism (soldiers have duties to their compatriots, not their enemies), and to democratic respect (to substitute one's decisions for the democracy's is unjust) (Estlund 2007; Walzer 2006; Vitoria 1991). The last argument is also made in the broader context of political philosophy to apply to almost all state agents.[4]

---

[4] Proceduralists in political philosophy include Rawls (1999), Christiano (2010), Estlund (2009), Valentini (2012b), and Landemore (2020), among others. In legal philosophy, Waldron (2011) has an interesting discussion of trial procedures. There are important differences in these forms of proceduralism, but they take procedures to do much of the justificatory work, while allowing for the fallibility to be compatible with its justificatory power.

One proceduralist argument moves, in part, from the basic intuition that substituting one's own judgment for the democracy's anytime one thinks the democracy has erred is dogmatic and incompatible with political equality and agency. Since any actual political procedure is imperfect, a mistake cannot by itself undermine the legitimacy of the procedure's output. A "correctness" theory of political legitimacy, in which the decision or law is authoritative only when the decision is correct, renders political procedures incapable of performing their task (Estlund 2009, 99). The point of having political procedures is to handle the disagreements that arise in trying to live together. If our judgment that a procedure has erred meant that we should ignore the outcome, there'd be no reason to have them at all. There will always be some who regard an outcome a mistake.

The procedural fallibilism is thus a result of a certain view about democracy and the legislature, namely *legislative supremacy*, at least over the executive. John Locke argued that because the legislature is the way *we* make decisions, it cannot transfer decision-making powers to others, and it must *direct* the executive (Locke 1690/1980).[5] If the executive didn't take marching orders from the legislature, we'd bypass the only thing that justifies the inequalities inherent in political power, where some members of society have power over others (Buchanan 2002). Philosopher Robert Goodin argues in this vein that the interpretation of rules by executive bureaucrats in their enforcement is often an "arrogation of what is properly a legislative function" (1988, 219). By relying on their own interpretations of the law, bureaucrats can supplant their own goals and interests for those of the legislature. And if interpretative discretion is objectionable, priority discretion concerning how and whether to enforce is even more so.

Additionally, political legitimacy is usually thought to flow "downhill" or transfer *down hierarchy*. Voters elect legislators (or pass referenda) and executives; legislators pass legislation and executives create systems of enforcement and delegate enforcement power; the ground-level members of the executive (in this case police officers) are subject to administrative guidelines and pressures in the enforcement

---

[5] Locke explicitly defends legislative supremacy in §135 and rejects the transfer of "making laws" to others in §141 of the *Second Treatise*.

of the legislative power. Legitimacy passes from one stage to the next. Accountability, in contrast, flows "uphill" (Heath 2020, 53). When political bureaucrats act in objectionable (though legal) ways, their boss is or should be held accountable (e.g., voted out of office). At the bottom of the hierarchy, police must faithfully enforce the decisions that were made above them. Any problems of justice, therefore, must be addressed via the legislature and other electoral processes.

Another related argumentative route to legalism can be found in rule of law considerations. The rule of law is a characteristic of government where political power is exercised in accordance with legal rules, rather than the whims of individual political agents. This allows for stable, predictable societies that respect the governed, enable and protect liberty, and so on (Waldron 2011; Pettit 1997, 174–177; Fuller 1969, 162; Hayek 2011, 312). To achieve that, rules must have certain formal characteristics and enforcement institutions must meet procedural requirements. If government by law, and not individuals, is required, this plausibly commits us to a legalist orientation to police legitimacy. We'll look at three rule of law problems for discretion: unpredictability, arbitrariness, and the persistence of unjust laws.

To get a sense of the value of the rule of law, consider two important formal requirements: generality and publicity (Fuller 1969, 46–51; Hayek 2011, 315). The generality requirement implies that there must be general rules to guide decisions, rather than decisions being made on a case-by-case basis. Further, the rules must be public, rather than hidden. Generality and publicity enables people to conform to them. For example, while a referee might be able to use their judgment to determine whether the defense should be penalized in a game of American football for too aggressively preventing a receiver from catching a pass, an actual publicly available rule is required to make the game competitive, fair, and enjoyable. Without specifying what counts as pass interference and letting everyone know about it, teams can't optimize their strategies and players can't play aggressively for fear of being penalized. Further, referee performance can't be evaluated without independent standards of pass interference.

When it comes to the enforcement of the rule, similar values will apply. It is objectionable for a referee to call pass interference randomly, only against the team they dislike, or for Bill Binovich to ignore pass interference against the New Orleans Saints in playoff games. A good referee will also inform players about what they are looking for when they call certain penalties, especially since they can't call them all. Equal enforcement of law is valuable in much the same way that generality of law is valuable. No one, says philosopher Philip Pettit, "should have discretion in how the instruments [of political power] are used" (1997, 173).

Full and equal enforcement, the argument goes, is required to avoid unpredictable and arbitrary, and therefore unjust and illegitimate, power. Full enforcement also has the advantage of preventing unjust laws from being passed, and might expedite the removal of bad laws (cf. Hayek 2011, 318). Allowing officers to exercise discretion will result in groups to whom police are sympathetic getting a pass, while the unsympathetic group bears the burden of the injustice. It is commonly remarked that if we arrested white college students for drug possession at the same rate that we arrest black men, the legislature may have an incentive to end the drug war.

To the extent that what happens to a person who violates the law depends on discretion—whether he is arrested and how prosecutors respond to the case—the *law* is not what determines what one can do and how they will be treated in response. This, says philosopher Douglas Husak, produces injustice; "the *real* law ... cannot be found in criminal codes" (2008, 27).

3.1.3. Faithful to the Law

To recap: legalism is characterized by commitments to proceduralism, fallibilism, legislative supremacy, and a preoccupation with full obedience and full enforcement of political decisions. These commitments amount to a plausible justification of the legalistic commitments of police administrators. Respect for democracy and the rule of law means that the legitimation of political power comes from the *impartial* enforcement of criminal law, not from the satisfying the perceived interests of the policed. Of course, no one thinks that the executive is *always* prohibited from exercising discretionary power. Pettit, for instance, concedes that the best we can hope for is to reduce manipulation of political power, and that "the best sort of law may have to leave some discretion in the hands of government agents" (1997, 175). Legalist commitments are weakened to produce a *good faith enforcement* requirement. The good faith enforcement requirement of legalism is a response to various facts about the non-ideal world. Locke recognized many of them:

> for since in some governments the lawmaking power is not always in being, and is usually too numerous, and so too slow, for the dispatch requisite to execution; and because it is impossible to foresee, and so by laws to provide for, all accidents and necessities that may concern the public, or to make such laws as will do no harm, if they are executed with an inflexible rigour, on all occasions, and upon all persons that may come in their way; therefore there is a latitude left to the executive power, to do many things of choice which the laws do not prescribe. (1690/1980, §160)

John Stuart Mill similarly warned that bureaucratic governments usually "perish by the immutability of their maxims," and hilariously, that "a bureaucracy always tends to become a pedantocracy" (1861/1977, 439). When we combine these considerations with legalist values, legalists must resign themselves to accepting whatever discretion can't be eliminated from the system (cf. Goodin 1988, 207). In practice, discretionary governance is the rule, but it is done in a "wink-wink nudge-nudge" fashion (Heath 2020, 18; cf. Goldstein 1963, 143). Since full enforcement is impossible, but discretion is objectionable, police must exercise their power in a way that is faithful to the legislature.

Philosopher Joseph Raz, acknowledging that discretion cannot be eliminated, advocates a good faith enforcement requirement:

> The discretion of the crime-preventing agencies should not be allowed to pervert the law . . . The police should not be allowed to allocate its resources so as to avoid all effort to prevent and detect certain crimes or prosecute certain classes of criminals. (Raz 1979, 218)

Philosopher Thomas Christiano similarly argues that the division of labor in large societies is necessary and that the police and other executive agencies have a kind of instrumental authority to determine the best ways to satisfy the aims and principles determined by the legislature. As long as "the various subordinate decision-making parts of the state are carrying out their duties in good faith and with reasonable competence," the overall system can be just and legitimate (2010, 257). Economist and philosopher F. A. Hayek likewise acknowledges that some discretion is often unavoidable. It is justified, he thinks, only when the decision is "deducible from the rules of law and from those circumstances to which the law refers and which can be known to the parties concerned" (1960, 322).[6]

Legalism is not authoritarian. It is, rather, rooted in procedural thinking about political legitimacy and political change. Such change should come from the governed, or from political bureaucrats and judges, through the appropriate democratic procedures. Looking to the police to take a more active role in navigating the injustices embedded in social and political systems is, on this view, objectionable. The police are and ought to be, on the legalist view, much more like the *conduit* through which the democratic will flows.[7] I will turn now to a critique of the view.

3.2. Ideal Theoretic Constraints and Real Institutions

Discretion deviates from the legalistic ideal of legislatures fully guiding executive agencies. Because ours is not an ideal world, we must try to approximate the institutions of the ideal world. To approximate most

---

[6] I should emphasize here that Hayek is more hostile to formal legislation than the others I've discussed under the heading of legalism. Hayek's preference for emergent common law over legislation makes him less vulnerable to the objections to legalism I raise.

[7] The strength of these legalistic commitments varies. Raz endorses a (seemingly) weak view in which police are required to spend at least some resources on all of the laws. Locke's views of prerogative are in places surprisingly expansive. He seems to think that uniquely talented "God-like princes" have a legitimate claim to arbitrary power as long as their subjects don't complain, and the power is exercised for good (§§162–166).

closely the ideally just society, police ought only to faithfully enforce the law. Some have argued, along these lines, that *mitigation*, not *exculpation*, is the acceptable response when we think a violation of law does not deserve full punishment. On this view, officers should make an arrest, and lenience (mitigation) should come from the courts rather than from discretionary non-enforcement (exculpation) (cf. LaFave 1965, 68–69). I'll argue that this misapplies constraints of ideal theory to our political institutions.

The problem with this argument is that it fails to take seriously the "problem of second best." It commits the "fallacy of approximation" (Estlund 2020, 272). To see that this is a fallacious inference, consider Estlund's pill example: it would be ideal for you to take all three of your prescribed pills, but this doesn't entail that you should take only two of them if for some reason you can't find the third. It depends on how the pills interact. Closely approximating the ideal course of action (taking two of three pills) doesn't mean you will, in fact, be close to the ideal outcome (health). To be sure, sometimes closely approximating ideal institutions does mean you'll be close to ideal justice. But that's not the case here. The effect of the police, much like the pills in Estlund's example, depends on interactions with other parts of society. Concluding that police discretion is unjust and illegitimate because it would not be part of an ideal world is similarly fallacious.[8]

The non-ideal parts of our world make this application of legalism an error. The view is far too optimistic about the chances of reform coming from legislatures or referenda. Recall that one source of failure in the criminal justice system is the democratic system that produces legislators who create bad laws. Relying on the (broken) system to fix itself might closely approximate the ideal legalist institutional structure, but it doesn't mean it will closely approximate justice.

This point is familiar in the tradition of civil disobedience. Thoreau defended civil disobedience over operating within "the ways of the

---

[8] Still, in some cases, the ideals of ideal theory do apply in our world. The ideal world might be one in which the police treat everyone with dignity according to a theory of liberal personhood. That constrains how police are permitted to respond to the non-ideal parts of the world they focus on as we move along the path toward the ideal (Hunt 2019). An anti-discretion principle, however, is unlike a respect for persons principle. I'll make the stronger case that there is nothing intrinsically objectionable about police discretion.

State" because the latter ways "take too much time" (Thoreau [1849] 2002). Martin Luther King, jr. echoed this sentiment a century later in the *Letter from Birmingham Jail*, justifying civil disobedience by appeal to the legal maxim that justice delayed is justice denied. An ideal world might have no civil disobedience—only political deliberation followed by obedience—but our world is not ideal. Police discretion is not rendered impermissible by its exclusion from the ideal world any more than civil disobedience is. Insisting on this particular ideal theoretic constraint serves only to exacerbate the problem. We should not insist that the problems of policing be solved exclusively with the mechanism that the policing subsystem has helped to break.

Even when there's widespread support for reforming a part of the criminal code, there is no guarantee that it will rank highly enough on the empowered party's agenda that they'll devote time to it. There's only so much legislative bandwidth. Garnering support for reform is only half the battle. The democratic process is slow and characterized by weak half measures. This means that fixes to the criminal justice system that employ only electoral mechanisms are destined, in most cases, to be slow and obtain only partial successes. The criminal code *emerges* from this process. It is not a *designed product* of a deliberative legislature.

3.3. Good Faith Enforcement

The second problem, I'll argue, is that "good faith" underdetermines the acceptable use of political power by the police.[9] To show that, I'll briefly canvass the reasons philosophers, theorists, and police scholars have for thinking that discretion is unavoidable. The primary reasons include legal vagueness, difficulties of oversight, and conflicting priorities.[10] Then I'll argue that these considerations undermine even weak good faith principles.

---

[9] And police, unlike other executive agencies, do not usually have explicit de jure grants of discretionary power from the legislature (Heath 2020, 266).

[10] They apply not just to the police, but to other administrative bureaucrats, and invoke similar normative questions. See Zacka (2017) and Heath (2020).

3.3.1. Legal Vagueness

Because language has an "open texture," judicial discretion is unavoidable (Hart 1961, 124). Not just laws; every set of rules will require interpretation for application (Goodin 1988, 190). One might be tempted to work on the problem by crafting ever more detailed rules for the police. But even the "general orders" manual for a police department, famously hundreds of pages long, does not amount to an actual how-to manual for policing.

Discretion is a necessary feature of patrol work for the same reason it is a necessary feature of deciding cases, but it is compounded by the complexity of regulating the use of space. Such complexity renders formal justice, in which like cases are treated alike, difficult to assess or achieve. The law the patrol officer must apply is in many places frightfully vague. Statutes that prohibit "loitering" or "disorderly conduct" are notorious.[11] Rosa Brooks's first call for service regarded teenage boys hanging out on the sidewalk and "talking shit" to passersby (2021, 7). "Shit talk" is not the sort of thing that admits of enough specificity to codify, but still might warrant an intervention. Someone menacingly panhandling outside of an ATM vestibule is not *exactly* mugging you, but they aren't exactly innocent either.

Or consider laws against gambling. While in spirit intended to prevent organized gambling rings, the complexity of the social world renders the statutes overly broad, making innocuous acts illegal. Flipping a coin to see who picks up the tab, or playing rocks-paper-scissors for a dollar, is illegal according to most gambling statutes (Goldstein 1963, 141). This is so even for the crimes of assault or battery. Typically, assault requires a credible threat, and sometimes unwanted physical contact. More precise categories sometimes include causing harm in the definition of assault. It is easy to imagine cases where an act clearly satisfies the requirements for assault (e.g., a shove

---

[11] So much so that many of them were ruled unconstitutional by the "void for vagueness" doctrine in *Papachristou v. Jacksonville*. But note that it's not just inherently vague statutes that pose a problem. Making them more specific isn't guaranteed to help. The decision didn't eliminate the abuse of loitering laws. Instead, "loitering plus" laws, those that make the statute more specific in some way, replaced the original laws in many jurisdictions.

with open hands that causes minor bruising before a fight is broken up), and yet it would seem inappropriate to always make an arrest for assault.

Therefore, police ethnographies find that officers tend to draw a distinction between the *behavior* and the *violation* (Brown 1988, 187). Flipping a coin to see who buys lunch is a violation of the statute for reasons of vagueness, but the behavior does not justify an arrest. This means that non-legal considerations will sometimes determine how an officer reacts to a situation. It is impossible for an officer's (or a judge's) actions to be fully determined by the text of the criminal law.

Finally, not all of the disputes that require resolving can be resolved (or are worth resolving) in court. For one or both reasons, the police inevitably must take on the task of bringing disputes to a resolution without the law or administrative guidance fully specifying what that looks like.[12] Making the shit-talker or the menacing panhandler leave, or telling the complainers to deal with it, is the resolution. Their decisions cannot be made by others further up the hierarchy or the law; in this way, they are "streetcorner politicians" (Muir 1979, 271).

3.3.2. The Myth of Full Enforcement

Even when there is no indeterminacy, there are often too many rules and only so many enforcement resources (Heath 2020, 269). There are so many rules that no one knows them all, and even after a couple years on the job officers often find themselves consulting with others on how to handle calls for service (Brooks 2021). Making an arrest takes an officer off the streets and makes them unable to respond to calls or detect criminal activity. Simple arrests, like those for loitering in which no evidence needs to be processed, can take an hour. They usually take longer (Moskos 2008, 123). Just as legislators or city council members must account for opportunity costs when determining a police

---

[12] To be clear, this argument applies to the work of the typical patrol officer. There are separate questions about discretion in investigative work, where a detective or federal agent might allow illegal activity to continue (or even partake in it) for the purpose of making a more impactful arrest. This raises important questions of its own (Hunt 2019).

department's budget, and just as administrators need to take them into account when determining how to distribute their resources across police functions, the individual officer must take them into account when determining whether to make an arrest. Thus, in some cases, enforcing even a clear violation of the law is undesirable. Police must decide *whether* to enforce the law and *when* to. This is the third reason that police discretion is necessary.

Patrol officers are, of course, keenly aware of this. Sociologist and former police officer Peter Moskos recounts his time policing drug corners in Baltimore's Eastern District:

> In high-drug areas, there is no shortage of drug offenders to arrest. (. . .) One officer described the scene around an open-air drug market: "[This is an arrest] free-for-all. (. . .) You can pull up to any corner and lock up everybody walking away [or] any white person you see. They're all dirty. (. . .) By the time we got the last, the first would be long out and we could start all over again." The decision to arrest or not arrest those involved in the drug trade becomes more a matter of personal choice and police officer discretion than of any formalized police response toward crime or public safety. (2008, 49)

As an illustrative exercise, it is worth thinking about what a set of rules would need to look like to eliminate officer discretion in the policing of an early 2000s East Baltimore open-air drug market. This highlights an important point: decisions not to enforce the law in a particular instance are typically decisions not to disregard the law, but rather to enforce the law differently, to solve some other problem.[13]

Even if full enforcement were practically possible, it is often unjust. Traffic enforcement is a useful example in part because traffic regulations are not usually regarded as unjust. They attempt to *fully specify* the scope of permissible behavior while driving. But the traffic code ends up being enormous, and typically harmless behaviors that

---

[13] Policing is so extensively characterized by discretionary non-enforcement that attempts to eliminate it have a name. *Zero tolerance* police strategies are one attempt to eliminate police discretion. They rely on saturating an area, typically a "hot-spot," with patrol officers who then attempt to make an arrest for every violation of the relevant laws.

need not be deterred end up illegal because in some cases we will want the behavior prohibited. To prevent speeding, we need some limit. But barely breaking the limit is, though technically a violation, not objectionable behavior. For this reason, traffic laws are a powerful tool for pretextual stops and instrumental law enforcement. If an officer wants to stop and search someone, all they need to do is wait for them to begin driving a car. They will almost certainly violate some traffic law. In this way, a large enough collection of (individually and in principle) just laws can, when taken together, amount to an unjust legal code *if maximally enforced.*

3.3.3. The Enforcement Dilemma

Deliberately vague public order statutes represent one extreme, and the highly specific traffic code represents another. This contrast produces a dilemma for views, like the legalistic one, that consider police discretion to be inherently unjust or illegitimate. Either allow (some) laws to remain indeterminate or make them highly specific. If they are indeterminate, they'll require interpretative discretion to determine *whether* the law has been violated. If they're highly specific, they'll require priority discretion to determine *when* the violation of a law would be justly enforced. In other words, we are always choosing between *interpretive* discretion and *priority* discretion, no matter where we are on the spectrum.[14]

Vague statutes like those prohibiting loitering or disorderly conduct require officers to determine whether some behavior meets their interpretation of whatever is prohibited by a loitering ordinance. Specific statutes like those prohibiting speeding require officers to determine whether some behavior is such that the statute is worth invoking or should be ignored. Reducing one kind of discretion means increasing the other (Thacher 2014, 139–140).

[14] Goodin (1988, 209) argues that the concerns one might raise about discretion are similarly in tension. For example, we can eliminate the unpredictability associated with discretion only by removing executive discretion by remaking the rules to be more specific, but that will also have the effect of increasing unpredictability (by making the procedure harder to understand).

That police must exercise broad discretion, and that law enforcement is but one police tool among many, is part of a "realist" understanding of the police and the "common wisdom" of policing (Goldstein 1990, 9, 11). Policing textbooks describe the view that the law is or can be fully enforced as nothing more than a myth (Berg 1999, 262). Once we see non-discretionary policing as a myth, we are better positioned to engage in more sophisticated normative thinking about policing.

3.3.4. From the Myth of Full Enforcement to the Myth of Good Faith Enforcement

Another important reason that executive discretion is unavoidable is that delegating enforcement activities down the chain of command in the executive branch of governments creates management problems (Heath 2020, 272). This is true both for the political management of the agency and the professional management of officers. These management problems amount to "breaks" in the transmission of legitimacy down the hierarchy because they introduce significant decision points that are not controlled by higher points in the hierarchy.[15] The result is that administrative oversight and the criminal code leave the actions of police officers surprisingly underdetermined, and this renders the "good faith enforcement" requirement underpowered.

Take the first gap between the police and the legislature. Police agencies must make decisions about how to allocate resources, and those decisions partly determine how policing manifests. Philosophers who worry about police usurping the legislative role are likely to find these decisions fraught. Recall that Raz's good faith enforcement requirement insists only that enforcement decisions do not "pervert" the law and do not entirely ignore a class of crimes. This might seem to give the legislature control over police agency. But in practice, keeping enforcement levels above zero would satisfy Raz's requirement without

---

[15] This problem applies mostly to patrol. Because criminal investigation goes through the courts (unlike patrol work), the decisions of prosecutors and judges more easily constrain detectives.

significantly constraining the agency's ability to make politically significant decisions.

For example, by allocating resources to the patrol division and tasking it with responding to calls for service, random patrol, and traffic enforcement, an agency devotes resources to much of the criminal code. But with scarce resources, only a small portion of the crimes will be deterred or detected. Having a general violent offenders unit versus having a specialized domestic violence unit, or having patrol officers serve drug warrants versus having a SWAT unit, both satisfy Raz's requirement but produce significantly different policing. Agency structures matter as much for policing as the criminal code, and police departments have a lot of control over agency structure.[16]

Additionally, the agency will need to settle on *strategies*, not just resource allocations and agency structure. The motivating problem here is that funneling people into the criminal justice system can be an act of injustice by kicking off a chain of events that can result in system failure. Different strategies, such as deploying a task force, or additional patrol units, to one part of town and not another, widen the filter there and narrow it elsewhere. It is hard to take legislative control over this, and democratic control over the executive doesn't reduce the scope of police decision-making as much as we might hope.

The adoption of quality of life, or broken windows, policing in the 1980s and 90s serves as a dramatic example. While police were devoting lots of attention to "hard" crime such as violence and property crime, they were devoting comparatively little attention to "soft" crime such as loitering, illegal parking, and so on. The broken windows theory enabled police to devote attention to soft crime without, in their view, giving up on policing hard crime (Thacher 2001, 776–779; Kelling and Wilson 1982). The key point, for our purposes, is that drastic changes in the criminal code are not the primary driver of the spread of broken windows strategies.[17] That a relatively constant

---

[16] Bratton and Knobler (2009, 229) describe making major agency changes upon coming to the New York Police Department (NYPD), including eliminating an entire level of hierarchy (the division, sitting between the borough and precinct levels).

[17] The development of broken windows policing followed a judicial crackdown, during the civil rights era, on racist, discretionary enforcement of misdemeanor laws (Meares and Kahan 1998). The shift to prioritizing quality of life enforcement happened *despite* attempts by the judiciary to constrain and reduce misdemeanor enforcement.

criminal code is compatible with such widely divergent kinds of policing shows that authorizing the code is not the same as authorizing its manifestation.

Rudolph Giuliani famously focused on the aggressive "squeegee men" who "washed" your windshield at intersections for compensation during his first New York City mayoral campaign. His newly appointed commissioner, Bratton, was ordered to eliminate the problematic behavior. He changed the department's response from issuing summonses (that were mostly ignored) to threatening arrest under a traffic statute. In practice, even where a policing initiative is at the forefront of political discourse, these fine-grained decisions are mostly left to the police.[18]

A second gap is present between the administration point in the hierarchy and the officers deciding to invoke the criminal code on the street. There are significant limits to the kind of control under which the patrol officer can be placed (Brown 1988; Wilson 1978, 227). Suppose the administrator (and even the voter) knows what they want the patrol officer to do; the complexity of the situation means that creating a how-to manual is impossible. Each situation is different, and there will be competing values at play. Psychiatrists, notes Wilson, don't use how-to manuals, and they typically have the luxury of decision-making without time constraints (1978, 65). If there is no fully specific how-to manual, administrators cannot use it to evaluate how an officer has spent their shift.

Possibly the most infamous policing strategy is the stop-and-frisk strategy in early 2000s New York City. Officers were instructed to increase their use of Terry stops in certain areas (Weisburd et al. 2014). Even in this case, where officers are issued a command rather than a prohibition, the instruction to make more Terry stops massively underdetermines which legally permissible stops will be made.

---

[18] See Bratton and Knobler (2009, 210) for a discussion of how this order came down to him from the mayor's staff. Noteworthy for our purposes: Bratton refused to let the mayor's office micromanage the department on grounds of professional expertise despite obeying the order. The upshot is "you must eliminate the squeegee problem" is very different from "you must adopt a strategy of threatening and making (pretextual) arrests."

Strategies—and their distributional effects—are not given by the criminal code or elected officials.

Political scientists Wesley Skogan and Susan Harnett note in their examination of community policing reforms in 1990s Chicago that "policing is one of the few organizations of the industrial age in which discretion increases as one goes down the formal hierarchy" (1997, 95). This, says David Bayley, makes policing "paradoxical." Whereas in most areas, discretion tracks one's place in the agency's hierarchy, and with it one's training, experience, compensation, and prestige, this is not the case in policing. The officer's rank and discretion, rather, are inversely related. The options for administrative oversight are limited. Thus, administrative oversight of patrol officers ends up looking like a "quota." Even if departments deny that they have quotas, there are known productivity expectations of how much officers are expected to stop and frisk, ticket, arrest, and so on (Moskos 2008, 152; Bayley 1996, 48).

To this point, one of the innovations in policing in the 1990s was New York City's CompStat, a program developed by Bratton, his colleague Jack Maple, and others in the late 1980s (Bratton and Knobler 2009, 99, 233). By 2006, over half of large U.S. police departments adopted CompStat or a program like it (Willis et al. 2010). The program collects data on crimes, their time, and location; senior administrators then use that information to evaluate the district commanders' strategies for dealing with the crime. This pushes discretion about police strategy down the agency hierarchy to district commanders rather than the police chief—it turns "precincts into mini–police departments"—and it clarifies administrative expectations (Bratton and Knobler 2009, 230; Weisburd et al. 2006).

Notice that even this technological innovation leaves serious strategic decision-making up to midlevel administrators, rather than the police chief who is directly appointed by an elected official. This deliberately separates (by empowering the precinct commanders) the legalistic source of legitimacy from the site of decision-making. Modern police agencies thus have "gaps" in the transmission of legitimacy between legislation and administration, and between administration and the officers tasked with carrying out the city or precinct-wide strategic focus.

The good faith requirement is ultimately concerned with maintaining the intent of the legislature: police can't ignore a class of crimes because doing so perverts the law. I've argued that even the spirit or intent of legislation does not determinately constrain policing. But is there a clear way for officers or police administrators to know what the intent of the legislature is in the first place? The overwhelming majority of laws that police enforce were not passed by the most recent legislature. The criminal code is a result of iterative changes over centuries. There's no way of knowing how the legislature prioritizes various statutes. And asking for a full and consistent priority ranking is probably impossible even if we could achieve more managerial control over enforcement strategies and decisions.

Because full enforcement is impossible, legalists opt for a good faith enforcement requirement. Unfortunately, these gaps in transmission and lack of clarity about legislative intent mean that widely divergent kinds of policing can be in good faith. If the answer to "When is policing just and legitimate?" is "When it is faithful to the legislature," we haven't given much of an answer.

3.4. Concerns about Discretion, Revisited

Before we get to my account, I want to revisit the legalistic concerns about police discretion having now offered a basic critique of the view's good faith requirement.[19] Is the situation a tragic one in which we have good reason to endorse the values but no hope of realizing them? I don't think so.

3.4.1. Taking the Military Analogy Seriously

Recall that legalism is motivated by the view that state agents need to leave decision-making power up to the democracy (via the legislature), and that is incompatible or in tension with executive discretion. The

---

[19] I make several of these arguments in more detail in Monaghan (2018; 2022).

military analogy is useful in this respect, because soldiers are often in a position where they are asked to do things of questionable justice by a rather far removed legislature or commanding officer, and yet obedience looks particularly important in these contexts. The justification for following unjust orders in war might extend to enforcing unjust laws in domestic contexts. If police officers have special permissions and obligations to do what would otherwise be unjust, and if they have good reason to avoid relying on their own decision-making, then my case for police discretion as crucial for just policing is undermined.

One argument along these lines appeals to the value of patriotism and related duties of partiality. Another argument appeals to the weak epistemic positions soldiers are in. Michael Walzer has argued that partiality grounded in patriotism and co-nationalism override competing values that would prohibit soldiers from following orders in an unjust war. According to Walzer, we should "draw a line between the war itself, for which soldiers are not responsible, and the conduct of the war, for which they are responsible" (2006, 38). On this view, soldiers have no special permission to employ unjust tactics, but they do have a special permission to aggress against innocent people if ordered into a war without just cause. Analogously, we might draw a line between the criminal code itself and the conduct involved in enforcing it, only the latter of which are police responsible for. So police may enforce an unjust law against pants-sagging, but they may not fire their service weapon to enforce it.[20] The epistemic argument holds that soldiers (and other agents of the state) are required to defer to their commanding officers because they are not in a position to know better (Vitoria 1991). In the context of policing, this would have to be translated to include not just orders from supervisors but "orders" from the criminal code as well.

This first argument faces two problems. One is that *patriotic* partiality is dubious. There may be strong moral reasons grounded in partiality, like those that permit parents to devote extra resources to their own children. But the relationship of co-nationals hardly reaches this

---

[20] Shreveport, Louisiana had a law against sagging pants from 2007 until 2019; 699 black men and 12 white men were arrested for violating the law in that time (MacNeil 2019).

level of moral significance. Patriotic partiality cannot bear the weight that an argument like this requires of it. The more serious problem is that, while in contexts of war soldiers are exercising political power over those to whom they lack any relationship of partiality, police officers typically exercise power over co-nationals. So any permission the values of patriotism might create for a soldier in contexts of asymmetric partiality are going to be nullified by the fact that police will also be constrained by partiality in their professional interactions.

The epistemic argument faces the problem that soldiers are clearly on the hook for assessing the justice and legitimacy of their orders. Soldiers, like police officers, are not incompetent moral reasoners, and so they are not permitted to simply defer to commanding officers or legislators in all cases, even supposing that were possible. Notice also that *other* governments make different decisions. In the context of decisions to go to war, that other, high-quality democracies decline to enter a war weakens the *epistemic* force of one's own government's decision (Tadros 2020). If the decision of one's government is to count as evidence, the decisions of other, reasonably high-quality governments will, too. That the political process in Idaho has produced laws allowing the "Idaho stop" in which cyclists may treat stop signs as yield signs is a reason for officers elsewhere to overlook Idaho stops in their jurisdiction.

Soldiers and police officers alike must engage in moral reasoning and thoughtfully mediate political decisions. If the mere fact that a political decision was made doesn't settle the issue of whether they are permitted to enforce it, then there is normative room for discretion.

3.4.2. Government by Laws and Not People

Police discretion clearly looks to be government by people, and so in violation of the rule of law. The rule of law, however, must not make impossible demands (Endicott 1999). We've seen that legalists attempt to weaken the demands of the view, in the form of the good faith requirement, so that they're not impossible. But police discretion is philosophically significant in part because the police agency's generalist character means priority discretion is unavoidable and produces extensive non-enforcement. Can priority, as well as interpretative, discretion be compatible with the rule of law?

Yes. Discretionary policing does not amount to a free-for-all. Just as legal precedent serves as a tool for guiding behavior in line with the rule of law for judges, *clear patterns of enforcement* can play a similar role for the police. Crucially, given the infinite uses of public space, expectations about how space may be used cannot come primarily from open textured law. That *real* law is never found on the books but rather in enforcement practices that create patterns and expectations reflects a fact about law rather than a problem with realized law enforcement.

Emergent patterns of enforcement are familiar. Traffic officers rarely give speeding tickets for slightly exceeding the limit or for many traffic offenses, no doubt motivated by the injustice of fully enforcing traffic laws. Another example of bottom-up "law" gleaned from clear patterns of enforcement can be found in the subway system of 1980s Manhattan. There, Transit Police officers worked out an informal agreement with unhoused men: they were permitted to sleep on the subway if they all slept in one subway car (Duneier 1999, 126). This left most of the cars on a train available for the intended and majority use of that public space, while also allowing them to avoid sleeping outside or in shelters. The threat to the rule of law comes not from this kind of clear pattern of non-enforcement, but rather from unexpectedly stringent enforcement as a tool for pretextual stop strategies or from bias in decisions to be lenient.

Law professor India Thusi's research on policing sex work in South Africa, where the complicated and ambivalent attitude toward sex work criminalization has resulted in de facto decriminalization, shows how police forces sometimes must take it upon themselves to create patterns of enforcement but also how those patterns emerge from the non-coordinated decisions of police administrators (2022, 71).[21] The patterns aren't approved by any legislative agency, but they are apparent to customers, police, and ethnographers alike. Different neighborhoods in Johannesburg have different kinds of sex markets;

---

[21] Sex work is illegal, but police are also expected to respond to sex worker complaints about human rights violations from clients. The criminal code offers little guidance in resolving this tension.

some are visible and street-based, others street-based but more discrete, and still others brothel-like establishments only. Clear patterns of police discretion render it compatible with the predictability element of the rule of law.

In other cases, departments announce their enforcement strategies, satisfying the publicity requirement in the same way that publicizing trial outcomes does. The Burlington, Vermont, police department, in conjunction with the state's attorney, announced in 2018 that they would stop arresting and prosecuting misdemeanor possession of unprescribed buprenorphine (del Pozo et al. 2020). The New Orleans Police Department, ahead of the entirely novel situation of a COVID-19 locked-down Mardi Gras in 2021, announced their enforcement strategy ahead of time (absolutely no one allowed walking on Bourbon Street!).

Good faith enforcement requirements have to allow for priority discretion, but I've argued that priorities aren't forthcoming from the legislature or criminal code. Just because we can read priorities off clear patterns of enforcement doesn't mean those patterns are justified. We need, then, a way to determine whether police power is arbitrary or discriminatory. How can we tell? Raz offers the following:

> an act which is the exercise of power is arbitrary only if it was done either with indifference as to whether it will serve the purposes which alone can justify use of that power or with belief that it will not serve them. (Raz 1979, 219)

This is useful, though notice that much of police discretion would not be deemed arbitrary on this view, *even if* it doesn't satisfy the good faith requirement discussed at the outset. Determinations of arbitrariness are made on the basis of the *justification* of political power, not the content of law. The decision not to make a traffic stop for speeding 1 mile per hour over the limit is not done with indifference to what justifies political power over traffic. Nor is it typically done with the belief that it will thwart the purposes of political power over traffic. The decision not to arrest two diners for gambling their tab on a coin flip comes from recognizing that whatever justifies political power doesn't justify intervening in that kind of behavior. As we'll see throughout the next several chapters, much discretionary police power is not rendered arbitrary on this understanding, because much of it is in service of an officer's sense of how to best do their many jobs.

Of course, police discretion can be (and often is) inconsistent with the rule of law. When old vagrancy laws, or more recently disorderly conduct or loitering laws, were selectively enforced to preserve oppressive, racist social hierarchies, it was clearly inconsistent with the rule of law. In our pants-sagging example, the decision not to enforce the law is a decision not to exercise political power. In this respect, concerns about the rule of law don't *directly* arise. They arise only insofar as they set up the conditions for violating the rule of law by later enforcing it in a way that upsets communicated policy or clear patterns of enforcement. This happened in 2013 in one South African neighborhood where a period of several months of non-enforcement of sex work laws was upset by officers seeking bribes by arresting clients of sex workers (Thusi 2022, 107). But here the objection is not exactly against the non-enforcement, but against the later enforcement.

3.5. A Proceduralist Argument for Discretionary Non-enforcement

Before concluding, I want to show that the fallibilism and procedural deference underlying the resignation theory of police discretion can be marshaled in support of a strategic model (as opposed to a conduit model) of just and legitimate policing. According to the *instrumental proceduralist* argument, political agents, like jailers, executioners, soldiers, or cops, must defer to the outcomes of the procedure so long as the procedure is an appropriate one. The procedure is appropriate if it is sufficiently reliable (hence the *instrumental* nature of the proceduralism) and if it meets certain non-instrumental criteria. Relevant procedures include elections, lawmaking procedures, jury trials, referenda, and so on.

For a procedure to transmit legitimacy to its outputs, it must satisfy several appropriateness conditions in addition to the reliability requirement. The procedure must be publicly justifiable in the sense that there is publicly available evidence of its reliability that reasonable people must be able to recognize (Estlund 2009, 41). Additionally, the output must be in principle justifiable. Capital punishment may be in principle justifiable, but death by deep-frying is not; a criminal trial that produced such a verdict would not be legitimate even if it met the other requirements (Estlund 2007, 229).

This case against discretion is appealing because of its modesty. Whereas the epistemic and patriotic partiality arguments rule out discretion at the cost of justifying far too much, the proceduralist argument justifies enforcing unjust or mistaken political decisions only when the procedure meets normative criteria, rendering the unjust outcome an *honest mistake*.[22] Thus, according to this argument, police must enforce even unjust political decisions if they're produced by appropriate political procedures so as to not substitute one's personal judgment for the public judgment.

Now, to be clear, this is not a direct argument against discretion in the administration of law. The argument is supposed to amount to a justification, a requirement, for following certain mistaken, unjust orders (or enforcing unjust political decisions), not that police administrators or individual officers should have no discretion in deploying resources. But the argument naturally lends itself to the legalist, resignation theory of discretion and the related conduit model of policing. Justification of political power comes from our legislative and criminal procedures, not police decisions.

The argument appears to rule out "corrective" reasons for exercising discretion in particular. Consider again a police chief, such as the one from Burlington cited above who takes "correcting an error" of the criminal law as one reason for discretionary non-enforcement (del Pozo et al. 2020, 373). The proceduralist argument would appear to rule out this kind of justification. Even if the view doesn't rule out priority discretion in principle, it does appear to rule out in principle justifications of non-enforcement on the basis of police judgments that some activity would be unjust.

Proceduralism, however, can justify discretionary non-enforcement. The justification requires the premise, established in the last chapter,

---

[22] The term "honest mistake" comes from Estlund (2007, 221), but many political philosophers endorse a view like this.

that police agencies and their decisions are *part of* our criminal legal, political, and social systems. It also requires slightly more demanding legitimacy (or appropriateness) criteria for procedures, ones that proceduralists have independent reasons to adopt. We should modify one of the appropriateness requirements and add two. The one to modify is the reliability requirement. Proceduralists should also add a requirement concerning the distribution of procedural failures, and another concerning *predictable* failures.

One way of understanding "reliability" is rather permissive: "better than random" (Estlund 2009, 116). In some cases, this might be sufficient. We might, for example, accept a radar gun used in traffic enforcement that is accurate merely most of the time if officers usually give a verbal warning and not a traffic ticket. The burden is low enough here that we might reasonably require motorists to stop in such situations. On the other hand, if one will be arrested and funneled into the misdemeanor system, a field drug test that fails a third of the time is probably illegitimate in light of the burden associated with that kind of political power.[23] This is doubly so because even if the case goes to trial, the field drug test will likely go unchallenged and end up as decisive evidence at trial. We should understand the reliability requirement to track the gravity of the political power the procedure legitimates.

Indexing reliability requirements to the nature of the situation is common outside of politics as well. Meteorologists consult multiple hurricane models in making a forecast and before issuing guidance in light of the gravity of evacuating a city. Surgeons follow demanding procedures to ensure that they're cutting open the right part of a patient's body and removing or repairing the correct organ. In these cases, what counts as *negligence* versus an *honest mistake* depends on the importance of getting the right result. In criminal legal contexts, then, the reliability requirement will often be more demanding than better than random.

We typically also concern ourselves with the distribution of failures, not just the rate. This is familiar in the criminal trial system. The evidentiary and burden of proof rules are set in such a way to select for

---

[23] It should not be surprising at this point that field drug tests have a high failure rate (cf. Gabrielson and Sanders 2016).

false findings of innocence rather than false findings of guilt. It is harder to justify wrongful political coercion than a wrongful absence of political coercion. Such reasoning easily applies to other aspects of the criminal legal system and goes beyond the false-positive/false-negative issue. Distributional concerns should extend to demographics as well. If one politically relevant group bears the burden of most of the political system's failures, they would reasonably reject the procedure. Even if field drug tests are highly reliable, for instance, but their small number of failures falls overwhelmingly on one group in society, there are proceduralist grounds to reject the legitimacy of the outcome. As we saw in the context of mandatory arrest policies, procedures can fail disproportionately for a variety of politically relevant groups.

Lastly, procedures do not confer legitimacy on their outputs in circumstances of known failure. That is, when the procedure can be predicted to fail, predictable failures are not honest mistakes. Consider hurricane models again. There are a variety of models (epistemic procedures) to predict the strength and path of a hurricane. Certain models perform better in certain circumstances than others. Global models are best suited to predict a storm's interaction with atmospheric conditions, and thus best suited for predicting a storm's track. They are less useful for predicting the structure of a storm, and thus its intensity. Using only a global model to predict a storm's intensity, then, is to use a procedure in circumstances of known failure. The output, if it fails, would be a predictable failure. It would thus not confer justification on its output (in this case a belief about the intensity of the storm).

Analogously, the necessarily crude nature of the criminal code renders its enforcement in certain cases predictable failures. Political demonstrations, especially spontaneous ones, typically violate loitering or public disorder laws. Those laws are not supposed to prohibit political participation, however, and so their enforcement would be a predictable failure. Similarly, if an officer knows that judges in her jurisdiction typically set high levels of bail, arresting an indigent person and confiscating their bike for riding at night without a light would predictably result in unjustly severe punishment, and would be a predictable failure (cf. Moskos 2008, 140). In these cases, the procedure does not meet legitimacy requirements and thus fails to legitimize its output.

We've seen that the misdemeanor system is characterized by widespread procedural failure. The system is not clearly better than random, its failures fall disproportionally on the poor and marginalized communities, and it does so for predictable reasons. These are not honest mistakes. Once we include the decision to make an arrest in this system, it is difficult to understand why instrumental proceduralist arguments would imply that police must make arrests even when doing so would be substantively unjust.

In sum, if the enforcement of an unjust law, or a just law that will be enforced in an unjust manner, is legitimate, then it will be the result of (1) a highly reliable procedure which (2) distributes its failures in a relatively uniform way and that (3) has not failed predictably. Realized political procedures can fail. And if they fail in certain ways, they don't count as reliable in the way the proceduralists require for justification. The motivation laid out earlier for taking discretionary non-enforcement seriously as a tool for increasing justice is precisely that it is a response to procedural (or systemic) failure. Further, as we saw above, police discretion is often a crucial element of securing just criminal legal outcomes. Proceduralism, properly qualified, serves as a justification for discretionary non-enforcement.

3.6. In Search of Legitimacy

To briefly recap, the problem with the resignation theory of discretion and conduit model of police legitimacy is that it fits poorly with certain features of realized social institutions. The complexity of the social world and the vagueness of any system of rules to govern it, as well as the unavoidable resource scarcity and opportunity costs of policing, render full enforcement impossible and undesirable. The dilemma between vague and highly specified systems of rules, where we trade off on interpretation and priority discretion, means that police cannot be a conduit for democratic decisions. Further, good faith enforcement requirements seriously underdetermine how police agencies and agents exercise their power. Surprisingly, the criminal code looks ill-suited for legitimizing police power. Indeed, the scary interpretation of these conclusions is that law enforcement agencies are simply an uncontrollable, and so unjustifiable, government agency. The legalist model of policing leaves us with a need for a theory of just and legitimate policing.

Philosopher and former Federal Bureau of Investigation (FBI) agent Luke William Hunt has developed a more complete and determinate account of when police officers may exercise discretion in the context of "otherwise illegal activity," such as when an FBI agent breaks the law or instructs an informant to break the law during a criminal investigation. The view has four requirements for legitimate discretion. First, the *purpose* constraint: the power must be wielded for the public good of security. Second, the *prudential* constraint: there must be no viable legislative solution to the problem. Third, the *personhood* constraint: the power must not violate deontic constraints attached to liberal personhood. And fourth, the *emergency* constraint: the power must be necessary to avert an acute threat of harm (Hunt 2019, 197).

The prudential and personhood constraints are worth focusing on. One way of putting a conclusion of this chapter is that the prudential constraint is much easier to satisfy than one might think. There is no viable legislative solution to many of the problems that give rise to police discretion. In light of this fact, the emergency constraint is too demanding. It is an entirely ordinary feature of policing that police discretion will be required to justly respond to some problem. I must emphasize that Hunt is concerned with justifying extremely risky otherwise illegal activity and does not claim that patrol officers are prohibited from exercising discretion except in emergency cases. So this is not a criticism of his view. Rather, I bring it up to serve as a contrast to the ordinary policing context. In that context, we should not view police discretion as an exception requiring justification. We should view it as the norm, and we should take developing principles for police discretion to be a primary task of developing a theory of just and legitimate policing.

As a result, I think we should not resign ourselves to (police) discretion. It is not a de-legitimizing aberration. It is a normal feature of governance that is neither inherently good and just nor inherently bad and unjust. Justice and legitimacy require, instead, a thoughtful application of the rules. If I am right that in certain cases the executive will need to disregard the legislature, a theory of just policing will need to be more permissive than the good faith enforcement requirement allows. And if I am right that this is an ordinary feature of policing, the theory must also be more permissive than allowing departures from the legislature only in emergency situations. But it must also be more demanding than the good faith enforcement requirement in that it must offer principles of justice beyond "don't pervert legislative intent."

Still, should police officers really decide which laws are just and only enforce those? Surely, that's an unattractive position. Maybe police discretion is unavoidable, but why would we give them *that* much discretion? Declining to enforce a procedurally legitimate political decision is offensive to democratic sensibilities. When politically conservative sheriffs, for example, decline to enforce newly passed gun control legislation, this strikes most as objectionable (Kaste 2019). It also presses a particular kind of concern: Should the police really be taking sides in contentious political disputes?

At this point, I've argued only that discretionary non-enforcement is permissible in principle and at least occasionally. This changes the dispute from one about whether discretionary non-enforcement is an acceptable tool for combatting criminal injustice into one about what just discretionary non-enforcement looks like. With that established, we can turn to the more pressing issue of what sorts of considerations ought to guide individual officers and administrators.

4

Legitimacy Risks and the Separation of Police Powers

Justice requires police discretion with an eye toward ameliorating the many injustices of the criminal system while responding to the problems that demand some kind of social control. So we need an account of just police discretion. Yet, even if well-exercised discretion is necessary for just policing, people will still tend to meet the expectations of their role. Not only will people typically be unwilling to go outside the confines of their role—it is often psychologically and otherwise personally demanding—roles exist for good reasons.

Part of what makes policing a moral morass is the lack of clarity over the policing role. The tensions between deterrence and detection, and law enforcement and order maintenance, have long been part of policing. The questions unanswered by the criminal code also leave the police role underspecified. Are—or should—the police be warriors fighting crime or guardians protecting the vulnerable? Vigilante-like sheepdogs or social workers with tactical hardening? Ordinary members of the local community or professional agents of the state enforcing the democratic will?

To make progress on the question of the police role and its relationship to just policing, I'll briefly sketch an argument for the importance of using rules and defined roles to organize our social lives. Then I'll make the case for a separation of executive powers that is more fine-grained than the Montesquieuian legislative, executive, and judiciary taxonomy. This is in service of the main goal of the chapter, to offer a framework for understanding the risks to just and legitimate policing.[1]

---

[1] As a reminder, I use the term "legitimate" to refer to permissible (but not necessarily perfectly just) power. On this usage, legitimacy is a precondition for justice.

Just Policing. Jake Monaghan, Oxford University Press. © Oxford University Press 2023.
DOI: 10.1093/oso/9780197610725.003.0004

Understanding the various risks and how they interact motivates conceptual and institutional boundaries for police power.

4.1. Roles and Rules

The adversarial trial is an easy example of the significance of roles and the normative division of labor. To oversimplify for illustration, by aiming to win—rather than aiming directly for accuracy and thus justice—prosecutors and defense attorneys are part of a system better able to secure those goals. No one would deny that the criminal trial ought to aim at justice. But that is in principle consistent with the individuals occupying particular roles within the system aiming at something other than justice.

Examples abound. Philosopher David Schmidtz has argued, with reference to a tongue-in-cheek example of drivers comparing who deserves to get to their destination first in determining who may proceed first, that whatever role we think desert plays in justifying the distribution of resources and opportunities, it can't be as simple as all of us aiming to act according to desert in our individual interactions (Schmidtz 2006, 31). It would be good for our traffic infrastructure to allow people to satisfy their transit goals as efficiently as possible. Some destinations are more important than others, so we'll want to be sensitive to that in our determinations of efficiency. But if we all aim directly at that goal by stopping and deliberating, none of us will satisfy it. We are also unlikely to get things exactly right. The costs associated with everyone aiming directly at justice in the criminal trial, or desert in the distribution of resources, are prohibitive. We're much better off setting up a system of (inevitably imperfect) rules that allow for predictability and to let people live their lives within the system.

So we've got two kinds of considerations pulling in opposite directions. On the one hand, rule-based systems with defined roles are often necessary to overcome our inability to directly aim at (and hit) whatever our target is. On the other hand, I've argued that this is not a decisive case against police discretion. We want to avoid government by what Mill called a "pedantocracy." In an ideal world, dutifully satisfying all and only the formal requirements of your role might produce justice. But, in our world, the pedantocrat strikes fear deep into the hearts of sensible people. Considerations about the virtues of rule- and role-based systems don't prohibit discretion in the occupation of those roles. But they do suggest that we need to attend to how agency structure determines the roles within the agency, and how those roles shape the professional behavior of their occupants.

One way to think of the arguments so far is that police should take seriously the separation of political powers. Montesquieu thought that it was important for nobility to say no to the king's dishonorable orders (Levy 2021, 8). A badly erring legislature can be checked by an executive that refuses to enforce the laws that they pass. Similarly, the jury is a crucial part of the criminal trial because it injects the say of the governed into an additional part of the political procedure that leads to punishment. If the jury so chooses, they are permitted to undercut the decisions of the legislature, the police, *and* the prosecutor (Barkow 2006, 1015).[2] But we need more than just veto points.

Separations of power are, in part, tools for reducing the risks of coupling to justice and legitimacy in political systems to avoid system accidents. This chapter goes a step further in this direction. Not only ought we to take seriously the police role in the separation of powers, but we ought to take seriously the need for more fine-grained separations of power. One of the reasons to separate power, institutionally, is to decentralize it and make it more difficult to wield. Another reason is to isolate particular kinds of risks to justice and legitimacy that arise in exercising power.

4.2. Executive Powers

Before Montesquieu, Locke defended a different separation of power. Instead of distinguishing judicial from legislative and executive power, Locke distinguished the *federative* power: the outward-facing power to manage foreign relations and provide national security. The executive

---

[2] It is worth contrasting this way of thinking with the legalist approach to the separation of powers which takes these kinds of departures from the legislature to be objectionable if not outright illegitimate.

power is the inward-facing power of enforcing domestic decisions. Locke insisted these are distinct powers, but they are to be placed in the same institution. He thought "it is almost impracticable to place the force of the common-wealth in distinct, and not subordinate hands," and that having the "force of the public under different commands" would lead to conflict (1690/1980, §148). I'll rely on this insight, that not only the goal of some political power, but also facts about its implementation, inform separations of power.

It has turned out not only to be practicable to place military and domestic law enforcement power in distinct hands but also valuable. Contemporary policing is partly a result of urbanization and the inability of growing cities to effectively police with a combination of volunteer watches, vigilantism, and private investigators. But police departments were not the only possible alternatives. Recognizably modern policing, and much of the United States' early political history, is a reaction to another: using the military for domestic policing.

Domestic policing by soldiers influenced the formation of the United States. Though cities like Boston and New York created night patrols in the 1600s, British soldiers were increasingly used for policing, and with general warrants were permitted to enter colonists' homes and seize property basically at their whim. While actual quartering was rare, violent disputes between citizens and soldiers were commonplace (Balko 2013, 13–14). Eventually, the U.S. Bill of Rights prohibited these practices. Americans were once skeptical of standing armies, and domestic law enforcement by soldiers was especially controversial. Consequently, early opposition to professional police focused, in part, on the military-like uniform. Some critics took uniformed police to amount to a standing army (Monkkonen 1981, 41, 45).

The professionalization of London's watch groups followed Peel's creation of a permanent police force in Ireland, which also involved a similar opposition to policing by the military.[3] The first Peelian principle commits the London Metropolitan Police to obviating the need for policing by soldiers: "To prevent crime and disorder, as an

---

[3] Though Peel's motivations weren't exactly benevolent (Monkkonen 1981, 43).

alternative to their repression by military force and severity of legal punishment."

While skepticism toward standing armies in the United States eventually waned, the United States' relationship to policing by soldiers has been more complicated. The original skepticism was drawn on to undermine Reconstruction by expelling soldiers from the South. National Guard units have been called upon to quell riots with some regularity—often, as in the 1992 Los Angeles riots, a response to terrible policing. More recently, the Pentagon ordered National Guard helicopters to "buzz" demonstrators in Washington, DC, who were a part of the wave of Black Lives Matter protests in the summer of 2020 (Gibbons-Neff and Schmitt 2020). Buzzing, a show of force tactic used in war zones, involves low-flying planes or helicopters passing over combatants to intimidate and disperse them. Using soldiers for domestic policing has never entirely gone away.

Despite this complicated relationship, opposition to policing by soldiers is well-founded. We don't want soldiers to police citizens because it is likely to result in the exercise of illegitimate power. Militaries are likely to produce illegitimate policing because an institution organized around national defense is not suited to securing peace, order, and enforcing domestic law. The organization's normative constraints are different, as are the organization's needs from its members. The structure of an institution or agency can be as influential on its activity as its explicit goals.[4] In the context of political institutions, that means that structure influences whether it is likely to exercise power legitimately. A legitimate domestic police agency needs to be structured differently.

Beyond the shape of an agency's hierarchy, there's the simpler matter of what we expect from occupants of its roles and what it takes for

---

[4] Other examples illustrate the significance of institutional form and its relationship to the powers associated with a role just as well. It is dangerous for physicians, for example, to skip important steps in a medical procedure; for this reason, we flatten the hierarchy in some respects and explicitly allow individuals further down the professional hierarchy to raise questions or concerns. Hospitals allow nurses to call for ethics consults when they are concerned about a course of treatment. In a similar vein, Peter Pronovost, a physician at Johns Hopkins Hospital, developed a checklist to reduce the occurrence of central line infections, and he convinced the hospital administration to empower nurses to prevent doctors from skipping steps on the checklist. The result was a drastic reduction in the infection rate (Gawande 2010, 38).

them to be proficient. Militaries exercising legitimate power provide national defense and wage wars for the defense of others. If we assume that the political bodies authorizing the use of military power make good decisions by only waging just wars (jus ad bellum), then we can assume that the military will be engaging in defensive, last-resort violence rather than preventive or punitive military action (Frowe 2016, 64, 77, 85). Given this relationship, once the requirements of jus ad bellum are met, the rules governing conduct in war (jus in bello) can be less restrictive than constraints on other kinds of force. The result is that not only may soldiers be trained to be aggressive, lethal fighters, but there are powerful normative reasons for them to be. All things equal, shorter, more decisive (just) wars are to be preferred.

In other words, given the defensive nature of just wars, if going to war is justified, then in most cases a particular side had better win. Ideally, separations of power allow for the just creation of aggressive troops, an important tool for successful defensive military action. But letting those eager for combat decide whether we engage in combat is likely to result in more of it, so we separate the power of decision-making from the aggressive military force.

We also must keep in mind other practical details. Given the practical realities of military force, militaries engage in massive collective action. Only a handful of people have the full military plan in mind. Tactics typically require the soldiers put themselves in danger; the mission objective often takes priority over troop safety. These facts increase the need for a hierarchical institution, reduce the need for individual soldiers to make their own decisions, and increase the moral latitude for acting aggressively and simply following orders. This further motivates the need to separate the decision of whether to go to war from those who make tactical decisions in war.

These same considerations show the need to separate police power from military power. The attitudes and abilities needed to win a war detract from the attitudes and abilities needed to make good decisions about whether to go to war. Similarly, the qualities needed to win a war detract from those needed to respect the various normative constraints on policing. Locke thought the executive and federative powers were distinct in part because the latter is less capable of prior control by the legislature. We should add to the list of considerations that count in favor of recognizing a conceptual and institutional separation of power facts about successfully exercising those powers. Police power is not simply defensive. It is often preventive. It also facilities punishment and, ideally, rehabilitation and restitution. It is used to create a certain kind of society, rather than merely preserve its existence against violent threats. The "targets" of police power are citizens, not combatants. For this reason, Peel thought that the permanent deployment of domestic police was a necessary element in public acceptance, and cooperation, with the police (Monkkonen 1981, 38). But as we now know all too well, a permanently deployed but military-inspired police force will not secure public acceptance or cooperation. Policing has not only different goals, but it has also more stringent legitimacy requirements.

The now-standard separation of power between legislative, executive, and judicial branches does not, then, exhaust justice- and legitimacy-relevant separations of power, institutionally or conceptually. We must separate military from police power because the risks to legitimacy that arise when militaries engage in domestic policing are simply too great.[5] But, I'll argue, we also have good reason to create further separations of executive power. To see why, we'll need to consider the various conceptual and institutional risks to legitimacy involved in policing.

4.3. Legitimacy Risks

The long-standing distinction of the inward-facing executive power between deterrence and detection has been institutionalized in the patrol and investigative divisions. That division is usually thought to track the order maintenance and law enforcement distinction as well. But this separation of power has proven insufficient for various reasons. To better foster and protect legitimacy via institutional form, we need an

---

[5] The exception is the *gendarmerie*, or a military unit with domestic policing responsibilities. In most cases, the gendarmerie and normal combat forces are under the control of the executive in the way Locke had in mind but are still institutionally distinct. Gendarmeries are rarely used for actual military purposes; and when deployed, they are often deployed for humanitarian, not combat, purposes.

account of the risks to legitimacy in a domain. Particular government roles are more likely to be characterized by certain legitimacy risks, or risks that political power is exercised impermissibly. When we assemble them, we have a "legitimacy-risk profile" for a role, and this will help us mitigate risks to legitimacy by separating the high-risk elements.[6]

Legitimacy risk is a useful framework, I think, because it captures some of the uncertainties of policing. There is the risk that certain institutional arrangements or governing strategy will actually produce illegitimate and unjust political power. Governments that lack basic separations of power, and use standing armies to provide domestic policing, are both highly risky in this way. They are likely, but not guaranteed, to produce illegitimate power. It is also useful because if the level of risk is high enough, it can be impermissible to subject people to it, even if we get lucky and the risky outcome does not obtain. In this way, if the legitimacy risk is high enough, an institutional arrangement can become illegitimate just because of the risk levels.

Legitimacy risks also provide an epistemic function. There are some kinds of political power that are illegitimate, but the prevailing or majority opinion does not see it that way. Military conscription, for example, is probably a grave injustice. Most now accept that. But at other times and in other places, most thought that conscription is an acceptable practice. It's possible that I am wrong about the injustice of conscription, just as it was possible at other times that the majority was wrong. Having an independent measure of legitimacy risk provides a tool for thinking about whether our assessment of the legitimacy of an institutional arrangement or governing practice is correct. The risk profile I develop here offers evidence for thinking that aggressive vice enforcement, for example, is likely to be illegitimate on grounds independent of the more common, first-order arguments against vice policing.

I'll focus on four legitimacy risks in the remainder of this chapter. They are the magnitude of the burden associated with policing, the distribution of the burden, the initiation (proactivity or reactivity) of police activity, and finally the activity's level of democratic authorization. This list is far from exhaustive. I selected the risks I focus on here

---

[6] The arguments of this chapter, and the notion of a legitimacy-risk profile, were originally presented in "Boundary Policing" (Monaghan 2020).

for their generality, because they can be assembled into a risk profile, and in part because they are useful in diagnosing some of the institutional ills of contemporary policing (a task I return to in Chapter 8). After outlining them, I'll explore their interactions before concluding. Different laws, as well as police strategies, have different legitimacy-risk profiles, and those profiles are important for understanding where to draw the boundaries of power.

4.3.1. Magnitude of Burden

We've seen the importance of the magnitude of the burdens associated with policing already. The higher the burden associated with police activity, the higher the legitimacy risk. This follows naturally from the view that political power is burdened by justification: the more power involved, the more demanding its justification. We're in the habit of distinguishing the "amount" of force involved in various kinds of punishment and self-defense to determine whether it is justified. A similar notion is useful for evaluating policing.

The night watches that preceded urban police departments in the Northeast often involved low-burden tactics. Watchmen carried lanterns and called the time, providing low-burden deterrence against property crime. This practice has survived in a different form. Today, officers in patrol vehicles will often leave solid blue lights on as they drive around, announcing their presence from a distance.

Other patrol practices are more burdensome. Contemporary examples of high-burden policing can be found in Los Angeles's skid row, where patrol officers "prowl" before interacting with suspects. Officers drive slowly down a block, announcing on their loudspeaker that people should make use of the nearby shelters' rehabilitation programs, and that people who are in skid row to engage in illegal activity will be arrested (Stuart 2016, 101). This typically causes most of the people on the block to disperse. This is, of course, a burden to the people who would prefer to stay where they are. But notably, it is a lower burden than being arrested, or, say, the aggressive stop-and-frisk strategy in 2010s New York City, or other even more burdensome practices.

In the next chapter, I'll argue that a principle of proportionality using considerations of the magnitude of burden is an essential principle of just policing. For now, we'll turn to how we typically compensate for higher burdens of political power by manipulating decision-making procedures to increase barriers to the use of power and to shape its distribution.

4.3.2. Distribution of Burden

We also need to select for certain *distributions* of burden across the innocent and the guilty, as well as other "police-relevant groups" (i.e., subjects of enforcement). This is well exemplified in the criminal trial. Criminal trials are, at least in principle, designed to make conviction difficult in an attempt to make sure that only the deserving experience the burdens of punishment. We should "distribute" the burden only to the guilty. They aim not at accuracy alone, however, since errors are unavoidable, but also to select for certain kinds of errors. We would prefer to erroneously let guilty parties off than erroneously convict and punish innocent parties. False acquittals are unjust, but (because political power is burdened by justification) false convictions are more unjust. We do this by setting high standards of proof, which is just a "mechanism for distributing errors" (Laudan 2006, 68). A standard of proof that distributes errors toward the innocent (false convictions) is *harsh*, and one that distributes errors toward the guilty (false acquittals) is *lenient*. Harshness makes for risky policing.

The commitment to lenience is an old and cross-cultural one, ranging at least from Moses Maimonides in the twelfth century to Voltaire, William Blackstone, and Ben Franklin in the eighteenth century, and into the present day. Disagreement on this principle is typically reserved for the "justice ratio" of false acquittals to false-positive ranges rather than whether some ratio is required. The famous "Blackstone ratio" has it at 10:1; Maimonides put it at 1000:1 and Voltaire at 2:1 (Laudan 2006, 63).

Why think the lenience requirement applies only to the trial and not the policing portion of the criminal legal system? A legalist-friendly line might hold that an acquittal leaves the defendant unscathed, so as long as the arrest satisfies the legal requirements, it is not a mistake (cf. Laudan 2006, 70). So the distribution of errors in the policing stage of the system is of less concern. Yet as the literature on the criminal justice system has decisively shown, an acquittal (or even non-arrest Terry stop) leaves defendants far from unscathed.

In some cases, the (subjectively) justified interactions are errors, such as when an officer effects a Terry stop on the reasonable belief that someone is carrying a weapon, but the suspect turns out not to be. In other cases, there will be (subjectively) justified interactions which are not necessarily errors, but in which the suspect is innocent. For example, when an officer conducts general surveillance from her patrol car, most of those who come under her surveillance are innocent. In some sense, this is an error: an innocent person is subjected to police power. In another sense, it is not an error: the officer is intuitively permitted to exercise power in this way. Plausibly, what makes the difference is the magnitude of the burden associated with the exercise of power. Visually surveilling an innocent person in a crime hot spot is a much lower burden than a system of comprehensive surveillance. So, for the sake of efficiency, we can say that a harsh distribution of political power is one in which there are more false positives than false negatives, while recognizing that the false-positive category is not composed entirely of all-things-considered unjustified political power.

The fallible nature of any human endeavor means that police administrators are making decisions about who will bear not only the burdens of policing but who (generally speaking) will bear the errors of policing. The individual police officer, we hope, only initiates contact with someone if they have reason to believe that doing so is justified. But sometimes they'll make mistakes. The administrator selecting strategies, on the other hand, is explicitly shaping the distribution of unjustified interactions (false positives) and would-be-justified non-interactions (false negatives) with the knowledge that their officers will make (sometimes blameless) mistakes. Harsh policing, like a harsh trial system, is typically illegitimate.[7]

---

[7] A complication: in some cases, it seems as though we pass a threshold at which we want police power to be harsher. Given the choice between searching lots of people at the airport and searching everyone, a commitment to equality and an aversion to profiling

In addition to the distribution of errors in policing across the innocent and the guilty, the distribution of burdens across politically relevant groups is clearly a concern of justice and legitimacy. When one
group bears most of the burden of a policing strategy, the risk that the
strategy is illegitimate is significant. Such enforcement strategies are
more likely to be discriminatory or abusive or represent an empowered
group's control over a marginalized group. Those who think justice
requires societies to protect and enable diverse ways of living should
extend that burden-sharing, neutral approach to policing. Naturally,
this comes into conflict with majoritarian political procedures
(discussed in detail later).

4.3.3. Initiation of Power

The third element of the risk profile concerns the initiation of police power. Police-initiated power we can call proactive, and citizen-
initiated power we can call reactive. This use of terminology is
slightly different from the way it is used in police scholarship. There,
it is common for random patrolling, in which an officer drives around
their beat, to be considered proactive. They're not at the station waiting
for a 911 call; they're out looking for crime. I follow police scholars
in considering rapid response to 911 calls reactive, but use "proactive"
in a slightly idiosyncratic fashion to demarcate deterrent patrol tactics
from enforcement tactics such as stings, buy-bust operations, or more
targeted surveillance. The latter is proactive in a way that patrolling a
neighborhood is not. Responding to a call for service involves citizens
initiating police power. Intervening in a burglary in process that an officer comes across while patrolling, I also consider reactive. Posing as a
sex worker to arrest "Johns," on the other hand, is proactive. Officers in
this scenario are not responding to a request from a citizen or reacting
to criminal activity they happen to come across. Rather, they are taking

likely entails that everyone should be screened (which means even more innocent
people subjected to invasive political power). But in most cases, we will be far below the
threshold for harsh, universal screening. This suggests a plausible test: a harsh enforcement strategy involving statistical discrimination is likely justified only if an *exceptionally* harsh strategy for the same goal that burdens everyone would be.

the initiative to find criminal activity, even to encourage it, to make an arrest.

Generally, proactive, police-initiated power carries a higher legitimacy risk than reactive power. In some cases, reactive power, like just and legitimate military power, is defensive. An officer sees someone violating another's rights to bodily integrity or property and responds with defensive force. Reactive police power that responds to an actual threat is clearly legitimate. Proactive power that is intended to be defensive (by responding to a threat in the making) is less likely to be legitimate.[8]

It would be foolish for police to only intervene when a threat is in progress. So proactive, preemptive police power can be justified. But again, it is risky: whether a threat is developing is often unclear, and easy to misinterpret. Stopping people for "furtive movements" to search for weapons or concealed narcotics is likely to result in police power exercised against the innocent. More proactive policing is more likely to be harsh simply because it increases police contact, and more police contact means more opportunities for error. It also means more opportunities for things to escalate, increasing the risk of high-burden interactions.

Indeed, I think this is conventional wisdom in policing. This is Bratton's explanation for why complaints against the New York Police Department (NYPD) went up during his tenure: "Was there more abuse than in previous years or administrations? I don't believe so. The rise in complaints was commensurate with the rise in contact" (Bratton and Knobler 2009, 291). Oddly, he doesn't take the predictable nature of an increase in complaints following an increase in proactive policing (more police contact means more complaints) to count against the strategy as long as *individual* police interactions aren't becoming more brutal and abusive.

---

[8] To see why, consider the well-worn issue of preventive or preemptive wars. Whereas most just war theorists agree that nations need not wait until they are being attacked to justly respond—they may *preemptively* attack a battalion staging near their border and preparing an assault—a *preventive* war is much more controversial. A preventive war intends to eliminate the capacity to generate a threat rather than responding to an imminent harm (Frowe 2016, 76–77).

Finally, one of the risks of police-initiated power is that they might be exercising power that they have not been asked to exercise. Police initiated power is a departure, in some ways, from self-policing (as analogous to self-governing). Despite the problems with today's 911 systems, police scholars describe the move to rapid response to calls for service as a way of increasing democratic control over the police (Moskos 2008, 92–97). The shift means that the "demand for police power no longer emanates from the state ... and the police developed a new set of masters" (Bayley 1996, 120). Police-initiated power is state-initiated power.

4.3.4. Strength of Authorization

Initiation's counterpart risk factor is the strength of authorization. Not all laws have the same kind of authorization even if they are all equally on the books. This is because of the pathologies of the actual electoral and legislative procedures that produce the criminal code. It is also because some laws were passed more recently, or with more support, or with more pluralistic support as opposed to across party lines, and so on. Because democracies are fallible, weakly authorized police activity could be legitimate and strongly authorized activity could be illegitimate. Still, the strength of authorization partly constitutes the legitimacy risk of police activity.

Measuring the strength of democratic authorization is a challenge. I assume we have an intuitive sense of which laws are strongly authorized and which aren't. More numerical support for a policy (or a larger "manifest normative mandate") generally entails stronger authorization (Guerrero 2010). But a concern for persistent minorities requires something more, ideally agreement across diverse perspectives. I'll have more to say about determining the democratic authorization of policing in Chapter 7. For now, I'll offer some illustrations.

Policing of the "index crimes"—those half-heartedly tracked by the Federal Bureau of Investigation to create a crime index—are paradigmatic strongly authorized activities. There are strong mandates, across perspectives, for policing homicide, rape, aggravated assault, robbery, burglary, larceny, vehicle theft, and arson. Policing physical harm anchors the strongly authorized side of the spectrum, with police protection of property close to it. Perhaps some anti-car urbanists would prefer to hasten the demise of the personal vehicle by removing vehicle theft from the criminal code, but even that is unlikely. And even communists will mostly approve of protection of personal, nonproductive property.

Vice crimes occupy the other end of the spectrum: many of them have comparatively weak support, and those that are more strongly mandated are likely not mandated across relevant minority groups. Religious conservatives or certain feminists might want police to arrest and incarcerate sex workers, but sex workers, their customers, and those committed to pluralism or neutrality will generally favor a more hands-off approach. Police activity that enforces absurd laws (or explicitly racist laws), such as those against pants sagging, anchor the weakly authorized side of the spectrum. Even if they're part of the criminal code, and even if there are no other pressing concerns, police ought not to enforce them.

Order maintenance statutes fall somewhere in the middle, not least due to their vagueness and the inherent conflicts over the use of public space. The police department's or officer's sense of what counts as orderly or disorderly, just like anyone's personal sense of order, will be a contentious one.

4.4. Legitimacy-Risk Profiles

The collection of legitimacy risks associated with policing strategies amounts to a legitimacy-risk *profile*. The overall risk of a profile is determined by the interactions of the individual risks. A profile made up entirely of low risks will itself have low legitimacy risk. One of the main virtues of the framework, though, is that it highlights the importance of offsetting high-risk with low-risk characteristics. In turn, it motivates a certain institutional separation of powers to avoid objectionably high-risk policing.

The magnitude and distribution of burden are natural counterparts: they interact in an important and intuitive way. High magnitude and harsh power are extraordinarily likely to be illegitimate.

The commitment to lenience in the criminal trial is, again, a reaction to the magnitude of the burden associated with conviction. The higher the burden, the more procedural safeguards are put into place. Some burdens may be so high that *any* risk of error renders imposing it illegitimate. It is common for appeals of the death penalty, for example, to go all the way to the Supreme Court, and some find the risk of error here enough to make it illegitimate. On the other hand, if the burden of power is quite low, then legitimacy does not require as much lenience. This plausibly explains why the burden of proof in civil trials (preponderance of the evidence) is lower than in criminal trials (beyond reasonable doubt). So the legitimacy risk of high-burden political power needs to be paired with a lenient system for approving the exercise of power.

This point generalizes to policing. For example, the burden of lethal force is so significant that police are permitted only to use it in self- or other-defense. And although the accountability mechanisms for police use of lethal force have been corrupted by the so-called scared cop rule (in which an officer essentially only has to articulate fear for their life for their use of lethal force to be ruled constitutional), most agree that a legitimate use of lethal force by police can only be justified by an immediate and obvious threat to the life of an officer or bystanders. One of the things that makes policing a dangerous job is that, in some cases, an individual will pose a threat to an officer that is difficult to detect (e.g., someone approaches an officer with a gun in their hand and their hands in their pockets). Or a suspect will resist arrest by trying to strike an officer. Yet justice and legitimacy require officers to live with this risk rather than neutralizing every conceivable risk to the officer's safety. The police are not permitted to force every passerby to remove their hands from their pockets at gunpoint or to incapacitate everyone from a distance before handcuffing them. This, in other words, requires police use of lethal force to be lenient.

On the other end of the spectrum, the general surveillance of an officer patrolling a beat involves subjecting everyone in the area to a kind of political power. But, again, the patrol officer's visual surveillance is typically low burden enough that the harshness of the distribution does not intuitively render it illegitimate. Occupying a middle ground are "filtering" strategies like "stop and frisk" or pretextual vehicle stop regimes. The burden is significantly higher than being looked at by an officer and significantly lower than being shot. Whether these tactics are legitimate will depend on how frequently innocent people are stopped (and what they're stopped for). The infrequency with which officers in New York City found guns during the stop-and-frisk heyday suggests that the practice was objectionably harsh in light of the magnitude of its burden.[9]

Alternatively, consider the "Baltimore miracle" in which arrests dropped while crime fell. Anthony Barksdale, architect of the Baltimore Police Department's strategy during that time, sought "proactive focused enforcement." He claims that a "relentless focus on repeat violent offenders," not mass-arrest, zero-tolerance strategies, is responsible for the drop in crime (Barksdale 2020). I won't take up the causal question here. Rather, what's noteworthy is the strategy's deliberate pairing of proactive, high-burden enforcement, with a "precision" focus on repeat offenders. Strenuously avoiding harsh distributions of burden—in other words, actually being precise—allows higher burden but legitimate policing.

Initiation and authorization are also natural counterparts. If a police activity is strongly authorized, then intuitively, there is low risk in police initiating it. If police activity is weakly authorized, there is something objectionable about police initiating it. And one way to accommodate the risks associated with weakly authorized activity is for police to reactively, rather than proactively, exercise their power.[10]

Take the Los Angeles ordinance against "aggressive panhandling" as an example. A perennial focus of quality-of-life enforcement, there is a real concern about aggressive panhandling shading into robbery. There is a fine line between someone assertively requesting spare change in front of an ATM vestibule and someone coercing you with a threat of violence into handing over some money. Police agencies

---

[9] I cover this example in more detail in Monaghan (2021).
[10] Some will worry at this point that proactive policing is an important development in the profession. Recall that I am using "proactive" in a slightly idiosyncratic way; I am not arguing that legitimacy requires a return to the old, ineffective rapid-response strategies or that police cannot be proactive in problem-solving. Though, it bears emphasizing, there are legitimacy requirements that reduce the efficacy of policing. That is an unavoidable tradeoff.

might reasonably take this to be an area for them to focus on. There is a constitutional right, however, and I presume most people would endorse the right, to merely ask for spare change. That suggests that in light of the level of democratic authorization for policing panhandlers, a sensible approach to managing this risk would be for cops to react to reports of genuinely aggressive panhandling instead of seeking out potentially aggressive panhandlers. Doing so increases the risk of overly sensitive judgments, since the officer is looking for potential threats, and thus harsher enforcement. Carrying out panhandling stings, in which "plainclothes officers pose as 'decoy pedestrians' to better observe and arrest individuals who beg for spare change in and around Skid Row," on the other hand, is much riskier because it combines proactivity with at best moderately authorized police power (Stuart 2016, 78). Panhandling is low enough on the priority list of problems people expect police to solve that, if I had to guess, I would imagine most people would think you were joking if you told them that panhandling stings are an actual police practice.

For similar reasons, the weakly authorized nature of drug prohibition suggests that buy-bust tactics, in which police proactively seek out drug dealers, are much more likely to be illegitimate than a similarly proactive sting against child pornographers.[11] If drug prohibition is illegitimate, then seeking out the opportunity to enforce those laws is highly objectionable. In fact, police-initiated power often coincides with weakly authorized power *precisely because* no one involved wants the police to intervene and so no one reports the crime. Crimes without direct victims typically go unreported, and this means that police need to take the initiative by conducting stings and using other proactive strategies (Bayley 1996, 83). Proactive policing in response to activity without a victim, rather than a "quiet" victim, is high risk.

Risk interactions occur across the natural counterparts, too. Harsh pretextual traffic stop tactics used for narcotics interdiction are even riskier, all things considered, than the NYPD's stop-and-frisk strategy because their purpose has considerably weaker democratic authorization. The prevention of violence is strongly authorized and removing

---

[11] Luke Hunt (2019, chapter 5) reaches this conclusion via an appeal to the emergency condition on the police prerogative power.

illegal guns from the streets is at least a prima facie attractive way of preventing violence. But policing the substances people consume for recreation is controversial, and a large minority if not a majority reject that as a legitimate police activity. Harshness, high burdens, weak authorization, and proactive initiation interact to produce high legitimacy risk.

4.5. Institutional Roles and Political Powers

Above, I mentioned that the framework serves an epistemic function. Applying the framework to a case helps to clarify this point. One might reject liberal neutrality and think using political power to enforce their controversial conception of the good life is a legitimate function of the state. Therefore, one might think, (certain) vice laws are legitimate. But, when we think about what goes into vice enforcement, we are also thinking about legitimacy risks. In most cases, the enforcement is weakly authorized. To have any chance at success, it will likely have to be proactive. Police will have to search for those engaging in vicious behavior, either through stings or through filtering strategies. And because it is difficult to tell from looking at someone whether they are engaging in vicious behavior, those filtering strategies are likely to be quite harsh. More contact means more burden. Finally, to successfully deter such behavior, people will be inclined toward punishment. The kind of policing we can expect from vice units looks like exceptionally high legitimacy risk. This should give us serious reservations about the legitimacy of enforcing prohibitions on recreational drug use or sex work, for example. It also gives the police administrator and the police officer reason to focus their efforts elsewhere: *there's plenty of low-risk policing to be done.* This point applies widely: police should generally focus their scarce resources on low-risk policing, and their discretion should reduce risks to legitimacy.

This conclusion makes progress on the question of police priorities. But what this argument does at a more basic level is highlight that the vice unit in patrol, the narcotics unit in the investigative division, the homicide department, the patrol division, and so on are doing fundamentally different kinds of work. They're not merely different police *tasks*, handled by different role occupants. They are exercising distinct political *powers* placed awkwardly under the same agency that expects many of its members to take up different roles at different times of the day. They're exercising different kinds of political power even if they are all kinds of inward-facing executive power. But as we've seen, to say that they're all kinds of executive power masks the different kinds of decision-making involved in the role; the patrol officer's decision-making looks more legislative than the homicide detective's. And a point to which we'll return, it masks the different legitimacy-risk profiles attached to different kinds of policing a patrol officer can take up on their shift (Brown 1988, 288).

Crucially, the legitimacy-risk profiles don't carve the police profession at its existing joints. They crosscut them. This is important because police priorities influence police legitimacy, and professional roles are tools for shaping professional priorities. Whereas it is common practice to distinguish the investigative from the patrol division according to their respective goals of *law enforcement* and *order maintenance*, it is not true that all patrol or investigative activity has basically the same legitimacy-risk profile. The profiles usefully distinguish the homicide from narcotics detective, but they also differentiate what James Q. Wilson (1978, 69) called the "undifferentiated patrol division." The undifferentiated patrol allows officers to take up widely divergent operational styles and professional priorities, and only limited opportunities for oversight. And officers who spend their time proactively seeking out unlicensed vendors, sex workers, or drug dealers, for example, are engaged in a different kind of activity than those who put their effort into effectively mediating domestic disputes or patrolling for burglaries and muggings.

To make policing more just, we need to attend to these different kinds of policing. This will inform our thinking about how different officers should exercise their different legal powers, and it should also inform our thinking about institutional structure. In the remainder of the book, I'll offer more thorough defenses of the principles that make up the legitimacy-risk profiles, starting with the issue of burden and proportionality in the next chapter, before returning to the topic of institutional form and police roles.

5

To Protect (and Serve), Proportionally

A theory of just policing will be partially constituted by principles that guide police discretion. The arguments of the last chapter motivate a highly abstract principle: *officers and administrators should avoid high legitimacy-risk policing.* I'll turn now to exploring and defending a substantive (as opposed to procedural) principle of proportionality that embodies concerns about the (magnitude and distribution of) burdens of political power. The proportionality principle says, roughly, that an act of policing is just and legitimate only if it is *worth it.* The principle deliberately foregrounds the systemic, dynamic features of policing canvassed in Chapter 2. Unlike many principles of political philosophy, the proportionality principle has found proponents in policing throughout its history.

The motivating thought is that policing is primarily, though not entirely, defensive. Deterrence and detection are both, though in different ways, aimed at defending people from threats to (some of) their interests. To the extent that policing is defensive, it will be constrained by principles of just defensive force, including a proportionality principle. I begin by characterizing the relevant principle of proportionality in contexts of self- and other-defense. Then, I apply the principle to two problems: predictably disproportionate police power and systematically encouraged violations.

5.1. The Night Watch and Defensive Force

This defensive role is at the heart of the legitimate state, and it is necessary for its legitimacy, even if we think there are other important state functions. The minimal state of classical liberalism and libertarianism

Just Policing. Jake Monaghan, Oxford University Press. © Oxford University Press 2023.
DOI: 10.1093/oso/9780197610725.003.0005

is referred to, disparagingly or approvingly, as the *night-watchman* state (Nozick 1974, 26). The basics of policing—preventive patrol—are thus largely justified on defensive grounds. Like all defensive force, it is constrained by a proportionality requirement.

The proportionality principle is philosophically useful because it is, I think, the most widely endorsed substantive principle of justice that, in other contexts, justifies departures from political decision-making procedures. One of the things we hold soldiers responsible for, despite their orders, is proportionality (they may not kill too many civilians). We should, and often do, accept a similar conclusion in the context of policing. This is significant because one of the major sources of skepticism about police discretion, recall, comes from privileging procedural principles (e.g., the police must faithfully enforce the appropriately reached decisions of the legislature) over substantive ones (e.g., the police must not make arrests when doing so predictably results in over-punishment).

Like actual night watchmen for centuries, the defensive force used by police is often aimed at diffused threats and deterrence; much of policing involves problems besides ongoing direct threats of physical violence. Those involve threats to certain uses of public or private property, as well as threats to the successful functioning of the criminal legal system (e.g., failing to appear for trial). For this reason, critics sometimes worry that thinking about policing in terms of exercising a monopoly on defensive violence encourages a harmful warrior culture in policing and elides other important values and principles. This is a reasonable worry. Evaluating police power with a proportionality principle from theories of defensive force is nevertheless useful because, I'll argue, when properly applied, it serves to constrain policing and make it gentler. If it turns out that a focus on defensive force undermines the warrior conception of policing and the thin blue line culture, so much the worse for them.

In competition with the profession's legalism, we also see commitments to proportionality in policing. Cleveland police chief Fred Kohler, in the reform era of the early 1900s, adopted a "Common Sense Policy or Golden Rule" for his officers. This policy instructed officers not to make "arrests where the arrests would do more harm than good, in cases of minor offenders." The policy ended arrests for public drunkenness for a time (Monkkonen 1981, 74). The commitment to proportionality is not isolated to early police reformers. Fifty years later, Egon Bittner's classic ethnography of skid-row policing uncovers a reliance on proportionality in officer decision-making:

> It is difficult to overestimate the skid-row patrolman's feeling of certainty that his coercive and disciplinary actions toward the inhabitants have but the most passing significance in their lives. Sending a man to jail on some charge that will hold him for a couple of days is seen as a matter of such slight importance to the affected person that it could hardly give rise to scruples. (Bittner 1967, 713)

The problem here is not taking into account what happens after an arrest in deciding whether to arrest, but rather a mistaken view that the arrest causes only a trivial burden.

A sensitivity to proportionality is evident in what sociologist Forrest Stuart calls "therapeutic policing" (2016). Therapeutic policing involves, contrary to Kohler's Golden Rule, making arrests, usually for minor offenses, to facilitate therapy (or, as I'll expand the term, paternalistic protection) rather than punishment. Bittner describes a case of therapeutic policing in which an officer arrests an intoxicated man to prevent him from bringing a sexual partner back to his room where the officer is confident he will likely be robbed (1967). The more recent version of the practice that prompts Stuart's name is the collaboration of officers and the "mega-shelters"—under the "Streets or Shelters" program—to push people into rehabilitation programs by forgiving misdemeanor citations in exchange for a skid row resident's participation. In other cases, officers appear motivated by what happens when they aren't aggressively making arrests, namely death and destruction. The incredible danger amassing on the other side of the thin blue line *morally demands* aggressive policing in the way national security threats demand aggressive soldiers. Charles Remsberg's critique of 95 percent of the police profession, those "retired on duty" who lack the aggressive nature of those with the "5%er Mind-Set [*sic*]" is not merely that they waste taxpayers' money. It's primarily that they are a danger to themselves and others. They're too "service oriented," they resort to too little force, they wait too long to use it, and are too quick to find "good in other people" and relax their tactical posture. The small minority of *real police* "personalize Criminal Patrol as protecting [their own] family," because they know that any illegal drugs that make it past the police "might have resulted in an officer getting hurt or killed" (1996, 25–44).

This contrast in the results of applying a proportionality principle to policing over the last century, whether it encourages or discourages minor arrests, whether it motivates a service or warrior orientation, reveals that we could use further reflection on the matter. To see how proportionality guides policing, I'll flesh out the principle and its role in a more general theory of permissible defensive force.

5.1.1. Self-Defense

For defensive violence to be permissible, most philosophers agree that it must satisfy proportionality and necessity requirements, among some others. Some also think that causing the need for defensive violence undermines its justification (though this is controversial). My focus throughout will be on understanding how these requirements come together to produce a determination about whether and how much defensive force is legitimate.

For defensive force to be proportional, the "good you are protecting must be worth the harm you are inflicting" to protect it (Frowe 2016, 53). You are not permitted to kill someone if it is the only way to prevent them from pinching you. Nor are you permitted to give someone permanent brain damage if it is the only way to prevent them from stealing your wallet. When the goods and harms get closer together, things get trickier. It is plausible that you are permitted to break someone's arm to prevent them from stealing your car. Proportionality does not require the good you are protecting to be worth the same or more than the harm you are inflicting. You are certainly permitted to kill someone to prevent them from raping you. Proportionality requires a kind of fittingness; the good merely must be *worth it*.

For the force to be permissible, one must not have less burdensome alternatives available. If you can obviously stop a would-be car thief by punching them instead of breaking their arm, breaking their arm is impermissible. If you can stop a would-be rapist by non-fatally stabbing them, lethal defensive force would be impermissible. This intuition produces the related *necessity* requirement (Frowe 2016, 12). Though this is a distinct requirement, it factors into judgments about legitimate self-defense by setting a ceiling on the amount of force within the set of proportional defensive options.

In cases where police officers are threatened, they are permitted to use defensive force subject to a proportionality constraint. If an officer is about to be fired upon, they may use lethal defensive force. If a suspect is fleeing, on foot or in a vehicle, they are not permitted to fire (unless the fleeing suspect poses immediate risk to third parties). Of course, one of the major controversies in policing now concerns its frequent lack of proportionality; officers claim to see someone reach for their waist band and take that to be justification for (often lethally) firing their weapon in defense. Or someone is brandishing a knife, and officers fire their weapons in defense. Criminologist Franklin Zimring (2017) argues that because officers have "hardened" their defensive posture with better equipment, knives are in fact rarely a lethal threat to police officers. Therefore, he concludes, police policies must be revised to prevent the use of a firearm as a defense against a suspect with a knife. The point is not to settle this issue, but rather to show that the proportionality and necessity principles are essential to a theory of just policing.

One more thing to consider in contexts of permissible individual self-defense is the issue of *provocation* or *self-generated self-defense* (Jones 2021; Ferzan 2013). Plausibly, if one intentionally causes the threat against which they now need to defend themselves, this impacts the justification of their defensive force. There's a menu of options for explaining this. The permissive option, found in the Model Penal Code holds that *deadly* force "is not justifiable if . . . the actor, with the purpose of causing death or serious bodily harm, provoked the use of force against himself in the same encounter" (§3.04(2)(b), cited in Ferzan 2013, 598). The stringent option, found in Arizona's self-defense statute, denies that provocateurs are justified in defending themselves and only allows "an initial aggressor to regain a self-defense justification by withdrawing or communicating their desire to end the conflict" (Jones 2021). A similar position, defended by philosopher Kimberly

Ferzan, holds that by intentionally causing the threat, the provocateur forfeits their right to *any* self-defense against the amount of force they anticipated causing.

So, if Ida would like to kill Betsy, and encourages Betsy to stab her by initiating a punch, she is not then permitted to use lethal force to defend against Betsy's stabbing. The permissive account would imply she is permitted to use non-lethal force (and is guilty only of the initial assault), whereas the stringent account would imply that Ida is not permitted to use any force to defend against the stabbing (unless she intended to provoke a less response than the stabbing).

In both cases, these provocation principles serve a similar function as the necessity principle: further removing options from the set of permissible defensive force created by the proportionality assessment. The purpose of bringing up these contrasting accounts is to motivate a moderate one: *if one intentionally causes a threat, they lower the ceiling on the amount of permissible defensive force.*[1]

Why endorse the weaker principle? I don't have space to offer a full defense, but here are some reasons. If you think that Ida might be permitted to use some small amount of *non-lethal* defensive force, and it seems to me that she might, you'll find the stringent account too stringent. If Ida is about to be stabbed, but she can slap Betsy in the face and then retreat, it's plausible that doing so is permissible, even though she provoked the stabbing. The Model Penal Code gets us the non-lethal part, but not the small part (any non-lethal force is apparently justified). We might begrudgingly admit that Ida is allowed to use *some* defensive force to defend against the threat that she intentionally provoked, but it's not as if she's in the same position as a non-provocateur with respect to non-deadly self-defense. So it is too permissive. If Rita innocently finds her life threatened by Betsy, and an open-handed slap could avert the threat while costing herself a black eye, she plausibly can opt for a more harmful close-handed punch

---

[1] Another option for a moderate principle, discussed by Jones (2021), moderates the violation attached to the lethal force. If Ida provokes Betsy and then kills her, his self-generated defense is not justified, but nor is he guilty of murder; he is guilty of manslaughter. My interest here is in determining what amount of self-generated defensive force is permissible, if any, so I won't take up the issue of how serious the violation the unjustified force is.

to prevent the black eye in addition to death. But if Ida provoked the threat, given the same choice, she plausibly cannot opt for the punch (let alone the deadly force she intended) and must simply accept the black eye from Betsy. If that's the case, then consistent with the moderate principle, self-generated threats lower the ceiling for what counts as an acceptable amount of defensive violence in a wider range of cases than the permissive account but without lowering the ceiling to zero as does the stringent account.

Ultimately, the cases most requiring analysis do not involve police officers intentionally provoking threats, but rather generating threats in less intentional, more indirect ways. What's important for present purposes is just establishing that having a certain causal role in the creation of a threat morally closes off options for defending against it.

5.1.2. Other-Defense

Not only do most of the relevant cases involve something other than provocation, the force that police officers use is more often than not aimed at *other*-defense. While policing, an officer might have to defend herself, but that almost always occurs in the process of contributing to the defense of third parties. And, as I've said, the police facilitate the state's defensive role by participating in a legal system that aims (in part) at deterrence. The deterrence is highly diffused. As we saw in the first chapter, this means that the effects on bystanders are also highly diffused, and these are crucial for evaluating policing. The other-defense nature of police force, and the far-reaching effects of policing on bystanders, introduce some complications in understanding the proportionality requirement.

These points highlight the need for the proportionality requirement in policing to take into account more than officers and suspects. Philosopher Jeff McMahan introduces a distinction between *narrow* and *wide* proportionality that will be useful (2009, 20). Narrow proportionality concerns only the effects on the one liable to harm (typically the aggressor), and wide proportionality concerns those not liable, typically bystanders. Narrow proportionality prohibits, for example, shooting at fleeing suspects in most cases, even if the probability of a later peaceful arrest is small, because that is too much force. Wide proportionality prohibits high-speed vehicle pursuits in many cases (even if we think that subjecting a fleeing suspect to the risk of a crash is acceptable) because the risk of harm to bystanders is too great.

The wide proportionality requirement motivates an additional one. Some philosophers think that permissible defensive force has a "reasonable chance of success" requirement. Even if force is defensive, proportional, and necessary, if it has no chance of neutralizing the threat it may still be impermissible. This principle strikes me as highly implausible unless we are considering wide proportionality. If Edna is attempting to kill Felix, and Felix is guaranteed to be unable to successfully fend off the attack, whether Felix is permitted to fire a gun in futile self-defense depends on the circumstances. If Edna and Felix are in a secluded area where firing a gun has no chance of harming bystanders, it is hard to see why Felix would not be so permitted. Alternatively, if they are on a crowded street, and the bullet has a high probability of passing through Edna and striking an innocent bystander, Felix is plausibly not permitted to fire his gun. If, alternatively, Felix is extremely likely to successfully fend off Edna's attack and has some *small* risk of accidentally striking an innocent bystander with a stray round, it is at least not obvious whether Felix may resort to defensively firing his weapon.

However much partiality toward one's own interests is permitted will help determine how much risk we are permitted to subject bystanders to. But in cases of other-defense involving impartial state agents, there is less room for giving more weight to the interests of the threatened than the bystander. Thus, how likely an officer is to succeed in defending others will play at least some role in determining what kind of force (and relatedly, how much risk to bystanders) she is permitted to use. The reasonable chance of success requirement is most compelling when grounded in wide proportionality considerations of other-defense.

Permissible other-defense is also influenced by self-generated threats. Just as one can cause the need for one's own defense by intentionally causing another to become a threat, one can cause the need for another's defense by causing a third party to become a threat. Insofar as it is criminogenic, bad policing generates a need for other-defense.

And if we accept that causing a threat can reduce the amount of force one is permitted to resort to in defending against in self-defense cases, we should accept that in other-defense cases as well, though the duty to provide security complicates matters. The point is that *state-generated violations* are analogous to self-generated threats: the state must respond with a lighter touch to the problems it has created. This implies that the defensive force an officer might use *now* is constrained both by the possibility that it was generated by the state in the past, and that it will generate a need for defensive force in the future. Thus, the sense of proportionality relevant to policing is exceptionally wide. It shows that policing must appropriately balance risks across a community.

In resorting to defensive force, most people are subjected only to the ordinary requirements of morality. Ordinary morality prohibits us from intentionally provoking a deadly threat against ourselves or others. But police officers, and agents of the state more broadly, have special obligations in light of their role. Not only may they not intentionally provoke threats, they may not *negligently* do so, where negligence is filled out in part by professional norms. Part of the expectation is that officers take on more risk to themselves to reduce risk to bystanders while providing security. These special obligations have the effect of making the necessity requirement more demanding. Whether a defensive option is necessary is a function of the risks involved to the defender. I might be able to keep you from killing me by telling a funny joke that allows me to abscond while you laugh. But since I'm not that funny, given the choice between firing my trusty pistol or relying on my not-so-trusty wit, surely morality does not require me to take on the risk of defense-by-joke. Firing my weapon is necessary here only in light of facts about me. Likewise, whether some force satisfies the necessity requirement for police officers depends on facts about them, their training, their tactical hardening, the risks they voluntarily take on, and so on.

To recap, permissible defensive violence must be widely proportional and necessary. The wide proportionality requirement entails a reasonable chance of success requirement for the police. Necessity is determined by a variety of facts about the police, such as their special obligations and training, that lower the ceiling on permissible defensive force. And finally, in light of considerations about self-generated threats, when the state or police are responsible for the threats (state-generated violations), the amount of permissible defensive force they may resort to is reduced. These elements come together to determine how much defensive force is permissible. Though they are distinct elements, for convenience, I'll treat them all as part of an expansive proportionality principle in what follows.

5.2. Predictably Disproportional Policing

The proceduralist argument for police discretion made earlier relied in part on the notion of "predictable failures." The thought was that if a procedure fails predictably, in the sense that the failure is a result of a known problem with the procedure, then the procedure does not transmit legitimacy to its output. Fallible procedures have success conditions, and the normative status of failures depends on whether those conditions have been met. There are many predictable failures in our current criminal legal system. They include excessively punitive, ineffective, and counterproductive policing and punishment. In these cases, we have two complementary political justifications for discretionary non-enforcement. First, the source of the political power's legitimacy is called into question if not undermined outright. Second, the principle of proportionality generates a reason for non-enforcement.

5.2.1. Excessively Burdensome Enforcement

The unavoidable reality is that the cost—to us, the bystanders, and to the suspect—of enforcing many laws is not worth it. Some laws, like those against recreational drug consumption or wearing sagging pants, are likely never worth it in light of the implementation details. But I'm also interested here in more mundane examples that are characterized by broad discretion.

The proportionality requirement implies that in cases where, for example, an arrest will lead to excessive punishment, police should refrain from making an arrest, or they should make an arrest on less burdensome charges. In Chapter 3, I offered as an example of a predictable procedural failure arresting someone for riding their bike without a light. Unlike helmet laws, these are not objectionably paternalistic. Riding a bike without a light can be dangerous to others. But it's typically not *seriously* dangerous and does not warrant seizing one's mode of transportation and putting them into the misdemeanor system. Thus, this law is rarely enforced.[2]

Not all officers ignore such violations. Moskos describes a tactic of one of his former colleagues:

> In March, after a series of low-arrest memos, Bricknell decided he was going to set the record for number of arrests in one month: "The major wants stats, I'm going to give him stats. (. . .)" Bricknell decided that the easiest way to make lockups was to arrest people for violating bicycle regulations. Many bikes, at least late at night, are used by drug runners and drug lookouts. At night, all bikes are required to have a light. Bricknell would stop bicyclists for this violation. If the rider had identification, he would write a citation. Most people didn't have identification. These riders were locked up. (2008, 140)

Arresting cyclists without a light to get "stats" that will further one's career (or mock the administrator's low arrest memo), in addition to being repugnant in terms of personal ethics, hardly seems worth the cost in most cases. A ticket is likely a substantial financial burden to the cyclist. An arrest and time in jail, plus the bureaucratic hurdles needed to reclaim one's bike (likely one's primary mode of transportation), is obviously a more substantial burden. Burdening people with the cost of a ticket or incarceration is simply not worth it, particularly in the East Baltimore Bricknell policed. This explains—and justifies—the *clear pattern of discretionary non-enforcement*. Bricknell acted unjustly in upsetting this pattern and in subjecting Baltimoreans to too much

---

[2] While writing this I witnessed a cyclist cross a busy street late at night without a light. They were nearly struck by an NOPD police cruiser. The officers, to their credit, did not stop the cyclist.

punishment even if his behavior has a legislative and departmental stamp of approval.

Because there are circumstances where riding without a light is not merely a nuisance but is a genuine danger, it is not clear that the right response is to take the law off the books. In situations dense with bicycle traffic, there can be good reason to empower this kind of social control. It is plausibly better to let officers use their judgment about when enforcement is worth it.

There are plenty of other examples that would serve this same argumentative purpose. Officers should prefer to mediate a conflict between two people instead of making an arrest (cf. Herbert 2006, 84). Officers should not "fish" for suspended licenses by running the plates of decrepit vehicles in poor parts of the city on the expectation that poor motorists are more likely to drive on suspended licenses (cf. Herbert 2006, 105). Proportionality does not restrict enforcement only in such minor matters. It extends to more serious criminality. On this point, compare the divergent attitudes of three police officers regarding proportionality:

> I've seen batteries occur right in front of me, where I could take him to jail, but I'd be doing more harm putting him in jail. (. . .) Maybe it's on the basis of I know people are getting away with so much more. We have organized crime, and the poor little guy on the street is getting caught. I can pinch him for a red light, but I won't. I can justify it by realizing there is so much more that is below the surface. You have the feeling that you have only a little fish. It's all disproportionate to what he's doing and how he's affected. (Muir 1977, 214)

On the other hand, here's Officer Bricknell's justification for arresting cyclists without a light:

> I lock up bicyclists. It's called zero tolerance. If you're biking in violation of the law, I'm going to write you a ticket. At 3 am, you need a light. (. . .) It's legal. And I'm gonna do it. (Moskos 2008, 140)

And finally, a third officer's justification for engaging in a dangerous vehicle pursuit:

We were rolling down Kercheval, and we see this '69 Mustang filled with kids. Significantly, it had no front plate. We do a U-turn, and the driver spots me. We chase them for almost ten minutes. We are almost on them at Boulevard and Elm, and he runs a red light. This little old lady came. So I hit the building and totaled the car. And I'm on the carpet [in front of the department safety officer, being investigated]. . . . "Is there something you could have done to prevent the chase?" I said, "Look, if you don't want us to chase, put it in an order. The criminal code gives us the power to use necessary force." I was completely justified in what I did. (Muir 1977, 218)

In the last quote we see an officer's peculiar sense of when force is necessary, as well as well-founded skepticism from the police administrator. But also noteworthy in both cases is the appeal to the criminal code and the lack of an order forbidding the pursuit to justify a likely disproportionate use of force. The third incident occurred decades ago, and many large departments now have orders to prevent exactly this kind of accident. But the appeal to proportionality made by the first officer, one sorely lacking from the perspective of the second and third officers, would have likely justified calling off the pursuit. A commitment to an inchoate version of legalism *unconstrained by a proportionality requirement* produces repugnant policing.

5.2.2. Inefficient Enforcement

Consider now the necessity and the reasonable chance of success conditions. Enforcement can be inefficient if there are less burdensome options reasonably available, and by being simply ineffective. Inefficient enforcement fails the broad proportionality requirement. This parallels an intuitively attractive requirement some philosophers argue constrains the criminal code. Douglas Husak argues that one of the (external) constraints on the legitimate criminal code is a success condition: a criminal law must be reasonably effective. This implies that, since drug prohibition does not actually advance the state's interest in deterring drug use, drug prohibition laws are not justified (Husak 2008, 147). I'll argue that the requirement applies not only to the enforcement of laws as a kind but also to individual decisions to exercise police power.

In a wide variety of cases, aggressively enforcing a law is virtually guaranteed not to succeed in deterring criminal behavior. Here, too, laws that create black markets are an obvious example. The goal of policing open-air drug markets is not, typically, the full elimination of drug crimes. No one can reasonably hope for that. The police strategy in light of this is merely to constrict the market by dissuading casual users (Harocopos and Hough 2005). And since moderately reducing the size of a black market leaves it, and all of its attendant problems, intact, this hardly looks like effective policing. Policing open-air drug markets, then, is virtually guaranteed to be ineffective if the goal is ending drug use.[3]

Or consider the problem of shoplifting. People shoplift for many reasons of varying degrees of injustice; because they need some essential good they can't afford, because they cannot afford to purchase gifts for family, and because they like the thrill. In these cases, the police have authorization from the criminal code to make an arrest. But in at least some of them, making an arrest will funnel people into the crowded, overly punitive misdemeanor system without any deterrence effect. This burdens shoplifters (and those who rely on them) with significant costs, but with no protection of property rights to show for it.

What are police to do in such situations? For one, they ought to consider what it would take to create an effective approach to protecting the rights of the shopkeepers. Making an arrest might, in principle, be proportional, but it is often not necessary. The Home Office Prevention Unit in Great Britain once recommended shifting resources away from fully processing arrested shoplifters toward catching (but not fully processing) more shoplifters. The rationale was that since shoplifters tended to steal low-value goods—for which they thought they would not be seriously punished—they did not expect to be caught, and increasing the likelihood of being caught would disabuse people of this notion. That, in turn, would reduce shoplifting (Goldstein 1990, 136).

---

[3] And if we redo our proportionality assessment to evaluate the goal of *reducing the size* of illicit drug markets, the costs of drug prohibition are plainly much harder to view as proportionate.

In this case, shoplifters reasoned from the disproportionate nature of prosecuting someone for trivial shoplifting to the conclusion that they wouldn't be caught. In response, a tactic of detaining people, but not turning them over for prosecution, appeared attractive to at least some law enforcement professionals. Just catching and giving a stern talking to shoplifters appears to be the tactic that satisfies both the necessity and reasonable chance of success requirements (cf. Muir 1977, 192). This is likely a better strategy than decriminalizing shoplifting outright (below some threshold), at least if decriminalization in fact exacerbates the shoplifting problem (Fuller 2021).

5.3. Counterproductive Enforcement and Systematically Encouraged Violations

Let's turn now to applying considerations of provoked threats to policing by looking at systematically encouraged violations of law. The motivating thought is that if criminal activity is systematically encouraged, police have good reason for discretionary non-enforcement on the grounds that they would be exacerbating an already clear failure of political procedures. I am not permitted to cause a threat intentionally or negligently against myself or others and then resort to the full suite of defensive options that would be justified in other contexts. The same goes for the state.

Again, that police are embedded in complex, coupled systems must inform the political ethics of policing. If, because of the injustices of the criminal legal system, many people distrust or are hostile toward the police, there is a good chance they will bristle at police interactions, especially non-voluntary ones. But the police are often in the grips of a norm related to perceived ability to maintain the upper hand in their work:

The code of the street allows one to avoid confrontation, but the code also states that to enter and back down from a conflict is a loss of face. Nobody wants to be "punked," least of all the police. Police play by these street rules with the assumption that any sign of weakness on their part will make future interactions much more difficult and

dangerous. Police, quite simply, cannot afford to lose confrontations.
(Moskos 2008, 104–105)

This state of affairs predictably heightens the tensions of these
interactions; the risk of escalation is serious. If police (generally)
are in some way responsible for necessary elements of this scenario,
then they must not let perceived disrespect result in escalations. This
systematic risk of escalation entails that, as a basic moral requirement, police must be capable of navigating interpersonal tension and
refraining from allowing interactions to spiral out of control. People
must be given some leeway in their interactions with police. Like retail
work, the job unfortunately requires being able to take verbal abuse
without losing one's cool. And, crucially, the risk of the interaction
causing such escalations raises the justificatory bar for initiating one
in the first place, a point seemingly lost on many. This point applies
widely.

5.3.1. Exacerbating Vice

The criminal law must not be counterproductive (Surprenant and
Brennan 2020, 48; Husak 2014, 228). Unfortunately, one of the failures
of our criminal justice system is its tendency to contribute to crime.
When that happens, we have to take into account the complication of
state-generated other-defense. In these cases, not only is the police use
of force typically ineffective, it also predictably generates a need for
further defensive force.

Take policing illegal markets in sex as an example. Aggressive
vice enforcement frequently makes that purportedly vicious activity
worse along a variety of dimensions. Goldstein points out in a discussion of the limitations of police work aimed merely at enforcing the
law (as opposed to genuinely solving public safety problems), there
are several potential reasons for enforcing laws against sex work.
Enforcement could be aimed at protecting the moral sensibilities
of a certain segment of the community, eliminating a nuisance, reducing opportunities for organized crime to flourish, protecting the
well-being of sex workers by reducing the likelihood of assault and

transmission of sexually transmitted infections, and so on (Goldstein 1990, 40–41). "Because there is a law" is a troubling justification for exercising power; the actual goal will recommend certain tactics over others, in part by delineating the proportionality assessment.

Imagine, for example, that some in a community find the thought of sex work upsetting because it communicates certain attitudes about sex and gender, and they make their perspective well known through 911 calls for service, complaints to the mayor, and complaints during community policing meetings. If this were the department's motivation, we would have good grounds to worry about failing the requirement that police power be worth it. Like crackdowns on drug markets, the best we can reasonably hope for is a smaller but probably more harmful market, so we'll be exercising a huge amount of power with little to show for it. But beyond that, to the extent that cracking down on forms of sex work (such as those that take place in brothels) pushes sex work outdoors onto the streets, or into less dignity-compatible forms of sexual labor, the moral sensibilities of (some of) the community are likely to be further offended, *directly* undermining the police goal.

Or suppose the justification for prioritizing the enforcement of laws against sex work is to reduce the opportunities for organized crime to flourish and to protect the well-being of sex workers by reducing the transmission of sexually transmitted infections. The problem is that cracking down on sex work is likely to backfire on both fronts. Illegal markets predictably raise prices, but such participation is also riskier in virtue of the fact that the state can no longer settle disputes peacefully. These are precisely the background conditions that invite organized crime. They also tend to make risky activity riskier. If a sex worker cannot call the cops after being sexually or physically assaulted, or to force a customer to leave if they refuse to use a condom, then assault and unprotected sex (or a dispute over protection escalating into violence) is more likely. And because people worry that carrying many condoms might be used as evidence in prosecuting a suspected sex worker, they are less likely to carry enough condoms for fear of them being taken as evidence if arrested, thereby increasing the amount of unprotected sex. In both cases, the police activity is not only ineffective but counterproductive.

Likewise, unlicensed vendor crackdowns are unlikely to eliminate unlicensed vending, and they are also liable to push vendors into more problematic illegal activity (cf. Duneier 1999, 261). There are plenty of other examples of counterproductive enforcement, and some of them are counterproductive in a surprisingly broad way. That is the lesson of descriptive work on perceived police legitimacy: aggressive police tactics that people perceive to be unfair will not only depress cooperation with the police, it will also reduce compliance with the law (Fagan et al. 2016; Tyler 2004).

5.3.2. Induced Speeding

Counterproductive enforcement is unjust because it is ineffective and lacks a reasonable chance of success, usually while burdening bystanders. It also introduces the complication of state-generated "threats" or violations. We noted above that policing sex work sometimes has the effect of making it worse, for example, by making it more harmful or a greater nuisance. In those cases, the state has contributed to the violation it then forcefully polices. When the state is integral in causing some violation, the burdens associated with policing it are less likely to be fitting.

Perhaps a less controversial example can be found in traffic enforcement. Speed limits are intentionally set in such a way that some motorists will routinely violate the law. This is the "85th percentile rule" (Taylor and Hwang 2020). Often, these speeders are dangerous, and their behavior should be deterred. But in other cases, speed limits are artificially low. When a road is designed with wide lanes, sweeping curves, concrete barriers between travel lanes, and nothing placed near the side of the road to narrow a motorist's field of vision, driving fast is nearly irresistible. These conditions *induce* violations of the law.

In 2015, a motorist traveling on a short stretch of highway with these characteristics that runs through Delaware Park in Buffalo, New York, fell asleep and crashed into a mother and her two children who were walking in the park. One of the children, a three-year-old boy, was killed (Epstein and Popiolkowski 2020). There was plenty of blame to go around; policymakers foolishly put the highway through the city's major park, and then negligently decided not to install barriers between the highway and the rest of the park, and the motorist couldn't manage to control his vehicle. In response, the Department of Transportation erected barriers and reduced the speed limit from 50 to 35 mph, a speed appropriate for a boulevard that bisects a public park. But they didn't do anything else to turn that road into a boulevard. The new barriers encouraged speeding, as did the wide lanes, wide field of vision, and so on. From that point on, speeding was induced, or systematically encouraged, by the combination of the infrastructure and the speed limit that did not match it. And people responded predictably by routinely speeding around 20 mph over the limit. While the accident was tragic, speeding on that highway is hardly blameworthy, given that it is systematically encouraged and (now) poses only a small risk to bystanders.

It would be unjust to set up a "speed trap" on that section of highway. Doing so would not improve public safety much. Beyond the efficacy requirement, the standard punishment for speeding does not fit the behavior, even if the law regards reckless speeding and induced speeding as violations all the same. Officers policing the highway therefore have strong reason not to make traffic stops for speeding in that area unless a motorist was substantially exceeding the original speed limit. To do otherwise would typically be unjust, even though the Buffalo Police Department played no role in encouraging the illegal activity. As agents of the state, they are part of the "agency" encouraging it.

5.3.3. Open Container Violations

There are many other systematically encouraged violations of law. Like the induced speeding example, some of them are largely and wisely ignored by police. Open container violations are one clear example. In most jurisdictions, having an open container of alcohol outdoors is against the law. This criminalizes a relatively popular activity. This illegal activity is systematically encouraged. Wealthy people can regularly consume alcohol with friends in a bar. People who cannot afford to drink in a bar are more likely to drink on their stoop or to congregate on the sidewalk or the bus stop shelter. Given the systemic failures that unevenly and unjustly distribute poverty throughout society, enforcement of open container laws compounds these systemic failures.

This is loosely analogous to the induced speeding example: political officials (and others), through honest mistakes or misconduct, create a scenario that increases the likelihood of criminal behavior. Poverty, combined with school spending characterized by feedback loops in which already wealthy areas have better public schools, exacerbates things and makes poverty more difficult to escape (readers can substitute their preferred causal story). As a result, some people turn to certain kinds of recreation that have been criminalized. But to the extent that this criminal activity is induced by bad governance, officers have good reasons to opt for non-enforcement.

Further, the behavior is not overly dangerous or detrimental to bystanders. Though a city without open container laws is hard to imagine for most people, it works fine for New Orleans (or, at least, the open container law is not responsible for the city's manifest inability to self-govern). Of course, alcohol does cause order and safety problems. But there's nothing stopping police from enforcing *those* laws if the need arises. One of the problems is that public drinking leads to glass litter. Thus, New Orleans has decided that in parts of the city where open containers are legal, they must not be glass. Since most tourists do not consult the local criminal code before visiting, the background environment induces this violation: if drinking in public is fun and legal, drinking in public out of glass must be, too. New Orleans Police Department (NOPD) officers would act unjustly, then, if they were to enforce the open container violation instead of instructing tourists to empty their beverage into a to-go cup.

In New Orleans and elsewhere, police officers regularly decline to enforce open container violations (glass or otherwise). If people are discrete, the police typically look the other way. Here is Kelling and Wilson on this practice in a busy transit corridor in Newark, New Jersey:

> One beat was typical: a busy but dilapidated area in the heart of Newark, with many abandoned buildings, marginal shops . . . and, most important, a train station and several major bus stops. Though the area was run-down, its streets were filled with people, because it

was a major transportation center. . . . The people were made up of "regulars" and "strangers." Regulars included both "decent folk" and some drunks and derelicts who were always there but who "knew their place." Strangers were, well, strangers, and viewed suspiciously, sometimes apprehensively. The officer—call him Kelly—knew who the regulars were, and they knew him. As he saw his job, he was to keep an eye on strangers, and make certain that the disreputable regulars observed some informal but widely understood rules. Drunks and addicts could sit on the stoops, but could not lie down. People could drink on side streets, but not at the main intersection. Bottles had to be in paper bags. (Kelling and Wilson 1982)

Whether the officer was *motivated* by a sense of justice or mere expedience, that such criminal behavior is systematically encouraged justifies the decision not to enforce the open container law. Enforcing the law would put people into a congested misdemeanor system, excessively punishing people, all the while doing basically nothing to eliminate the "problem" of drinking in public. And, of course, interactions with the misdemeanor system are often criminogenic, making such enforcement counterproductive. But the element to focus on here is that the state partially caused the problem, and that lowers the ceiling on the amount of force that can be justly used in response even if we set aside the interests of bystanders.

5.3.4. Diverted Buprenorphine Possession

Possession of unprescribed (or diverted) buprenorphine, a case we've briefly touched on already, is our final example of systematically encouraged criminal activity. Whereas our first two examples concern the built, social, and political environments' ability to induce crime, this highlights the criminal legal system's ability to induce crime. It is especially interesting because it resulted in a public commitment to discretionary non-enforcement on the grounds that the criminal law has failed, and because it involves a change in agency strategy rather than an individual officer's discretion. Earlier I relied on this example to argue that discretionary non-enforcement need not conflict with the rule of law and to highlight the stakes of responding to the proceduralist argument against police discretion. Here I want to argue that such a decision is an example of public officials being strategic in imperfect political systems.

The criminalization of the recreational use of prescription opioids, we saw in Chapter 2, is likely a cause of the heroin and fentanyl overdose death crises. People with opioid addiction substituted heroin or fentanyl for the prescription opioids that became harder to acquire. Because these substances are less predictable in terms of potency, opioid overdose deaths skyrocketed.

Buprenorphine, like methadone, is used to treat opioid use disorder (OUD) by reducing the severity of withdrawal symptoms. It carries a low risk of fatal overdose and is much more successful at treating OUD than behavioral strategies for many. Those suffering from OUD turn to buprenorphine for a variety of reasons, including self-medication for OUD and recreational use when alternatives are unavailable. But most diverted buprenorphine possession is consumed therapeutically, not recreationally (Allen and Harocopos 2016). Nevertheless, possession of buprenorphine without a prescription is treated by the law like heroin or fentanyl. Due to concerns about diversion, policymakers have made buprenorphine treatment harder to access. Unsurprisingly there is a robust black market in buprenorphine.

This prompted the police chief and the state's attorney of Burlington, Vermont, to stop arresting and prosecuting people for possession of diverted buprenorphine. Two years later, district attorney of Philadelphia, Larry Krasner, followed suit. They offer three justifications:

> first, to correct the error of criminalizing a person struggling with opioid addiction for possessing an effective means to treat it, second, to reduce stigma against the use of partial agonist medications to treat OUD, and third, to compensate for a serious gap in medication-assisted treatment capacity. Government officials with the discretion to enforce laws should not underestimate their ability to shift critical societal and public health norms with the choices that they make. Our use of discretion was an effort to save lives. (del Pozo, Krasner, and George 2020, 371)

The change was one of many that preceded a 50 percent reduction in opioid overdose deaths in Burlington, Vermont. While determining causation is difficult, this was a promising experiment. The criminal law in this case is a failure of nearly unparalleled proportions, and the gap in medication-assisted treatment capacity is but a small part. It causes people with OUD to break the law. It is unfitting and unjust for the state to then harm opioid users further by subjecting them to the burdens of the criminal legal system. Interestingly, this error is one of the justifications offered for the de facto decriminalization. The framework so far developed in this book, and in particular the broad proportionality principle defended here, implies that they got this right.

There are a few final issues to take up. First, even though theories of punishment often appeal to a principle of proportionality, I should emphasize that I am not advocating for police officers to take over the role of punishment. Police force is not directly punitive, and proportionality in defensive force is different from proportionality in punishment. The police should not detain suspected shoplifters and give them a "physical" warning, even if it is likely to succeed in deterring criminal behavior. Taking up a punitive role would violate our right to legitimate punishment, which usually requires a trial or (non-coercive) plea deal (Hunt 2019, 161).

Second, does this position imply that officers should stop arresting murderers when we can attribute the murder to conditions created by the state? I think in most cases the answer is no. The reason that state-generated violations, as analogous to provoked threats, permit lower levels of defensive force is that the violation is to a large degree innocent or excused. One would need to make the case that a behavior is a reasonable response to the background circumstances for the broad proportionality principle to recommend non-enforcement. But the standards for excusing extreme violence are demanding.

Finally, there is the issue of police priorities. Prioritizing enforcement initiatives that are likely to be disproportional is unjust. It bears emphasizing that since decisions about how to enforce the law are also decisions about which violations not to enforce, the proportionality principle is essential. It helps to distinguish, in a principled manner, the *behavior* from the *violation*, something the criminal code cannot do. If we take proportionality to be a principle of justice for wielding political power, justice requires police to take up a more strategic role than merely making legal arrests and letting the courts adjudicate matters to ensure proportionality.

6

Maintaining Order in the Face
of Disagreement

In this chapter, I'll motivate and characterize another substantive principle of just policing before turning to procedural, democratic matters
in Chapter 7. The principle that concerns us here is a variant of the
principle of liberal neutrality, according to which the state should
avoid "taking sides" in disputes about the good life. The principle of
neutrality is contentious, with those skeptical of liberalism holding the
principle to be incoherent or infeasible (nothing is neutral, the charge
goes). It might even seem like a nonstarter for policing—taking sides is
seemingly at the core of what police do. I'll explore the principle in the
context of managing conflicting uses of public, urban spaces.

Why think neutrality is feasible or desirable? It is feasible as long as
the principle doesn't require *perfect* neutrality. There's the traditional
defense of its desirability: if we try to use state power to enforce our
comprehensive moral theory on a diverse population, the result is inevitable conflict. There's also the "new diversity theory" defense that
finds value in fostering diversity rather than begrudgingly accepting
the need for tolerance in light of our persistent moral disagreement
(Gaus 2018; Muldoon 2016). More and more diverse people means
better problem-solving and more opportunities in life. So we should
opt for more neutrality, or governance that respects and enables diverse ways of living, by enacting fewer prohibitions on contentious
behavior.

The significance of neutrality is heightened in contexts of persistent
and marginalized minorities. Under these conditions, the burden of
non-neutral rules is likely to fall on minority groups that are vulnerable because of their lack of social and electoral power. This phenomenon is not isolated, and certain groups end up bearing a huge burden
compounded across many dimensions of social and political power.

Just Policing. Jake Monaghan, Oxford University Press. © Oxford University Press 2023.
DOI: 10.1093/oso/9780197610725.003.0006

This basic point motivated the legitimacy-risk framework: burdensome enforcement of weakly authorized laws is likely to be illegitimate. Enforcement initiatives like those during Prohibition, or the anti-homosexual policing of the mid-twentieth century, or the responses to the crack epidemic later in the twentieth century, give us reason to worry that the burdensome enforcement of weakly authorized laws today is illegitimate and unjust.

Why focus on the use of public space? Practically, because managing public space and professional policing are intimately linked. Cities have made us amazingly efficient and capable of being ever more productive. They have also proliferated opportunities for crime and made us capable of being ever more annoying and noxious to neighbors. Cities were figuring out how to manage their public space, transit infrastructure in particular, as they were professionalizing their police forces, and the two processes were tightly connected. Philosophically, this confluence of factors (diversity and marginalization in dense environments) is a fundamental concern of political philosophy. The order maintenance function is deeply controversial: uses of public space are often disorderly only on contested conceptions of public order. A common charge against policing is that what counts as order reflects simply the most powerful ideology in society. But no one, even those who are skeptical of order maintenance policing, think the government should exit the social control business of maintaining order or keeping the peace. Even before the police were uniformed and professionalized, they were called upon to settle disagreements and conflicts over the use of space. And a world with non-police alternatives will have some agency managing the use of public space.[1]

This chapter argues that the just maintenance of order requires judicious use of police discretion informed by the principle of neutrality, and it often requires declining to invoke police authority, in service of protecting pluralism and diverse ways of living. First, I argue that there are ineliminable disagreements over the acceptable use of public space, and that such disagreement is an example of pluralism that diverse societies must tolerate or even embrace.

---

[1] As Brandon del Pozo (2022) points out, even police abolitionist protestors occasionally find themselves taking up the order maintenance role (e.g., directing traffic).

This, I argue in the second section, implies that police must opt for strategies of *containment*, rather than dispersion with the intent to *eliminate*, contentious uses of space. Finally, I argue that the dynamic nature of cities requires a presumption of deference to the established uses of public and private space, something that an agency like the police is well-suited to accommodate. Neutrality, I'll argue, has an advantage over other considerations like fairness in dynamic, highly non-ideal contexts.

6.1. Disagreement and Disorder

Disagreement is the foundational problem of political philosophy. Our conflicts of interest lead many to conclude that we must have a state, and our disagreements over how to manage those conflicts have produced a liberal tradition concerned with protecting and fostering diversity. Although liberal approaches to policing (and politics more generally) have come under fire recently, we have powerful reasons to endorse this aspect of the view and enable diverse ways of living when those ways are grounded in sincere normative disagreement, even if only for self-interested reasons: to avoid endless conflict, because if our team loses power our way of life will be threatened, and because exposure to diversity provides us with new opportunities for satisfying and enlightening our preferences.

One familiar way of motivating neutrality and respect for diversity is the Millian notion of "experiments in living." We don't know how best to live our lives, and the difficulty of the question means people will need to try things out. But though we should enable an environment of experimentation, lots of purportedly disorderly behavior doesn't look obviously like an *experiment* in living. To its opponents, it looks either obviously misguided or it interferes with their activities, and so its wisdom is beside the point. I argue here that disagreements about the acceptable use of public space turn in part on intractable disagreements that fall within the realm of reasonable pluralism. Just as important, these disagreements often *appear* to be zero-sum: ultimately, one side must get its way and one side has to lose.

6.1.1. The Vicious Part of the City

Disagreements over the use of public space range from the mundane—how loud can my music be at the park; where may kids skateboard and adults congregate; is it ok to repair your vehicle while parked on the street—to the dramatic. Those include the use of space in skid rows and homeless encampments, vice districts, and some unlicensed economic activity. An important starting point is that, unlike the political philosopher, the police officer takes the world as it is. When they begin their work, the city and its prevailing patterns of use are already established. The police officer and the police department, then, cannot be required to establish perfect justice in managing the use of public space. So, even if we think, for example, homeless encampments are a result of seriously unjust policy, it does not follow that justice requires the police officer or agency to eliminate them. As we saw in the last chapter, sometimes justice requires living with a problem instead of opting for a bad "solution." To show that just order maintenance in diverse societies requires widespread discretionary non-enforcement for the sake of neutrality, we first need to establish some details about contentious uses of urban public space.

Skid rows were a feature of nearly every American city from the Civil War into the twentieth century (Garnett 2010, 112). Characterized by high densities of cheap housing like single room occupancy hotels (SROs) or "flophouses," and later unsheltered residents, early skid rows were also places dense with bars, burlesque shows, and sex workers (Stuart 2016). Employment agencies provided short-term work for some residents, and religious missions tried to save them (the missions have persisted, especially in Los Angeles' skid row). Skid rows began to decline around World War II, and many cities attempted to destroy them by razing and redeveloping the lots in the area. They have, however, remained in several cities. San Francisco's Tenderloin today has many of the characteristics associated with skid rows (Matier 2021). Los Angeles' skid row is probably the most well-known, in no small part because it was formally protected and maintained, whereas most other skid rows were the result of informal policies (hence their eventual elimination).

Most people think drug and alcohol abuse are over-represented on skid rows, though that is not clear. The "Bowery bum" or "skid row drunk" was the stereotypical resident of early skid rows. Yet mid-twentieth-century sociologists distinguished alcoholics from "skid row drunks," the latter not thought to drink heavily due to addiction as evidenced by their communal drinking and sharing of alcohol (Wallace 1965, 182). Research suggests that a minority of skid row residents were alcoholics in the early skid rows (Rossi 1991, 32). It is, however, common for illegal drugs to be easily available in today's skid rows. And, as SROs were eliminated, residents were increasingly unsheltered. So they often spend a significant amount of time sitting or standing on sidewalks, setting up chairs or tents, and storing their property in public spaces. But as we know, dense living creates familiar public order and public health problems.

More general vice districts, including red-light districts and "adult entertainment districts," represent a related but different set of problems. Manhattan's Tenderloin and, until the mid-1990s when Disney restored the New Amsterdam Theatre, Times Square, were both vice districts though not considered skid rows (Traub 2004). Boston's "Combat Zone," like Times Square, was an adult entertainment district in the 1960s, with a high density of adult book stores, strip clubs, and sex workers (Garnett 2010, 116).

Before World War I and the rise of pornography, several U.S. cities had red-light districts. New Orleans' Storyville was unique in that it was created by an ordinance allowing brothels only in that part of the city. The arrangement lasted from 1897 to 1917 and was a reaction to the fact that making sex work illegal does not eliminate the demand for it. As New Orleans Mayor Behrman noted, "you can make it illegal but you can't make it unpopular." Containment was thought more likely to be successful. But, of course, other cities had informal red-light districts that were the result of police looking the other way and in which solicitation happens in public instead of in brothels (Best 1998, 17). New Orleans now has a "mainstream" vice district, Bourbon Street, where heavy drinking and strip clubs remain common. A good Marxist might say, similarly, that Times Square's Disneyfication and elimination of adult book stores and peep shows merely changed the nature of the vice district from *sexual* vice to vicious *consumerism*.

Currently, one of the largest open-air drug markets in the United States is in the Kensington area of Philadelphia. It has some skid row qualities, including rough sleeping on sidewalks. Philadelphia's overdose deaths are concentrated there (Ratcliffe and Wight 2022).

Unlicensed economic activity also consistently produces disputes over the use of space. As of 2010, there were 850 licenses for "peddlers" with a waitlist 5,000 long and estimates of 10,000 unlicensed vendors in New York City (Garnett 2010, 58). Earlier, during the 1980s and 90s, Manhattan had a robust informal written material economy. Vendors would set up tables along Sixth Avenue in Greenwich Village to sell books and magazines, some of them scavenged, some bought used for resale, and some stolen. There was a protracted battle to eliminate them because the vending required tables that took up valuable sidewalk space, involved people "laying claim" to public space that wasn't theirs, panhandling, purportedly encouraged sleeping and urinating in public, and because the vendors competed with tax-paying bookstores (Duneier 1999). For a smaller example, Venkatesh (2006) details the off-book economic activity, including not only vending, but car repair, food preparation, and child care in one Chicago neighborhood. Since much of this occurs in public spaces, it crowds out other uses. New Orleans has a robust economy of unlicensed food and liquor vendors that follow the city's "second-line" parades or do business under the Urban Renewal–era elevated highway that travels through a historically black neighborhood. Though residents have made the best of things by turning the area under the highway into an informal gathering and commercial space, the city began cracking down on them in 2020, motivated in part by complaints from licensed restaurant and bar owners (Adelson 2020). These activities serve a crucial role in the lives of vendors and residents, but they also create social friction. What draws these together is that many think they are impermissible uses of public space that ought to be policed in some way.

6.1.2. Why People Live in the Vicious Part of the City

The reason for cataloging these controversial uses of space is to show that there are reasonable disagreements to be had about whether they are acceptable. This is significant from the point of view of determining what counts as just and legitimate political power.

Because skid rows or homeless encampments are typically where the unhoused go to live, and because their lifestyles are often very different from the majority, they have long been eyed with suspicion. Egon Bittner described the majority view of skid rows as a "primordial jungle, calling for missionary activities and offering opportunities for exotic adventure" and the typical resident as having "repudiated the entire role-casting scheme of the majority and to live apart from normalcy." And, as a result, cities have turned to the police to contain them and to others to "salvage souls from its clutches" (Bittner 1967, 704). Sociologist Nels Anderson attributed residence in skid rows to a handful of reasons, including the travel and unemployment that goes along with seasonal work or discrimination, the inability to secure or maintain employment in the industrial manufacturing economy, "defects of personality," life crises, and "wanderlust" (Anderson 1967 [1923], 61). Anderson describes the "intellectuals" residing in skid row as "a group of egocentric and rebellious natures who decry most things that are" and who are ill-suited to the normal work and family life environments and lack the discipline needed for "regular occupation" (Anderson 1967 [1923], 75).

Despite the popularity of the "repudiation and defect" theory, there is a more sympathetic interpretation available. Viewed through the lens of Millian experimentation, these people want something else from life. And as Anderson recognizes, many Americans were taken with "wanderlust," which he describes as "a social pattern of American life" (1967 [1923], 82). This sentiment was famously echoed thirty-five years later in Jack Kerouac's *On the Road* by Dean Moriarty, who romantically defended the itinerant lifestyle. The Beat Generation, and later the hippies of the 1960s counterculture movement who were heavily influenced by Kerouac, explicitly set out to challenge prevailing cultural norms in America.

Even today, as skid rows in most cities have been eliminated and then later replaced (though often not officially) with homeless encampments, the Millian experimentation view has defenders. Philosopher Alex Smith defends homelessness as a "viable lifestyle" (2014, 34). "Tent cities" are attractive to many residents because they allow for a lifestyle that is more secure, slower, less materialistic, and more autonomous than alternatives. They allow residents to challenge prevailing socioeconomic norms, and especially the individualism of contemporary life, by opting for starkly different collective or nonhierarchical living arrangements. This lifestyle allows people to achieve Thoreauvian self-sufficiency and deliberate living (2014, 41–49). Disputes about participation in illicit sex or drug markets have a similar shape.

I don't intend to romanticize the itinerant or unsheltered lifestyle or to ignore the difficulties faced by people who live this way. Surely many of the people living unhoused or who turn to illicit employment are victims of bad policy decisions who have not chosen the lifestyle. The point for now is that a minority of people do appear to find this experiment in living a worthwhile one.

6.1.3. Second-Choice Lifestyles

Many of the people engaging in purportedly vicious behavior are not pursuing a contentious ideal. Plenty of the residents of skid row or homeless encampments are just trying to get back on their feet. But although pro-diversity theorizing is in some ways concerned with people pursuing various ideals, there is more to be gleaned from thinking about imperfect societies and the various imperfect responses people have to problems. Various problems and shortcomings prevent us from living out our conception of the excellent life. But that our lifestyles are deficient in some respect does not mean that the state should interfere with our ability to muddle along. Just as diverse societies mean people will pursue different ideals, they will also pursue different responses to problems. We must also enable *non-ideal* experiments in living. This follows trivially from a commitment to fostering diversity since no one lives an ideal life in the first place. But the implications are worth emphasizing.

Ideally, the unhoused would make use of a shelter. But in reality, some places have insufficient capacity. In others, like Edinburgh, shelter capacity goes unused (Huey 2007, 44). New York City—which is governed by a right-to-shelter mandate where the Department of

Homeless Services is required to provide people with shelter—there are many who, for a variety of reasons, opt to sleep unsheltered. Surely some of these reasons are illegitimate (e.g., the shelter prohibits property crime). But some of them are legitimate (e.g., the shelter prohibits pets).

In many cases, then, purportedly disordered uses of public space are imperfect responses to an imperfect world. They are attempts at living the best life available to one, path-dependent problems and all. Ethnographic research finds much of value in these uses. For some, street vending is an alternative to racism in corporate America or to committing property crime because of a dearth of employment opportunities, and it can be an important step toward upward mobility (Duneier 1999). For others, operating as a nomadic "street hustler" performing off-the-books automotive repairs is a response to wanting to own one's own business while confronted with an inability to find creditors willing to finance an actual garage. Various social problems cause residents of "the ghetto" to view public spaces as areas not only for recreation (as middle-class communities view them) but also as economic opportunities (Venkatesh 2006, 166–172). Crucially, this work is a source of self-respect, dignity, and autonomy for the street vendors or hustlers (Duneier 1999, 108, 319–320). The vendors play what Jane Jacobs called a "public character" role, conveying local information and participating in informal accountability and social control mechanisms. They also participate in mentoring, community networks, and support for education and sobriety for others (Duneier 1999, 6, 79–80).

More recent ethnographic research features similar findings in Los Angeles' skid row. The vendors in Los Angeles also tended to engage in informal social control to prevent police being called to the area and forcing them to leave after responding to whatever incident brought them there (Stuart 2016, 164). There are also therapeutic benefits. Several of the residents exercised together as a form of "self-directed recovery" to create systems of accountability. Members expected one another to show up for scheduled workouts in a public park and to avoid any behavior that might attract the attention of the police. Until, that is, the police prohibited that use of the park. Without their autonomous support group, several of the members recidivated (Stuart 2016, 136, 159, 161).

The self-directed recovery found in the social networks of the skid row residents is especially important because the "mega-shelters" that have come to have a monopoly over the rehabilitation and support functions in skid row are successful for an unfortunately small number of people. Residents of Los Angeles' skid row complain about the invasive, highly regimented, often infantilizing lifestyle available in the mega-shelters. Many compare them to jail or prison—and some regret opting for the rehabilitation programs there instead of incarceration (Stuart 2016, 4, 142). The median stay in the twenty-one-day shelter program is three days, a third leave within twenty-four hours, and under 10 percent graduate (2016, 72). These may be excellent programs given the difficulty of the problem, but they succeed for only a minority of the relevant population, and this success rate and distributional pattern demand alternatives.

Many of those involved in the sex work economies similarly find dignity and autonomy in their work, or at least take it to be the best option available to them. There is a robust theoretical perspective on which sex workers are workers like any other and on which people opt into the work because it enables a comparatively attractive lifestyle. According to these theorists, the sex work abolitionist position is either objectionably moralizing or it denies sex workers the agency they clearly possess (for discussion, see Thusi 2022, 140; Sanders 2005, 39). And here, too, people are making the best of their situation. Sex workers sometimes choose sex work over other options, and choose between working in brothels or outdoors in different areas. They have strategies for navigating according to their values and perceived risks (Thusi 2022, 145; O'Neill and Pitcher 2010, 204).

Finally, plenty of people think that the kinds of disorder discussed above are valuable parts of the city. This is especially the case for those who prefer laissez-faire approaches to rehabilitation in skid row (the dominant position in Los Angeles, at least, for several decades). It is also true for the customers of the informal, illegal, or purportedly vicious economies in these disorderly areas. As one long-time vendor in New York City put it, "If the community didn't want us in business, we wouldn't be in business" (Dworin 2008). That a vendor can make a living for over a decade is pretty good evidence that a substantial minority, if not a majority, value this use of public space. We can make similar arguments for those participating in the illegal sex and drug economies.

Many of the behaviors people find especially objectionable are also a result of people responding to the problems in their lives. Those who find unlicensed vending objectionable tend to worry about the outdoor sleeping and urinating it encourages. But people sleep outside for a variety of reason, including to protect a vending spot, to save money for housing through the winter, or—perhaps surprisingly—to increase their privacy by avoiding the situation in a shelter or hotel room wherein the manager can allow the police into the room (Duneier 1999, 162–169). People will sometimes urinate in public to save a spot, because if they leave their possessions unattended, the police are likely to throw them away, or simply because there are few options for public or private toilets (Duneier 1999, 173–187). Some tolerance (if not support) is required for even unambiguously problematic uses of space with high externalities when they are a response to problems created, at least in part, by democratic decisions about what to criminalize, whether we allow SROs or paid restrooms, what kind of options exist for shelter and therapy, and so on. A challenge for just policing is that there are legitimate conflicts of interest in a context where zero tolerance responses to even high-externality uses of space can be illegitimate.

The Millian commitment to experiments in living, and the related political commitment to protecting diversity, implies that our urban land-use policies should generally protect minority views about acceptable uses of public space when they are attempts at living a good life. Thus, when it comes to disputes between the Jane Jacobs–style urbanists who take a measure of *apparent* chaos and disorder in mixed-use areas of cities to count, deceptively, as a kind of valuable order, and the Le Corbusier–style rational planners who think that single-use zoning is necessary for the good life, there is a powerful case to be made against using the coercive power of city governments to prevent the apparent chaos of most cities.

6.2. To Disperse or Contain?

Early skid rows and many vice districts were contained. The police were given wide latitude to enforce vague order maintenance laws to keep disorder in certain sections of the city (Bittner 1967, 704). Attitudes toward skid row alternated from coercively therapeutic to harm reduction and back to coercively therapeutic, all the while adopting a containment approach. By the 1970s, however, many of the SROs that skid row residents lived in had been demolished and replaced by parking lots because of concerns about "unsightly flophouses" and to expand the central business district. They were eventually redeveloped. By the 1980s, homelessness increasingly meant sleeping in public rather than living unattached lives in skid row cubicles, and it had been mostly decentralized (Rossi 1991, 33–39). This led to "compassion fatigue" and an increasing reliance on police to eliminate the now-dispersed disorder (Garnett 2010, 113). Los Angeles' skid row, uniquely, was formally protected with the 1976 Containment Plan (Stuart 2016). After several decades of dispersion, the pendulum appears to be swinging in the other direction. Cities like Phoenix, Atlanta, and Sacramento have "recreated skid row" by creating homeless encampments or "human services campuses" (Garnett 2010, 104). But not everywhere: breaking up an informal homeless encampment moved many problems of public order to the Kensington area of Philadelphia (Ratcliffe and Wright 2022).

There's an important question about formal, citywide policy created through local legislation, about how to respond to these uses of public space. There's another, related question about how the police in particular should respond. Should police officers and departments take the initiative to disperse and eliminate, or to contain and regulate, contentious uses of space? How should they respond to the conflicts of interest that are essential to the use of public space in diverse societies? I'll argue that frequently, containment is the just strategy because it is the neutral (and more proportional) strategy.

6.2.1. Neutral Containment Strategies

To get an intuitive sense of the case for containment, consider another example concerning the use of public space. Many urbanists are proponents of "complete streets" projects where streets are redesigned to accommodate not just motorists but also pedestrians and cyclists. If a street is wide enough, you can "complete" it. Some streets, however, are too small for dedicated cycle, car, and pedestrian traffic, as well as parking, in both directions. One neutral option for solving these zero-sum problems is to leave the cars and pedestrians to one street and give another nearby street to the pedestrians and the cyclists. Wherever possible, we should not exclude any uses of the street. Where that's not possible because of unavoidable conflicts, however, streets should be allocated so that there is some high-quality infrastructure for more modes of transit. The non-neutral option would be to eliminate one of the conflicting modes of transit. Notice that the neutral containment approach means that prohibiting a particular kind of traffic from an area replaces the zero-sum nature of the conflict with something less zero-sum, reducing the burdens of the enforcement.

Instead of a destined-to-fail complete streets analog to order maintenance, you could give certain public spaces over to certain uses. We do this with formal policy, of course. But the taxonomy of uses is infinitely more fine-grained than the kind that can be reflected in written zoning policy. We need more flexibility in administering the restrictions. Order maintenance laws end up being analogous in some ways to zoning laws, enforced by the police. "Informal micro-zoning" is a non-negligible part of order maintenance policing, and understanding it that way illuminates many disputes.

Take some of the objections to the street vendors. Some of it is protectionism; merchants don't want competition. Some of it is not; merchants don't want their customers blocked from entering their stores. Nor do most want public spaces strewn with litter, as can happen from dense street vending. Further, people need to be able to use the sidewalk for transit or the local park for recreation.

On the other hand, some order maintenance policing relies on the kind of considerations police, and the state more generally, are simply not permitted to rely on. In a discussion of the issue, legal theorist Nicole Garnett remarks that:

> To some early twentieth-century New Yorkers, pushcart markets were an integral and picturesque part of urban life. Elite opinion, however, strongly disfavored them. As middle- and upper-class residents ceased their patronage of street markets, vending increasingly became identified with the poverty of the immigrant ghetto. (Garnett 2010, 60)

Aesthetic, class-based concerns are not usually a legitimate justification for exercising the amount of power that goes into shutting down established vending markets. On the other hand, containing street vendors to certain areas allows vending, and it allows others to avoid the practical inconveniences and the moral turpitude of pushcarts. In this way, containment protects diversity.

How should police implement this basic idea? Again, they can't implement an overarching plan. But they can focus on other problems when vendors are operating in areas where that is the established pattern, or where they are successfully avoiding conflicts with others (e.g., by operating in the unused space under elevated highways that are in some ways a greater nuisance or by using parks when kids aren't playing). They can enforce relevant laws where vending is not typically occurring and where it will be especially disruptive (e.g., busy transit areas, areas dense with retail) if they receive complaints.

Recall the issue of unsheltered people sleeping in the subway. Sleeping in a subway station or train means others can't use these spaces for their intended use. A neutral, informal solution to this problem, mentioned earlier, was settled upon in the 1980s:

> Between ten-thirty and eleven o'clock every night, [unsheltered men] would meet on the platform. The men say that there was an informal agreement between them and the transit-police officers assigned to the station that they would be left alone when they were in a single car, a claim that transit officials confirm is highly plausible.

According to one official, the MTA operates certain trains with ten
or twelve cars but uses only a few of them. The unhoused would take
over one of the closed-off cars. (Duneier 1999, 126)

This is not a stable solution or reflection of an established pattern, but
it is neutral and proportional. It was a valuable arrangement while it
lasted.

To return to another earlier example, police in Chicago encourage
people using parks to sleep or to engage in unlicensed economic activity to congregate away from children (Venkatesh 2006, 200). The
parks are attractive to children and adults alike, though for different
reasons. Police in both cases play an important role in allowing diverse
uses of the space at different times, and that is especially important
when residents of a neighborhood lack ample private space.

Of course, I don't mean to suggest that everyone will be happy with
these arrangements. But there is no complainer's veto. The following
exchange at a community policing meeting is unsurprising:

"I got many problems. People hooting at me if I wear a short dress.
People peeing on my lawn, people taking a shit right there in the park
where my children are playing. People selling things! If I want to buy
something, I'll go to the store." "Yes, Ms. Williams," the police official replied, his patience being tested. "We understand. Now, we can't
get all these people out, because they have the right to use the park
too. And, you know, they are going to sell things somewhere, and we
do try and get them not to harass people." (Venkatesh 2006, 201)

The legalist might reject this (clearly imperfect) balancing of interests
(the selling is illegal after all), but in addition to cracking down on
the vendors eliminating a plausibly legitimate use of space, it would
require disproportionate police force: the police response would have
to be aggressive. And, in the view of the police anyway, dispersing
and eliminating the vendors would very likely be criminogenic by
creating room for more disorderly, or even violent, uses of that space
(in this case by a local gang) (Venkatesh 2006, 203). The complaint is
obviously legitimate, but that alone does not show that police should
act on it.

Finally, another important benefit of these neutral containment strategies is that they can make certain errors in moral reasoning less damaging. Majority conceptions of vice and disorder, we know all too well, are often unjustified. In an ideal world, we would not make these errors. But in our world, they're inevitable. Containment has the ancillary effect of making the dispersion that does occur less objectionable by making it more proportional. Telling a vendor they'll be issued a citation or have their merchandise confiscated for operating *here*, rather than in general, forces those who'd like to vend to bear a smaller burden. We have a strong moral obligation to allow for some minority uses of space, so using the police to shut down vending is risky. It's not unjust, on the other hand, to protect some areas for the anti-vendors *if the vendors have space elsewhere.*

An immediate objection is that containment is not benign. Containment typically results in concentration. And concentration sometimes amplifies disorder rather than merely containing it. Concentration is thought to have exacerbated problems in Times Square and the Combat Zone (Garnett 2010, 116). It is not clear, however, whether that is true across the board.

We can grant that containment will, in some cases, amplify disorder. It does not follow that the just strategy is dispersal and elimination. Rather, in some cases, we might want to contain disorder to several parts of the city to allow for competing uses of public space while also keeping the density of disorder low enough to avoid amplification. In other cases, we'll simply have to accept amplified disorder and hope to combat that with harm-reduction programs. But recall that the police are not in the business of implementing an overarching plan of where to contain contentious uses of space. They are usually determining whether to proactively police disorder violations, when to initiate stops or make arrests and for which behaviors. Those marginal decisions should be guided by the legitimacy-risk framework, and neutral policing lowers the risks of poorly authorized, high-burden power. Frequently, dispersion does not eliminate disorder; it merely displaces it. In some cases, containment is the best we can do consistent with the requirements of neutrality and proportionality.

6.2.2. Fairness and Neutrality on Patrol

In addition to skepticism about the value of containment, as I've mentioned, there is considerable skepticism about neutrality. Some of that skepticism comes from the view that the state should not protect diversity, but should enforce a particular conception of the right and the good. A more plausible, and friendlier (to my approach) source of skepticism says that we should go further than neutrality and aim for *fairness*. We should protect not just diverse uses of space; we should ensure that there is a fair distribution of the resource.

David Thacher explains that on one conception of the order maintenance function of policing, it is justified when it targets unfair uses of public space. Uses of public space are unfair when they result in *accumulative harm* like littering or sleeping in the park or when they are *offensive* (in a technical sense) like verbal harassment (Thacher 2014, 133). This is an important insight because it helps to distinguish between patrol officers enforcing a controversial, parochial conception of the good life and helping us navigate shared spaces.

Contentious uses of public space clearly evoke concerns about fairness. People drinking in public spaces might bother some, but it typically doesn't interfere with their own use of the public space. Other common activities, like busking, vending, and unsheltered sleeping, *can* interfere with one's use of space. Vendors can block the sidewalk or access to your business, unfairly setting back your interests. If a group of unsheltered people move their belongings into a pavilion in the park and use it as their private space, this is intuitively unfair (what about the other people who'd like to eat their lunch in the park?). If older women gather to dance to music in parks so loud that other people can't enjoy the park, this is also intuitively unfair. Without some policing of the park, individual users will take matters into their own hands. If we're lucky, they'll turn to speaker-disabling stun-guns instead of violence, but we're not always lucky.[2]

The intuitive idea, however, needs specification. When is a use of space unfair? Fairness is often a distributional concern, and it is natural

---

[2] This is an actual order maintenance problem, complete with speaker-guns, in some Chinese cities (Lin and Davidson 2021).

to think of this in terms of having a fair share of space. But what is the just distributional pattern of access to space? Whatever it is, police aren't in a position to implement a particular pattern or to assess the relative quantity of space available to different people. Further, it is not clear that many of the relevant cases involve taking an unfair amount of space. We might have in mind a "duty of fair play," where we incur an obligation to restrict our activities because we've enjoyed the benefits of others restricting theirs. This more naturally accounts for why accumulative harms or offenses are unfair (we benefit from others not littering and shouting insults at us, so we must also refrain). But the diversity of uses of space, including the benefits we enjoy from technically illegal uses of space, makes determining which uses of space are unfair an extreme challenge.

If someone is obstructing a sidewalk by sitting down, they're not taking up much more space than someone who is walking. They're simply reducing a primary use of the space. And if there are many people sitting, they might each be taking up a comparable amount of space to the same number of people walking. Given that some people want to be able to sit on the sidewalk (or engage in vending), and that many residents find benefits in these purportedly disorderly, sometimes clearly illegal, uses of space, quantitative and fair play concerns seem not to get off the ground. Likewise for someone playing loud music in the park: they're taking up the same amount of space they would be if their music were quiet, but the other park-goers don't get to enjoy the park. But again, sometimes a use of space prevents other uses, and that seems not to justify police intervention. When picnickers take over the field, Frisbee throwers can't use the park. It seems that the police ought to overlook some uses of public space that take a larger share or crowd out other uses in some circumstances.

Neutrality, rather than direct concerns about fairness, then, strike me as the more central and capable principle. Instead of attempting to reason on the basis of a contentious view about the proper allocation of access to space across society or which activities are prohibited by the sacrifices others make in allowing us to benefit from using public space, police should aim to preserve diversity. People should not block the sidewalk entirely because then there's no walking, and police should preserve both uses. People should not play loud music at the park because they can listen or dance to headphones and not crowd out others' access, but if it's off hours, it may not matter. People who opt for sleeping outside instead of a shelter should avoid locations that prevent other, especially limited, uses of space. Because police should aim for neutrality, they should de-prioritize policing activities without significant externalities.

Like the proportionality principle, the neutrality principle appears to have some uptake in the profession. Because police tend not to have a specific distributional theory of fairness, we see evidence of the principle in the policing of externalities. Whether neutrality motivates these strategies, it contributes to their justification. The principle of neutrality instructs the police to preserve diverse uses of space in the provision of order or peacekeeping. These two demands of justice— preservation of diversity and orderly, broadly accessible public space— are in clear tension where people disagree about the acceptable use of public space. There's a related conflict between preserving orderly uses of public space (which usually requires preventing accumulative harms) and the proportionality principle; going to jail for panhandling really seems excessive (Thacher 2014, 136). Looking at some cases will help to connect the principle of neutrality with individual police decisions to focus on the externalities of various public behaviors.

One perennial conflict I've focused on so far is the dispute among vendors, panhandlers, and business owners. To address this dispute, police will occasionally target their enforcement of "disorderly" be- havior like panhandling to those behaviors that prevent people from accessing business (Gascón and Roussell 2019, 158). The "no-go zones" around businesses are an example of allocating space in such a way that everyone satisfies some of their interests instead of entrenching ma- jority (or dominant) preferences at the total expense of minority (or marginalized) preferences.

Criminologist William Sousa's fieldwork reveals a concern with this principle in other ways:

> While driving on a busy, slow-moving roadway, officers see a pan-
> handler walking in the street between cars. One officer turns on the
> car's public address system and tells her to stay on the sidewalk. The
> woman complies and the officers continue on. The officer explains,

"Technically, she can be arrested for that, but personally we would never do it. The arrest option is not meant for those people." Later in the evening, the same officer sees an apparently homeless person sleeping on the steps of a brownstone. Referring to the previous panhandler encounter, the officer says, "See, this is what I'm talking about. Look at this guy. Now what is he doing? Who is he really bothering? The 'homeless' enforcement is not meant for him—it's meant for the assholes." (Sousa 2010, 53)

Some have raised reasonable worries about the police having a category of "asshole" in their informal moral taxonomy (Zacka 2017, 161). But there is a more sympathetic interpretation available: the asshole makes no attempt to internalize the costs of their use of public space. The officer asks about the person's behavior—what are they doing and, especially relevant, who are they bothering? If the behavior doesn't bother anyone in the sense of producing an actual complaint, it is not disorderly in the sense that warrants police power.

In a different context, officers use discretion for similar purposes. Sousa recounts officers deciding not to make an arrest after finding a sex worker in the act:

In this particular case, prostitution was taking place yet the officers decided not to invoke the legal process, on the basis that they (the prostitute and john) were not "being obvious" and because the prostitute heeded the officer's warning and left the area. This of course implies that by not being obvious, the harm to the community had been minimized. It also implies if the prostitute and john were less discrete, the officers would have more strongly considered official action. (Sousa 2010, 51)

Neutrality justifies this decision. The police enable a contentious use of space in a way that does not come at the cost of anyone else's. In cases of *discrete disorder*, contentious uses of space that nevertheless do not interfere with others using the space, the police are better off looking the other way, or invoking their authority in the least burdensome way possible. This helps to satisfy two of the competing demands on patrol officers: protecting diversity while preserving orderly, minimal-conflict public space.

6.3. Dynamism and Disorder

The police response to disorder must be informed by the dynamic nature of our cities. Not only do people disagree over the acceptable use of public space, those disagreements have temporal and geographic elements, and different uses will prevail in different times and places. Beyond changing land-use patterns, the nature of the problems people have and the menu of solutions will change over time. Static and uniform policing cannot accommodate these practical realities.

These problems of disagreement over the acceptable uses of public space present, in less dramatic ways, in more typical urban settings. This is partially a result of disagreement over the use of public space but also partially a result of the fact that use of our private space is often not entirely internalized (fixing cars or living in RVs parked on the street, congregating on the sidewalk in front of one's house, etc.). In other cases the use of private space spills over (playing loud music audible from other lots, etc.). In some cases, the local government or homeowner's association will codify the acceptable use of space in such detail that it's funny. The local government might prevent you from keeping an unregistered vehicle visible on your property for extended periods of time. The Home Owners Association (HOA) might allow you to paint your home in one of three shades of blue or white and will give you the option of two styles of mailbox and fence. Some people appear to find these impositions on the way other people can live to be deeply valuable, so to the extent that one can opt into such safe spaces, there's good reason to allow certain areas to be so governed. On the other hand, others have a much more laissez-faire attitude and tolerate car maintenance on the street and even appreciate unlicensed vendors rolling their carts down the block or setting up nearby. As you move through a city, you'll see different informal land-use standards on the three-shades-of-blue/vice district continuum. And as we've seen, the laws governing this behavior are typically vague, or not capable of full enforcement. Thus, their enforcement needs to be sensitive not only to disagreements over the use of space but to the fact that those problems and their solutions are dynamic.

The HOA is, at least, a useful analogy for thinking about how police should accommodate such dynamism. The overbearing HOA rules are justified by consent-like behavior. Homeowners opt into the rules (and the community) by deciding to buy a home in an HOA with the knowledge that they will be subjected to a large set of rules. If you don't like the rules, the HOA enthusiasts can, with justification, tell you that you shouldn't have opted into them. Similarly, there are (or can be) clear patterns of behavior, and clear patterns of enforcement, on the hyperlocal level. These patterns of behavior, established with the help of policing, are plausibly opted into by those who move into new homes.

Just policing is sensitive to these established patterns of behavior. This is, again, because these problems are simply unlikely to be solved by top-down rule-making. For the reasons discussed above, if a several block area in a neighborhood widely accepts an idiosyncratic use of public and private space, and newcomers to the area call on the police to enforce a new idiosyncratic conception of order, the police have ample justification for engaging in discretionary non-enforcement.

Local knowledge is important in adjudicating the use of public space while accommodating the dynamic nature of local conceptions of the acceptable use of space. Without knowledge of the various informal relationships that govern the many uses of public space, it can be impossible for police to play a role in adjudicating disputes and assisting the community in maintaining order. The informal maintenance of order in the bourgeois West Village that Jane Jacobs lived in differs significantly from the informal control negotiated in a Chicago ghetto, or, as we've seen, the West Village that Duneier researched (Venkatesh 2006, 205–209; Duneier 1999, 115).

Cities have in the past responded to disorder by shifting its management from the police and onto land-use regulators. By engaging in formal zoning, regulators must make decisions ahead of time about what counts as disorder and where it is permitted. This kind of decision-making is necessarily blunt, and the lawmakers responded to that problem in the criminal context with vague ordinances and discretionary law enforcement. Land-use regulators do not have that option. The social costs of disorder management can be modulated with discretion in a way that land-use regulations cannot (Garnett 2010, 117). Of course, the patterns of behavior are not set in stone. The city is, if anything, dynamic. If enough change occurs, the established patterns of behavior will come to change, and with it, informal standards of acceptable uses of space. Similarly, the contained zones of disorder will, in some cases, be dynamic as well. This is an additional problem for relying on land-use regulators.

Los Angeles formally delineated the boundaries of their skid row, and there is something to be said for that as an explicit policy. But even then, dynamism is unavoidable. As the skid row population and the problems they face change, the options available for addressing them will as well. This is reflected in the changes to the community groups (and their strategies) that partner with the police to provide support for residents. What is especially objectionable about the kind of therapeutic policing we see in Los Angeles' skid row is that the rehab programs are not particularly effective in absolute terms. So police and their community partners are closing off other opportunities for rehabilitation. This has led to conflict over whether those groups actually represent the residents of skid row (Stuart 2016, 213). The unavoidably dynamic nature of cities and their problems underlies a need for neutral policing—to accommodate the changing sensibilities about the acceptable use of public space, to preserve diverse ways of life, and to accommodate non-ideal experiments in living.

The disagreements relevant to this chapter are inevitable and intractable. We can treat diversity as a problem and hope we win political battles to enact our preferred institutions and policies. Or we can treat diversity as a valuable resource to be protected by more neutral political power. I've argued that when it comes to policing, the use of public space, diversity, and experimentation—and so neutrality—are deeply important in light of the difficulties we face in our non-ideal world. Neutrality guides police to prioritize violations that involve high-externality behavior and to de-prioritize discrete, low-externality behavior. It also guides police to work to contain (in time or place) high-externality behaviors that are here to stay, as in the subway example, or in informal skid rows. Occasionally it means dispersion to protect certain uses of space like panhandling in front of an ATM. While I have pointed to real-world examples of order maintenance policing to motivate or illustrate these claims, our current police forces are not particularly well-suited to produce just policing so understood.

Further, there are significant procedural, democratic concerns about the principles of just policing I've defended so far. I take up procedural matters in the next chapter. Then, in Chapter 8, I offer a diagnosis of some problems in contemporary policing with an eye toward imagining police agencies that are designed to provide the kinds of just, discretionary policing covered thus far.

7

On the Democratic Authorization of Police Power

I must now finally take up procedural, democratic principles. I argued in Chapter 4 that when a law is weakly democratically authorized, police should de-prioritize its enforcement. This is doubly so when the enforcement has other high-risk characteristics. The appeal to neutrality in the last chapter is motivated in part by the view that laws that burden those with minority views and lifestyles are at much higher risk of being unjust and illegitimate. Does the account of just policing developed so far require us to adopt an anti-democratic view of justice and legitimacy?[1]

I'll begin by recapping the problem of democratic authorization of police power. Then I'll outline a Millian dilemma for democratic authorization. These conclusions set the stage for evaluating extant attempts at securing democratic authorization via participatory democracy mechanisms. I'll argue that they are either underspecified or do not address relevant procedural concerns about democratic authorization. The rest of the chapter is dedicated to a positive account of how policing can secure democratic authorization, one that relies on both electoral and non-electoral mechanisms. The choice between democratic, faithful enforcement of the criminal code and anti-democratic, discretionary policing is a false one.

---

[1] Plenty of theorists think so, in the sense that they think separating criminal justice decisions from politics is justice-enhancing (Surprenant and Brennan 2020; Rappaport 2020; Barkow 2019).

Just Policing. Jake Monaghan, Oxford University Press. © Oxford University Press 2023.
DOI: 10.1093/oso/9780197610725.003.0007

7.1. Two Problems of Democratic Policing

The first problem for democratic policing, understood as policing oriented toward securing democratic authorization, is the problem of legitimacy laid out in Chapter 3. The mainstream, broadly legalist view holds that police legitimacy flows from the authorization of voters to the leader of the executive branch, the legislature and criminal code, and down the police hierarchy to the patrol officer and detective. Police power is legitimate when the exerciser has been delegated power through the appropriate channels and when they act faithfully to the criminal law. But the enforcement dilemma that requires us to trade off priority and interpretive discretion, and the unavoidable fact of opportunity costs in enforcement decisions, both indicate the weakness of the command to faithfully enforce the law and the break in the transmission of legitimacy. Additionally, the current criminal code both lags changes in public opinion and is the emergent product of half-measures. It is not a comprehensively designed product of a legislature wielding delegated authority. Necessarily, in between the democratically emergent criminal code and the demos sits a bureaucrat making important decisions about how to enforce it and exercise police power.

We might respond to this problem by replacing the (liberal) legalist strategy of finding authorization in the criminal code with a participatory democratic strategy of injecting authorization elsewhere in the process, much like the jury trial is supposed to. That framework will need to be sensitive to a second problem for democratic policing. A simple motivation for democracy is to avoid tyrannical, arbitrary, or otherwise illegitimate government (tyranny of the *rulers*) by enabling the people to govern. If we govern ourselves, then we eliminate the problem of a small number of rulers impermissibly exercising control over us—the tyranny of the minority—in part by sharply limiting their political authority. But problematically, this is not guaranteed to secure political agency.

On John Stuart Mill's telling, after some time of periodic elections making political power "emanate" from the community, the concern with limiting authority waned. Now that the ruled are also the rulers, there's no risk of tyranny. We won't exercise it over ourselves (Mill 1859/1978, 3). The problem, noted Mill, is that latent in the solution of political liberties and the "consent of the community" to the "struggle between liberty and authority" is another equally significant threat:

> The "people" who exercise the power, are not always the same people with those over whom it is exercised, and the "self-government" spoken of, is not the government of each by himself, but of each by all the rest. (1859/1978, 4)

Mill, citing Tocqueville, called this the "tyranny of the majority." If you make government too responsive to all the rest, you disempower minorities and you risk empowering our worst impulses. Mill's focus in *On Liberty* is with how the "tyranny of prevailing opinion" can be coercive even outside of politics, but we'll see how it manifests in community control over the police.

It is obvious that democracies with various franchise extensions have enabled the control of some by all the rest. Majority support has, at various times, "justified" slavery and Jim Crow laws, prohibition of alcohol in the United States, and later recreational drug use in most democracies, bans on sodomy and same-sex marriage, bans on soliciting homosexual intercourse in public when the sodomy bans proved difficult to enforce for evidentiary reasons, bans on adultery (still on the books in many US states), bans on the construction of minarets on mosques in Switzerland, bans on burqas and niqabs in France, bans on pants-sagging in Louisiana, and on and on. Majorities have tyrannized minorities resulting in moral atrocities on one extreme and busy-body annoyances on the other.

So we have another dilemma. Allowing political power to be unconstrained by the interests of the governed via democratic mechanisms, risks illegitimate, tyrannical power. But allowing the majority, or more broadly, the winners of political decision-making procedures—not always majorities—to run roughshod over the minority also risks illegitimate, tyrannical power. One of the ways this happens is through persistent minorities—groups who rarely or never find their governments responsive to their interests. Persistent minorities are especially problematic when they are the result of *marginalization*. These two problems help us to frame a discussion of the popular accounts of democratic, community policing. The crucial point is that we can have procedural, *democratic* grounds (not just substantive grounds) for rejecting the legitimacy of even ostensibly democratically made decisions.

7.2. Community Policing Strategies

Just because some instance of political power is apparently approved by a democratic process does not mean the outcome enjoys genuine democratic legitimacy. If the procedural problem is that there is a gap between the demos and the police, the natural response is to try to shrink, or bridge, that gap. Police reformers have made several attempts. Recently, they have fallen under the heading of "community policing," an unfortunately ambiguous term. In what follows, I'll use the term anachronistically to see how community-oriented strategies fare with respect to securing democratic authorization. I'll focus on those policies that aim for formal community engagement rather than tactics like foot patrol and policies like residency requirements.

7.2.1. Peelian Principles

The London Metropolitan Police famously sought to secure democratic legitimacy. In addition to government by the governed, we should have policing by the policed. According to the seventh Peelian principle, the police must:

> maintain at all times a relationship with the public that gives reality to the historic tradition that the police are the public and that the public are the police, the police being only members of the public who are paid to give full-time attention to duties which are incumbent on every citizen in the interests of community welfare and existence.

And we've already covered the principle that holds that the appropriate way for the police to honor that relationship is for "public favor" to come from impartial and full enforcement of law, without regard to the substantive justice of each law. Professional policing serves the community as a replacement for amateur, volunteer policing, and secures democratic authorization, by deferring to the rule-makers. In fact, the Peelian principles rejected an approach to community policing that would later become ascendant. Impartial service to the law is achieved by the isolation of the police officer as an agent of the state rather than member of the community: the Peelian model viewed officers as representatives of the English Constitution (Monkkonen 1981, 37–39). This is a commitment to legalism. We've seen how impartial service to the law as a way of respecting separations of power is supposed to secure police legitimacy, and we've covered at length problems for the view. The contrast to the London model in U.S. cities in instructive.

7.2.2. Adjuncts to the Political Machines

Only some parts of the "London model" spread to early U.S. cities. The agency organization and especially the uniform, representing separation from the community, were adopted by U.S. cities, but not the central political control. Departments were originally "adjuncts" to the local political machines. Robert Fogelson's history of "big city" police departments details the widespread practice of political machines compensating ethnic groups for their political support with relatively lucrative jobs in the police departments. Fogelson writes:

> ward leaders influenced appointments, assignments, and promotions; and as many policemen who fought the system discovered, they arranged suspensions and dismissals. . . . But the machine's hold over the police did not depend exclusively on even primarily on [sic] insecurity or intimidation. Most officers were linked to the politicians by strong personal, familial, class, and ethnic bonds. (1977, 69)

This close relationship between local ethnic enclaves and police departments is one manifestation of the police also being the policed. Under this model, police legitimacy comes from reflecting highly local interests, not merely of the city, but of the ward or neighbor-hood. Police represent actual, local interests, rather than standing in as a representative for an impartial nation-state (Monkonnen 1981, 39). In Ireland and London, early police officers stayed in barracks like soldiers. In the United States, they lived at home or slept in the station house. Given the tight connection between the police were the policed, Fogelson reports that ethnic minorities were empowered by police tailoring their enforcement to preserve minority lifestyles (1977, 38). This is a win from a liberal, pro-diversity orientation, but I'll argue later that it was valuable for distinctively democratic reasons.

But the connection to the political machines was a result of factional in-fighting; the police were *some* of the public. The risk of the tyranny of the majority under the early American model is plain. Battles be-tween political factions, some empowered at the state and others the local level, over the early urban police departments, were a common experience (Monkkonen 1981, 43; Fogelson 1977, 14). Corruption was extreme and widespread. In New York City, officers of the Democrat-controlled New York Police Department (NYPD) intimidated Republican voters and tampered with ballot boxes. They protected gambling in local Democratic clubs (Fogelson 1977, 2, 73). To pay for appointments to the force, officers collected bribes for ignoring crime. This was not unique to New York City; similar problems plagued many American cities. The Lexow Committee released their report on NYPD corruption, initiating the first wave of police reform around the country in 1895 (Fogelson 1977, 5). Reformers sought to remove policing from local political influence. This involved centralizing police administra-tion and removing power from the more local wards, instituting civil service exams and more demanding hiring requirements, eliminating residency requirements, and applying a military analogy to policing to further remove policing from politics (Fogelson 1977, 82–89).

In broad strokes, American policing first adopted aspects of London's agency organization and technology, and only later did it adopt an orientation of legalistic isolation. The upshot is that the London and American models are differently sensitive to democratic values. The London model lends itself to legislative supremacy and finds democratic authorization in formal, electoral mechanisms. The early American model lends itself to "streetcorner politicking," despite its many glaring faults in finding a measure of democratic authorization in representing and making government responsive to (some) local, parochial interests.

7.2.3. The Beat Meeting

By the 1970s, the pendulum was swinging the other way again, against the core elements of professional reform (Fogelson 1977, 298). The term "community policing" attached to a variety of reforms characterized by bringing officers into closer contact with the community. This included a renewed appreciation for foot patrol (early reformers rejected foot patrol in favor of motor patrol; Seo 2019, 108). Many advocated for the reinstatement of residency requirements, hoping this would ameliorate the racial disparities in urban police departments and reduce the likelihood of the kinds of "race riots" seen in Watts in 1965 and elsewhere, though police officers and their unions predictably resisted such proposals (Fogelson 1977, 288). The wave of community policing reforms eventually sought opportunities for democratic authorization via community engagement in other ways, too. In the early 1990s, this came in the form of "beat meetings," pioneered in the early 1990s by the Chicago Police Department in a program called the Chicago Alternative Policing Strategy (CAPS). By 2002, many major police agencies were implementing police-community meetings, police meetings with community partner groups, long-term beat assignments for individual officers, and citizen "police academies," among other strategies for reducing police isolation (Cordner 2014, 61; Skogan and Harnett 1997; Kelling and Moore 1988, 12). These reforms were not always enthusiastically pursued, though many departments retained a nominal commitment to community policing with programs like New Orleans' "Police Community Advisory Boards," the NYPD's "Neighborhood Policing" initiative, or Boston's Bureau of Community Engagement.[2]

---

[2] In 2021 the NOPD rejected my application for membership in the First District's Police Community Advisory Board.

Police scholars have remained captivated by this kind of community engagement, as seen in the "Statement of Principles on Democratic Policing" from New York University's Policing Project. They take inspiration from the first of the Peelian principles cited above while also being sensitive to the wave of "community policing" reform over the last decades of the twentieth century. On their view, democratic policing has several requirements, but the "robust engagement between police departments and the communities they serve around the policies and priorities of policing" is the most important for present purposes (Policing Project 2015).[3] On this view, democratic policing is not achieved by impartial service to the legislature, but with policing in light of information gleaned from community engagement. It holds that democratic authorization must be *added* to policing by the department.

The Statement is right, I think, in taking the just police role to be a strategic one. Justice requires that police actively secure authorization through their work; it is not handed to them by the legislature. The challenge is what to *do* with the robust community engagement.[4] This is a long-standing problem in democratic theory, and we'll see that it is important in the present context, too.

Thomas Christiano has grappled with the problem, arguing at different times that democratic authority comes from procedures that *equally advance* the interests of the governed, or *equally consider* the interests of the governed (Christiano 2004, 269; Christiano 1996, 73). The challenge is that the latter requirement, though one that can be satisfied, appears insufficient. Sure, the police might *consider* my interest when responding to a dispute about the volume of music in a public park, but it is possible to consider an interest without ever doing anything to protect it. This matters because democracy is often held to reconcile the equality of persons with an unequal distribution of

---

[3] This statement's signatories include The Police Foundation, the Public Executive Research Forum, and the National Organization of Black Law Enforcement Executives, as well as several police chiefs and members of President Obama's Final Report of the President's Task Force on 21st Century Policing.

[4] I should emphasize that my goal in what follows is not to denigrate this widely endorsed statement; it is deeply important for the police profession to take up these kinds of self-reflective projects and welcome the input of scholars.

political power by giving everyone an "equal say" (Buchanan 2002). You might give me a say, but if I'm always in the minority, I may have no, or less, political power (Abizadeh 2021). It may never be acceptable to me. This is just the problem of tyrannical majorities and persistent minorities. Giving everyone an equal role in the decision-making procedure is no guarantee that it will produce laws that treat us equally or equalize political power. Presumably for this reason, Christiano's more recent work strengthens the requirement to *equal advancement* (Valentini 2012b, 195).

Yet the equal advancement requirement is too strong. The police regularly deal with zero-sum scenarios and will simply be unable to equally advance all of our interests. This is a general problem: while democracy might equally advance our interests in *political participation*, it does not equally advance our material interests (Buchanan 2002, 713). Setbacks to material interests must be compatible with democratic authorization and legitimacy, but if an individual or group's interests are unlikely to be advanced at all by the process, the process is unlikely to produce democratic authorization.

The problems of unequal participation and self-selecting representation in democracy are quite likely to generate procedural pathologies that undermine community engagement's production of democratic authorization. And community policing meetings are extremely susceptible to self-selecting representation. If community engagement is conducted via beat meetings, or something similar, the police will seldom have a representative sample of the policed. People with more free time than others, or people with especially strong preferences, or people who feel most comfortable with the police are more likely to attend the meetings. This makes equal consideration (let alone advancement) extremely unlikely. It's true that, at least in Chicago, there weren't massive racial disparities in the beat meeting attendance, but this is an overly simplistic way of determining whether all of the relevant political perspectives are being represented.

Unequal participation is compounded by mechanisms that produce unequal advancement of the represented interests. Ethnographic research finds that Chicagoans perceive the police to favor those community meeting attendees with greater "conventional social clout" (Venkatesh 2006, 72). Additionally, other cities tend to have much more prominent "middles-class bias" in meeting attendance with the highest rates of attendance in the lowest crime areas (Skogan and Harnett 1997, 159). Not only is there a middle-class bias, but racial biases also appear common, and the number of attendees is surprisingly small. In community meetings for a new police program in Seattle, Washington, police scholar Steve Herbert reports only six (white, property-owning) "regulars" attend most of the meetings, and that community-led initiatives are usually organized by a handful of the same people (2006, 5, 55). In Los Angeles' Lakeside community-police advisory board meetings, the majority Hispanic neighborhood's meetings are majority black (Gascón and Roussell 2019, 100).

The problematic mechanism, what we can call the "squeaky wheel problem," is built in (Heath 2020, 74). As the saying goes, the squeaky wheel gets the grease. And while we might hope that the normative significance of one's interests will determine how squeaky they are, we know that that is not true. Because the community policing meetings are a source of information, residents typically attend to complain. Given the meetings' purpose, their perceived legitimacy relies in part on police responding to these complaints (Gascón and Roussell 2019, 122).

The beat meeting dynamic, self-selecting representation combined with an incentive to respond to complaints, can produce tyrannical majority problems. In one case, residents of a Chicago neighborhood used a beat meeting to organize blocking the opening of a "halfway house" that rehabilitated drug users and housed parolees. While the community group was purportedly concerned about the fact that the people opening the halfway house did not effectively rehabilitate their clients, it is easy to see this is a typical case of NIMBYism. People want less punitive, more rehabilitative options, but just not in their neighborhood. In cooperation with the police, the group discovered that the building owed back taxes and had code violations and convinced the housing court to block further construction (Skogan and Harnett 1997, 177). While community–police cooperation is valuable, in this case the community engagement appears to have channeled the majority preferences through the relevant bureaucracies to tyrannize an underrepresented and marginalized minority.

Democracy is, in large part, concerned with political equality and self-governance, and majority rule is not always guaranteed to satisfy those political values. When an ostensibly democratic procedure is ill-suited to satisfy those values, such as when there are persistent and marginalized minorities, and especially when the purpose of the community engagement is to receive complaints about marginalized minorities, the justificatory force is attenuated or lost (Christiano 2010, 288).

7.2.4. Community Partnerships

Another approach to community policing, one that dominated the Los Angeles Police Department (LAPD)'s strategy for policing skid row, relies on community group *partnerships* instead of neighborhood meetings. This approach moves closer to *participatory* democracy than even the Chicago beat meetings. We'll see, however, that in practice community partnership strategies do not clearly empower the relevant groups. Similar problems of self-selecting representation and tyrannical majorities beset community partnerships.

Here's an illustration. As discussed in the last chapter, many cities employed urban renewal strategies to eliminate most skid rows. But in Los Angeles, community groups—especially the Catholic Worker Coalition—blocked redevelopment and convinced the city to formally establish a skid row in which police would take a hands-off approach. Eventually three "mega-shelters" opened within skid row (Stuart 2016, 52, 65). The mega-shelters set out to make participation in a rehabilitation program required for long-term housing, medicine, and food support. Residents became "service resistant" (Stuart 2016, 39). Partly in response, Los Angeles passed the Safer Cities Initiative in 2006, increasing collaboration between the mega-shelters and the LAPD. As mentioned, skid row was saturated with police, and they aggressively enforced ordinances against panhandling, sitting or lying on sidewalks, jaywalking, and obstructing the sidewalk. This enabled them to prevent other community groups from feeding residents, thereby concentrating resources within the mega-shelters. Programs were established to waive fines or jail time in exchange for joining a program. Private community groups were therefore crucial to establishing this strategy of "therapeutic policing" in which arrests were thought by police to benefit skid row residents (Stuart 2016, 121). The Initiative cost $6 million per year and produced 9,000 arrests and 12,000 citations in the first year (Stuart 2016, 6).

The democratic problem is that the initiative privileged cooperation with some community groups over others. The mega-shelter groups sought therapeutic policing, whereas the earlier Catholic Workers Coalition sought a more lenient approach that might now be called a "harm reduction" approach. In the years after the Catholic Workers Coalition lost out to the mega-shelter groups, the Los Angeles Community Action Network (LACAN) was formed to fight back against therapeutic policing and, indirectly, the influence of the mega-shelters (Stuart 2016, 204, 310).

This example highlights the justificatory difficulties associated with community organization partnerships. Which organization a police department partners with will play a major role in determining the kind of policing an area receives. Partnerships will elevate certain perspectives over others. The initial partnership in Los Angeles' skid row brought a hands-off approach. The later partnership brought an aggressive, coercively therapeutic approach. LACAN, the only group largely made up of skid row residents, fought back. All three groups claimed the role of community representatives. That the mega-shelters approved of the policing strategy does not mean that the *policed* did.

The fundamental problem is that if police seek community engagement by reaching out to community organizations, those whose interests are not embedded in an organizational infrastructure are less likely to be heard (Skogan and Harnett 1997, 111). When it comes to allocating community policing resources outside the context of the beat meetings, politically empowered communities are more likely to get them, just as they're more likely to get regular maintenance of their infrastructure. Community engagement strategies are likely to compound problems of marginalization.

7.2.5. Community Control

We must be cognizant of the fact that in many cases community policing serves to empower one part of the community over others. Some democratic theorists have responded to these problems of poor political representation by proposing non-electoral forms of democratic authorization and legitimacy. Instead of elections, deliberative bodies might be staffed by lottery. The nature of the deliberative bodies differs across proposals, but often they are envisioned as having narrow or single-issue jurisdiction (Landemore 2020; Guerrero 2014). There is growing interest in using these tools to solve the problem of police legitimacy. An even more ambitious approach moves beyond democratic participation to direct community control over police departments. According to one proposal, plebiscites would have direct democratic control (via a majoritarian vote) to abolish or restructure police departments (Táíwò 2020). This bold idea is difficult to evaluate without precise details about what it would look like in practice. A plebiscite could fire bad officers, for example, only if we also solve the legal problems that currently make it difficult for reformist police chiefs to fire bad officers. Allowing plebiscites to restructure departments or revise department policy plausibly empowers the community, though whether that will produce responsive, quality policing is an open question.[5]

This proposal improves upon the self-selecting representation problem of the earlier proposals by using a random selection method. Unfortunately, though it fixes that procedural problem, it does not make much progress on the general problem of police legitimacy because it does not offer guidance for the exercise of discretionary police power. The plebiscite will not be in a better position to craft rules that thread the needle of the enforcement dilemma. We're still left with the question of how to justify the police decisions that go underdetermined by the criminal code and oversight mechanisms. The policies and procedures might enjoy stronger democratic authorization, but many

---

[5] It is an important question, given the instrumentalism that underlies lottocratic thought. For discussion of the instrumentalist aspects of these views, see Landemore (2020, 147) and Guerrero (2014).

of those are routinely ignored in the field (and as we've seen, not always for unjust reasons). The plebiscite will likely be as frustrated as the police administrator at the difficulties of managing the patrol officer, even if they might be able to fire officers more easily.

Finally, and most important, the concerns about being overly deferential to majority positions are also relevant here. Empowering more local majorities struggles to address procedural concerns about majoritarian decision-making. Geographic areas can have group conflict, such as in Lakeside, Los Angeles, where street vending is primarily undertaken by one ethnic group and resented by others (Gascón and Roussell 2019, 75). Lakeside has undergone rapid demographic change, and this is a roadblock to "community" governance (2019, 84). Setting up a plebiscite there risks disempowering whichever ethnic group is in the minority. Ultimately, the communities relevant to democratic decision-making when it comes to policing are not always *geographic* communities. To better address tyranny of the majority concerns, we must think about authorization outside the geographic community framework.

Here's the interim conclusion. The "classic" models of policing and the major innovations in community policing alike, concerned at least partly with securing democratic authorization (or at least ostensibly sensitive to the demand), do not clearly succeed in that aim. Some risk enabling procedural pathologies that weaken authorization. Others leave the problem of police legitimacy intact by locating (democratic) legitimacy in the criminal code or in underspecified community engagement. We haven't figured out the social technology that makes possible the Peelian goal of the policed being the police. Even the adoption of 911 calls for service that democratizes the distribution of police power features the basic problem: people call the police *on others*. At the community level, the policed often lack a say. These problems exist independently of whatever police desire there is to thwart accountability.

The goal is not to show that policing or other parts of the criminal legal system should be separated from direct democratic control. It is, rather, a kind of expectation setting. Local, deliberative democratic solutions to guiding police discretion might be inevitably underpowered relative to theoretic desires. Community engagement is necessary, but "community support" is not the same as democratic authorization. We should not have overdemanding expectations about realized community policing initiatives.

7.3. New Community Policing and Police-Relevant Communities

One of the problems for injecting generating democratic authorization with the various community policing strategies is that they're susceptible to one group using the mechanisms to wield power over another. In real societies with group power imbalances, this is a pronounced problem. One source of the problem is difficulty in demarcating the politically relevant groups. "Police-relevant communities" don't neatly track geography or demographics.

A high-profile dispute over a Chicago anti-gang loitering ordinance exemplifies the problem. In *Chicago v. Morales*, the Illinois Supreme Court struck down an ordinance which had granted Chicago police more discretionary power to target gang activity. One element of the dispute concerns whether judicial control of police discretion, developed in the 1960s and 70s and motivated by concerns of racism, had been obviated by newfound political empowerment. True, the police strategies and tools from the criminal code ruled unconstitutional in the 1960s and 70s (curfews, anti-loitering ordinances to crack down on drugs or sex work, and warrantless sweeps of public housing) appear similar to the strategies employed by many police agencies in the 1990s. But the political landscape was much changed.

Legal scholars Tracey Meares and Dan Kahan argue that changes in the democratic procedure, namely political empowerment of black Americans, rendered both the procedures capable of justifying expanded police power and the old jurisprudence anti-democratic. While strict *judicial* oversight of policing once protected black minorities, it came to threaten their democratic self-governance once the procedures achieved appropriate representation (Kahan and Meares 1998, 1154). In fact, the return to these strategies—what Meares and Kahan call "the new community policing"—is actually a "testament to the growing political strength of African-Americans, particularly in the inner-city" (1161).

Albert Alschuler and Stephen Schulhofer reply that the claim that something has "community support" is hopelessly ambiguous (1998). They note that there was pushback against the anti-gang loitering law from Chicago's black residents; six black aldermen supported it, but eight voted against it. The local chapter of the National Association for the Advancement of Colored People (NAACP) and many of the city's newspapers also advocated against the proposal. Alschuler and Schulhofer conclude that the Chicago gang loitering ordinance was not well authorized.

To be sure, there was robust support from black Americans for "new community policing" in the 1980s and 90s. James Forman Jr. shows how the racially disproportionate effects of the drug war aren't entirely a result of tyrannical racial majorities. He notes that black Americans held municipal city power by the 1990s, with 130 black police chiefs and 300 black mayors nationwide (2017, 165). Prominent black community leaders, not just those in government, called for more drug enforcement. Part of the explanation for their support for brutal drug policing in the 1980s and 90s, he argues, is that the crack epidemic was so damaging in black neighborhoods that it was thought by some to be the biggest threat since slavery (2017, 158). Ta-Nehisi Coates explores this dynamic, describing the "vicious" police of Prince George's Country as a creation of majority black democratic procedures (2015, 53). There was not, however, unanimous support in the black community for harsh drug laws and policing (Forman 2017, 205). This was also true in Chicago, and Meares and Kahan take such disagreement to support their position because it shows that, unlike in the past, the law is not a result of white voters wielding power over an unwilling community (Meares and Kahan 1998, 251).

What should we make of this dispute? One upshot is that if we're appealing to "community support," the community we're appealing to matters. The discussion of community policing above shows that the relevant communities aren't always geographic. The dispute over Chicago's ordinance and the broader history of local control over warrior policing is evidence that the relevant communities aren't always basic demographic groups either. Who will be stopped by the police under the new ordinance? Who must bear the burden of wrongful enforcement? Intentions aside, should we expect the police to use the ordinance instrumentally and, if so, how and against whom? If the answer is some marginalized group(s), actual democratic procedures are unlikely to take those interests seriously. The "communities" relevant to procedural, democratic principles often do not match the taxonomies that we are inclined to draw. My claim is not that the ordinance lacked democratic authorization. It is rather that disagreement among black Chicagoans doesn't establish that the democratic procedure has secured authorization from relevant communities, even if it undermines claims of racial domination.

One unfortunately familiar reason for this is that people are eager to marginalize along a variety of cross-cutting dimensions. Another reason is a phenomenon described by political scientist Cathy Cohen, "secondary marginalization." According to Cohen, marginalized groups marginalize members who are taken to be a threat to the group's social standing (Cohen 2010, 28, 48). Though she argues that in the black community it leads only to a secondary reliance on "state intervention," it does lead to some reliance. We can find secondary marginalization in skid row populations where groups sometimes form according to their recreational substance of choice and want one another excluded (Stuart 2016, 132; Huey 2007, 24). Book vendors plausibly marginalized magazine vendors in New York City's informal written material economy (Duneier 1999, 327). This is in part because the magazine vendors more often scavenged their goods from the trash.

The upshot is this: popular "community taxonomies," for lack of a better term, are liable to overlook the kind of marginalization that produces persistent minorities. Marginalization helps to identify the persistent minorities that undermine democratic authorization. Put differently, in some cases we don't worry about persistent minorities. If those who would like to return to the gold standard never get their way, this doesn't look clearly anti-democratic. In other cases, persistent-*because-marginalized* minorities do pose a problem for democratic authorization since they can't really be described as "having a say." Those groups often bear most of the burdens of policing.

Sometimes police units are evidence of marginalization, such as when vice units in the 1950s and 60s proactively policed male homosexuality. Historian and legal scholar Anna Lvovsky (2021) argues that such policing was important for generating a politically active gay community. But even before it was clear that there existed a politically engaged gay community, policing created a community relevant to normative analysis. Police strategies in general create communities. The Chicago anti-gang loitering ordinance produces or reifies an existing community: gang members, those who police might think are gang members, and residents of public housing. The ordinance "creates" this community because they are the targets of the power enabled by it. The homicide department's work produces a community: those who commit murder or those who are suspected of killing other persons. The residents of a skid row or homeless encampment in a city, especially when cities increasingly treat homelessness as a criminal problem, are a politically relevant community as well. Sex workers and "Johns," drug dealers and buyers, the boisterous youth, and unlicensed vendors and their customers all count as politically relevant communities with respect to the police. "Create" refers not to a kind of gerrymandering, but rather a way to seek perspectives in accordance with enforcement strategies. This plays a role in evaluating claims of democratic authorization. It also instructs police to identify relevant communities (subjects of their power) to engage.

7.4. Responsiveness, Prioritization, and Non-Electoral Legitimacy

One measure for how democratic a government is the speed at which it responds to a newly formed majority will. Another is how equal the opportunity for political influence is (Arneson 2009, 199). Both are (in part) concerned with how *responsive* political power is to the preferences of the governed. Though there is some controversy over whether majority rule via elections is a necessary part of democracy, responsiveness is close to universally acknowledged to be essential (cf. Landemore 2020; Guerrero 2014; Saunders 2010; Mansbridge 2003). I've argued that one of the problems police must contend with is that the criminal code they enforce lags, in some cases considerably, public opinion. And in this chapter, I've argued that actual community policing initiatives fare poorly with respect to equalizing political influence and the opportunity for it. Policing secures democratic authorization, I'll argue, by being responsive to the police-relevant communities. Responsiveness tells us what to do with the information gleaned from engaging the community, and it also builds in concerns about marginalized, persistent minorities: if marginalized minorities never get policy decisions going their way, we can't say the system is responsive to their interests.

The argument draws on work in democratic theory on the ethics of political representation and non-electoral legislative legitimacy. Just policing, like legislating, requires a strategic role in producing responsive power. Police can take up this active role by wielding their power responsively, by setting their priorities according to what I'll call the *democratic prioritization principle*. The principle requires police to set their priorities, and thereby exercise their discretion, in light of the strength of authorization enjoyed by types of police power. This section clarifies and defends the principle.

7.4.1. Normative Mandates and the Strength of Authorization

My case for securing democratic authorization via strategic policing relies on two contentious claims. The first is that some political power is more strongly authorized, or has a stronger *normative mandate*, than other kinds of political power. The idea of a normative mandate is important for determining how political representatives should exercise their authority. Briefly mentioned in Chapter 4, the intuition is that a newly elected representative who won 75 percent of the vote is in a normatively different position from one who won 51 percent. Philosopher Alex Guerrero (2010) claims the former representative has a stronger normative mandate. This helps to explain, Guerrero thinks, answers to questions about the ethics of political representation (those with stronger mandates are more trustee-like and less delegate-like). Understanding the ethics of political representation through the lens of normative mandates is a response to a problem in democratic theory that shares similarities with the problem of police legitimacy I'm concerned with here. That a representative won an election underdetermines what she may do in that role, and notions of support and responsiveness help to flesh things out. I'll broaden the term and say that "normative mandate" refers to the degree of political support a policy or law (not just a candidate) has. The more support a law or policy has, the stronger the law or policy's normative mandate.

The second contentious claim is that democratic authorization can be generated by non-electoral and even non-majoritarian procedures. There are a variety of arguments for the conclusion. I'll highlight one from political scientist Jane Mansbridge, who claims that legislatures staffed by formal elections have normative properties that cannot be explained in terms of the standard principal–agent relationship (2003). According to that relationship, representatives go to Congress, for example, to do the business of the represented. But my representative may not be representing my interests (I voted for someone else, say), and there can be others, "surrogate" representatives, who are informally representing mine. As I've said, if my interests aren't represented in the process, I didn't really have a say, and the process is unlikely to be responsive. One strategy is to fix problems of representation (perhaps by replacing elections with lotteries). Another strategy is to hold legislatures responsible for strategically representing certain minority interests such that the overall process is sufficiently representative. The democratic credentials of a legislature and how strongly authorized its decisions are, on this view, depend on whether the representation of interests is *proportional* to the demos, and on whether the relevant interests are being highlighted in legislative decisions.

The possibility of non-electoral representation is important for understanding how the outputs of non-electoral, but still democratic, procedures like juries can be democratically authorized. But it is also important for making sense of how even our electoral, legislative procedures can overcome the problems of marginalization and representation we've been grappling with. We can broaden the scope of these theoretical approaches to answer questions about just political administration. Policing that is sensitive to normative mandates and proportional political representation can secure democratic authorization.

Again, laws, like political candidates, have different normative mandates. Laws against sexual and physical violence have very strong normative mandates. Laws against the recreational use of pharmaceutical opioids or stimulants, or some unlicensed commercial activity, have much weaker normative mandates. Not only are there fewer people who support criminalizing recreational pharmaceutical use, the decriminalization/legalization perspective is marginalized.[6] In the legislative context, a stronger normative mandate plausibly motivates a more trustee-like relationship; if everyone supports me enthusiastically, I can interpret that to mean that I have more discretion in pursuing the interests of those I represent. If I am a police officer, however, it is not me that has a normative mandate, but the various goals I can pursue and the various tools with which I can pursue them. Setting priorities according to one's sense of the relevant normative mandates is a way to increase the political agency and autonomy produced by a system of governance. By reducing the share of resources that go to the enforcement of democratically questionable laws, police power better satisfies the goal of proportional representation of interests.

The democratic prioritization principle, then, is justified by the same kinds of considerations that figure in explanations of the legitimacy and authority of legislatures. And, perhaps surprisingly, the principle is rather compatible with the principle of neutrality. That is, while it may seem that a principle instructing agencies to prioritize more strongly authorized initiatives risks devolving into crude majoritarianism, we'll see in what follows that it provides a democratic justification for de-prioritizing objectionable kinds of enforcement.

7.4.2. De-prioritizing Weakly Mandated Enforcement

Old, outdated laws that remain on the books are the analogical anchor. West Virginia made "lewd cohabitation" before marriage a misdemeanor in 1931 and repealed it in 2010. A West Virginia police

---

[6] It shocked many, for example, when Carl Hart not only critiqued American attitudes about drug use and prohibition but admitted to regular heroin use in his *Drug Use for Grown-Ups*.

officer would be acting substantively unjustly by making an arrest for violating the law in 1931. They would be acting *anti-democratically* by making an arrest for violating the law in 2005. Other cases are more challenging.

Let's return our case of Bricknell's bikes and the related problem of opportunity costs for policing. An officer who, as a matter of strategy, routinely and proactively invokes their police power in response to riding without a light is exercising power in a manner that is inconsistent with the relevant normative mandates. They are prioritizing the enforcement of weakly mandated laws over more strongly mandated ones. Such arrests are clearly non-responsive to the interests of the policed. On the other hand, when most officers decline to arrest a cyclist riding without a light, their decision is justified by considerations of democratic authorization. The fact that the overwhelming majority of these offenses go ignored by police is not a perversion of the criminal code but a way of making an imperfect criminal code broadly responsive to the demos.

Of course, I have no data to show that the law is weakly authorized. There are no public opinion surveys I know of. But that is not the only source of evidence regarding public opinion. There is no obvious clamor for better enforcement of the law, and this suggests that it is not an area of consensus entitled to great political effort. If a larger number of people begin riding bikes, there will be such a clamor (just as there was for better traffic policing as the adoption of the automobile ramped up). Determining with precision the strength of a normative mandate is challenging, but the judgment that *this* law is weakly authorized strikes me as not too epistemically demanding. After all, the tactic was bizarre enough for an officer-ethnographer to cover it in detail. In Norfolk, Virginia, a cyclist was tackled to the ground and their leg badly broken by an officer enforcing the law. Body-cam footage shows the cyclist claim, plausibly in my view, not even to know there was such a law (Harper 2021). Taking the initiative to enforce such a law looks more like an anti-democratic use of power than does the decision to continue patrolling for burglaries (or even scrolling one's phone from the police cruiser). It looks extremely inappropriate to make the stop when there are calls for service one might be responding to instead.

Take, for another example, the decision to de-prioritize arrests for cannabis or opioid possession. Here we have more solid evidence.[7] A growing majority of people now think that cannabis should be legalized (or at least de-criminalized). The reasons people cite include that it would free up police to focus on more important issues (Gallup 2019). Further, over two-thirds of people think that treatment, not incarceration, is the proper response to users of substances like heroin or cocaine. And if we take party membership or other demographic categories to be a weak proxy for one's perspective, then this majority persists even considering some measure of perspectival diversity; over half of Republicans prefer treatment to incarceration, and the proportion is even higher for Democrats. There is also majority support for this across all age groups, education levels, and ethnicity (Pew 2014). But as we've seen, the legislative process is slow, filled with half-measures, and has a narrow bandwidth. So, in the face of evidence that a perspectivally diverse majority prefers not to use the criminal justice system as a tool for attempting to solve the problems of recreational drug use, discretionary non-enforcement is again recommended not only by the principles of proportionality and neutrality but also because it satisfies the democratic prioritization principle. In so doing, the decision not to enforce the law—really, the decision to spend time on different kinds of policing—enjoys some amount of democratic authorization.

Let us consider again the example of Officer Kelly, in Newark, New Jersey, who engaged in discretionary non-enforcement of disorderly conduct laws instead of arresting the "regulars" who like to sit on the stoops and drink in a busy transit corridor. A crude majoritarian, full enforcement approach to this issue would likely recommend making arrests to (attempt to) stop the public drinking. The regulars are, often, breaking the law, and at least sometimes the majority of passersby would prefer not to allow that use of space. Were there a community policing meeting, attendees would

---

[7] Right now, it seems like the United States is close to national legalization of recreational cannabis. The example is hackneyed a result. Nevertheless, it is useful in highlighting the length of time between changing public sentiment on criminalization and changes to the criminal code.

plausibly complain about them. The "community" subjected to the police power, though, would prefer to spend their time that way. Fortunately, Officer Kelly enabled a compromise, one that is responsive to both "communities." Passersby go unmolested, the "offensive" use of public space is constrained in terms of use and location, and regulars get a claim on the use of space and are free from spending any time in jail before they take a plea deal. This arrangement affirms some (non-electoral) democratic values and therefore is not merely an affront to democracy, but indeed claims a measure of democratic authorization.

We see decisions that produce a similar kind of negotiated compromise elsewhere. The cases of police officers overlooking discrete sex workers and rough sleepers from the earlier chapters are cases of officers representing the interests of both "communities" in their deliberation about how to police and trying to ensure no one loses out completely. "Police-created communities" are thus a tool for enabling the normative mandate at the heart of the democratic prioritization principle to accommodate the problems of minority interests in democracies.

Recall one of the predictable dynamics of the community policing meeting: concerned citizens bring a complaint to the meeting, and both citizen and officer have a baseline expectation that *something* will be done to address the complaint. The way to reduce the risk of the community policing meeting devolving into a cudgel for the politically empowered to wield against the disempowered is for the police to be responsive to the targets of their power. The goal of democratic authorization is to make political power justified to those subjected to it. This can only be accomplished by making an effort to be responsive to the policed, not just those who request police services. The main problem discussed above is that incorrectly drawing the boundaries of community can produce tyrannical majorities. One remedy is for police to take an active role in drawing the correct boundaries. There is no guarantee that they'll succeed, but if they do, they can achieve democratic authorization outside existing electoral mechanisms by, like the legislature, enabling responsiveness and representation beyond the formal principal–agent relationship.

7.5. Accountability and the Opportunity for Electoral Authorization

Accountability is also necessary for democratic authorization. A benevolent dictator does not earn authorization just by wielding power responsively. I'll argue that the exercise of police discretion secures democratic authorization when it occurs within a system that allows for accountability. I'll also argue that the police administrator and the elected official have important similarities in some respects. They both must make *novel decisions*, or decisions made outside the confines of an electoral promise. Novel decisions can make a plausible claim to democratic legitimacy even if they haven't been explicitly authorized by the demos.

Note first that elected representatives sometimes face problems that were outside the scope of their campaigning and promises to their constituents. These problems require novel decisions. We don't conclude that these decisions are illegitimate because they're not democratically authorized. Rather, we rely on the fact that we can vote the representatives out to explain legitimacy. In fact, to whatever extent democratic accountability is important for authorization, that accountability is going to come in no small part from retrospective voting simply as a result of how much decision-making by elected officials is not part of either their campaign promises or the sort of thing one might be able to read off of the apparent qualities of the official. Elected officials will always have to make decisions that our reasons for voting for them do not bear upon. If those decisions are democratically authorized, it will plausibly have something to do with our ability to either punish or reward them when they are next up for reelection.[8]

Similarly, we can have democratic authorization over administrative decisions, too. This is clear enough in the federal context: a presidential

---

[8] An important qualification: the empirical literature on retrospective voting is mixed, suggesting in some cases that people do not engage in it, or do not engage in it well, and in other cases that it is rather effective. I don't take any stand on that debate here. My argument requires only that to whatever extent retrospective voting is normatively relevant to democratic authorization, it can also be used to authorize some police decisions.

candidate might not disclose their choice for Attorney General during the campaign, but frequently there is a short list of likely candidates, and motivated voters can rely on that information when casting their vote. Then, when they come up for reelection, if the president has appointed an especially morally repugnant Attorney General (or a series of them) who has enacted terrible law enforcement policies, motivated voters can cast their vote on the basis of that information. This mechanism extends to the local level as well. District attorneys (DAs) are often directly elected in the United States, and the police chief typically serves at the will of the mayor or city council. If the DA or the police chief makes decisions, or if the chief refuses to hold accountable officers who make decisions, that a voter dislikes, they can again cast their vote on the basis of that information.

Police chiefs in large departments sometimes can bypass city government and appeal directly to public for support. Police scholar Michael K. Brown argues that this is how the LAPD came to be so politically powerful and isolated (1988, 63). Indeed, this makes some mayors uncomfortable. Bill Bratton reports coming into conflict with Mayor Giuliani nearly immediately after they both took up their new positions because Bratton was getting too much favorable attention from the press (Bratton and Knobler 1998).

Police chiefs can harness their public support to make novel, responsive decisions. Recall the case of de facto buprenorphine decriminalization in Burlington, Vermont. Recall also that the justification was that they were correcting an error of the criminal code that the legislature had neglected and to contribute to more effective responses to the problems of addiction. This is not a change that makes their police and prosecutorial power less responsive. We've seen that there is majority support for turning to non-punitive tools for fixing the opioid crisis. And this decision brings to the forefront the interests of a marginalized, persistent minority: recreational opioid users. This decision responds to what can plausibly be described as a democratic procedural failure. And they announced their decision; it was not made in secret. Further, because voters in Burlington, Vermont, or Philadelphia, Pennsylvania, can vote against their DA or vote against their mayor unless she promises to replace the police chief, the decision has some of the democratic authorization that other novel decisions have.

Better yet, this looks like a realized democratic success story. In May 2021, years after de facto decriminalization, the legislature finally managed to make progress on the problem. H.225 was passed, eliminating penalties for possession of up to 224 milligrams of buprenorphine. Though dreadfully delayed, sometimes this is the best we can hope for from our actual legislative bodies (most of which, as I write this, have not managed to make even this modest change).

This produces a generalizable mechanism for electoral authorization of police decisions. An agency informs the policed of a decision to change their enforcement priorities. That can include the decision to de-prioritize enforcement of certain offenses or the decision to increase the priority of other kinds of enforcement. The informing process will typically occur formally, as in a press conference. But the information can also be common knowledge, such as when the agency opts to maintain the status quo. Voters then either care enough for them to vote for a different DA or mayor, presumably after a process of making their preference known through existing channels (e.g., writing op-eds in the local paper, calling the mayor's office, or protesting). If the voters do not engage in retrospective voting to punish the relevant parties, then the decision enjoys a kind of democratic authorization—certainly a weak one—that looks something like the democratic authorization for novel decisions made by elected officials.

My first goal in this chapter was to show that most of our real attempts to secure democratic authorization are predictably inadequate, and that we need to be aware of this when thinking about how to make policing democratic. My second goal was to show that there are things police can do to make policy more responsive to the interests of the policed. Although much of the conversation on political control over the police follows the fault lines of the "more or less democracy" dispute, judicious police discretion can overcome the problem of police legitimacy in a way that is perhaps surprisingly congenial to recent developments in democratic theory.[9] Ultimately, non-electoral

---

[9] Of course, the "less democracy" proponents will not necessarily find the democratic prioritization principle attractive, or recognize the problem it is supposed to solve, but then they are less likely to be worried about proportional and neutral but non-democratically authorized police discretion.

democratic authorization comes from producing reliable, responsive political power with an appropriately structured procedure (whether that involves an election, a jury, or some other democratic procedure). Next, and finally, we'll see how attention to agency form can enhance the justice and democratic authorization of policing.

8

The Form of Police Agencies

Plato raised a structural concern about selecting for political rulers in the *Republic*. Good people won't rule for money (to avoid being thought of as "hirelings") and they won't rule for honor (because good people are not ambitious "honor lovers") (347b–c). The challenge is finding a way to install good rulers and prevent the hirelings and honor lovers from gaining power. This Platonic worry is especially apt when it comes to modern policing, even if in our non-ideal world we're more concerned with preventing power-hungry authoritarian types from gaining power than with inducing perfectly virtuous people to.

Compare these two attitudes toward the Boston Tactical Patrol Force (a unit disbanded in the 1970s). First, journalist J. Anthony Lukas:

> The TPF [Boston Tactical Patrol Force] weren't like other cops. They didn't perform routine police tasks such as walking beats, checking locks, making arrests. They were there for only one purpose: to intimidate people. Their very appearance had been carefully calculated to deter opposition: jumpsuits and combat boots reminiscent of the Green Berets, leather jackets and black gloves to hint of a Central European police state. They were trained to inspire dread with Grand Guignol theatrics: rapping their riot batons rhythmically on cars and light poles as they advanced, emitting guttural roars when they charged. Many a demonstrator had thought to himself: Oh my God, these guys are really nuts! And when sheer terror didn't do the trick, the TPF could swing their clubs with fierce resolve, reinforcing their fearsome reputations. (1985, 461)

And second, Bill Bratton:

> The Boston Tactical Patrol Force [was] an aggressive unit that every cop wanted to get into. It was the crème de la crème. (1998, 65)

Just Policing. Jake Monaghan, Oxford University Press. © Oxford University Press 2023.
DOI: 10.1093/oso/9780197610725.003.0008

An aggressive use of force is justified in some cases, so there's reason to have a specialized unit to provide it. But the risk of injustice is pronounced. It is difficult to create agencies that are willing to be aggressive without having an overly aggressive disposition.

Selection isn't the only practical concern about the occupants of political roles. At least as important is the influence of institutional structure and the expectations and incentives it creates for occupants of political roles. During the era of volunteer and paid-replacement watch systems, for instance, the problem was ensuring that watchmen were sober, awake, and patrolling (Reynolds 1998, 54, 61, 120). In this chapter, I'll argue that a separation of powers can ameliorate the concern about selection and make policing more just by shaping the police role.

The argument begins with a diagnosis of the injustices of *criminal patrol*: the structure of police agencies contributed to the blending of high-legitimacy-risk police goals and tactics. The multifunctional, generalist nature of the police agency and the patrol officer enabled a plurality of officers to take up an unjust operational style. Earlier I argued that not only are preventive patrol and criminal investigation distinct political powers, we also have reason to make finer distinctions according to legitimacy-risk profiles. I'll argue now that the rise of criminal patrol motivates institutional boundaries to prevent the exercise of criminal patrol powers. I'll conclude with a discussion of agency reform and professionalism.

8.1. The Rise of Criminal Patrol

Earlier we saw a quick sketch of police history from the constable and watch system codified in 1285, the creation of paid watch positions in the 1700s, and the consolidation of these early police organizations under professional, uniformed departments. By 1900, nearly all U.S. cities had uniformed police departments. By World War 1, police began a second major transition, turning their focus to crime control, professionalizing, bureaucratizing, and adopting new technologies and strategies. Vollmer, and his protégé and eventual Chicago police superintendent O.W. Wilson, played major roles in the professionalization movement, also encouraging the adoption of technology—another hallmark of professional status—like the service weapon, radio, and the patrol bicycle and car, the last of which was highly influential in the rise of criminal patrol. The model lost some credibility over time. First, the received wisdom was that the strategies of the era did little to stop crime (Bayley 1996). Second, the 1992 Los Angeles riots made obvious the problems with the professional era's departments taking the Peelian non-pandering principle to an extreme. Surely, the Los Angeles Police Department (LAPD)'s problems included explicit racism and aggressiveness fostered by SWAT creator and police chief Daryl Gates. But the LAPD was the epitome of the professional model of policing, with its preoccupation with technology and isolation from the community (Sklansky 2008, 82; Brown 1988, 60). Professional isolation was important in preventing the corruption from the local machines, but the pendulum had swung too far. A bit over ten years after Daryl Gates had been forced out of the LAPD in the wake of the riots, Los Angeles hired Bill Bratton in 2002, marking a replacement of the professional model with a vague commitment to community policing, one that had become nearly as widespread as the professional model before it (Sklansky 2008, 74). This version of the story is probably too kind to policing's history, however.

The professionalization of policing occurred alongside the developments of Prohibition. Much of "crime control" was really vice control. In time, the specialized investigative and patrol units that formed to police alcohol consumption would be remade and deployed to police men seeking sex with men, and then again to police narcotics consumption. During the "community policing era" we also saw the rise of militarized, drug warrior policing. Daryl Gates was forced out of the profession, but deadly SWAT raids have proven an enduring legacy—his community policing initiative, DARE, not so much.[1] While departments were experimenting with beat meetings, they were also equipping their officers with surplus military equipment, deploying SWAT overwhelmingly to serve drug warrants, and

[1] DARE, "drug abuse resistance education," involves police-officer led sessions in primary schools to discourage drug use.

embracing the war on drugs (and in time the war on terror) with aggressive patrol tactics and surveillance equipment (Coyne and Hall 2018; Balko 2013). The end of the twentieth century into the present is also the *warrior policing* era (Forman 2017, 171–181; Balko 2013).

How can it be that the profession made real changes to adopt a more community-oriented model while also producing warrior policing? A partial answer can be found in the democratic pathologies discussed last chapter: the police were engaging a community, and that community wanted to wage war against some recreational drug users, or they didn't realize they were making things worse. But that can't be the full explanation given how much control over their work the police have. Misaligned financial incentives are a major factor (Surprenant and Brennan, 2019). Part of the answer is, I'll argue, poor agency structure.

The legitimacy-risk framework offers an alternative lens through which to look at the big-picture history of policing. The "warrior" archetype is plausibly a more illuminating model of the late twentieth/ early twenty-first century policing than the community police officer despite internal and external pushes to adopt an explicit community policing orientation because insufficient institutional boundaries allowed for a merging of the crime fighting and "service" aspects of policing. Police agencies encompassed both of these functions, and over time, the criminal patrol officer is using the patrol power to investigate crime.

Recall an argument from Chapter 4. At the very beginning of the police-as-crime-fighters era, police were tasked with a major law enforcement initiative: the enforcement of Prohibition. This turned the police into *weakly authorized* and *proactive* crime fighters. Proactive strategies increase *harshness* because they involve stopping people who might be guilty (as opposed to intervening in an obvious crime in progress). And because of the strategy's predictable harshness, a significant amount of *high-burden* investigative police–citizen contact goes unconstrained by the courts. Given the weakly authorized nature of the law, punishment is required to induce compliance, raising the burdens of policing.

This should be familiar by now as a justification for the view that vice enforcement is highly likely to be unjust. But it is also a dynamic that motivates justice constraints on police agency structure. Crucially, the change from police as engaged in order maintenance, to crime fighting, and then to a preoccupation with vice enforcement undermined the original separation between fighting crime and maintaining order. Patrol became *criminal patrol* and in turn officers became *warriors*. Criminal patrol officers want to "pull off make-a-difference busts" and "regard themselves as first-line criminal investigators . . . *total-commitment* law enforcement officers" (Remsberg 1995, 9). Given their motivation, they see evidence of crime everywhere. Criminals are, after all, trying to "lull you" into complacency with, for example, pro-police bumper stickers (1995, 55). The criminal patrol officer also sees danger everywhere, playing the sheepdog who guards the flock from wolves, notably at the urging of Dave Grossman (of the "Killology" Research Group). Criminal patrol is likely to be exceptionally harsh. You can't pull off make-a-difference drug busts without breaking some eggs. The criminal patrol model that began to evolve during Prohibition would continue to develop over the next century in response to the vice scare of the day. Put differently, police agencies have a risk of degenerating.

A large plurality of patrol officers came to reject the conceptual distinction between patrolling and proactive crime fighting, taking up a crime fighting operational style (Brown 1988, 288) The blending of high-risk factors would continue, enabled as we saw earlier by an unfortunate operationalization of the broken windows theory, the profession embraced instrumental enforcement and repurposed their tools to create new opportunities for searches and seizures to interdict prohibited substances, guns, and stop other vicious activity. As Bill Bratton recounts it, it took some convincing:

> We were working in partnership with the Drug Enforcement Administration [DEA] at the time, and Maple said, "Why don't we go after drug dealers with the quality-of-life violations?" The feds spoke to him as if he were just a little slow. "Well, Commissioner, we don't do things like that." Quality-of-life arrests were small potatoes to them. (Bratton and Knobler 1998, 227)

Federal enforcement officers thought of themselves as crime fighters, not beat cops. One gets the sense that Bratton thinks the DEA officers were being a bit precious. The change in strategy also pushed the authority to engage in vice enforcement—once housed in the department's investigative units—down to the precinct commanders (2009, 230). Even if Bratton and Maple were creating novel enforcement strategies, they were also embracing huge risks to justice by further undermining the long-standing separation between deterrence and detection. And there were no institutional separations to prevent the resulting injustices.

But obviously, "total commitment" can't mean total enforcement. In practice, it meant that officers began to enforce many laws only instrumentally in the service of make-a-difference busts. Traffic stops were intended to maintain safe traffic infrastructure. Many misdemeanor ordinances were intended to manage the uses of public space or interpersonal disputes. But those activities, the criminal patrol officer recognizes, don't directly fight the kind of crime they're interested in. So they avoid outright or put in less time and effort at them, or they wield their power according to statistical judgments about who is likely to be a real criminal. For example, they handle domestic calls for service quickly, and they exercise their interpretive discretion to push the boundaries on rules limiting high-speed vehicle pursuits in the hopes of making a high-profile arrest (Brooks 2021, 258; Brown 1988). This repurposing of much of the original patrol authority has the effect of de-prioritizing low-risk, high-authorization policing. When traffic enforcement and foot patrol are used instrumentally or pre-textually, priorities shift accordingly.

As is often remarked, when police are waging a war, they become an occupying force, breaking the identity between the police and the policed. But we don't need to imagine police officers as embracing the view that their targets are combatants rather than fellow citizens to see pernicious tendencies. A moderate interest in making arrests that enhance one's status in (some parts of) the department is enough to increase the reliance on high-risk strategies and to decrease the intentional order maintenance and service functions among a segment of the profession. There is some ethnographic evidence:

> By specializing in narcotics, these patrolmen believe they can demonstrate their proficiency in arresting "hypes," developing

informants, and making buys to narcotics investigators. . . . Through these informal relationships with narcotics investigators a patrolman enhances his chances, or so he believes, of being promoted to an investigative position. All of the patrolmen observed specializing in narcotics expressed, at one time or another, the desire to "get out of the bag" and into a narcotics unit. Given the ease with which many of these patrolmen picked up personnel complaints, the only way many of them would ever "get out of the bag" was by getting into a specialized investigative unit. (Brown 1988, 150)

The rise of criminal patrol embodies many of the problems with insufficient separations of police power.

They include not just these difficulties in maintaining appropriate agency and officer priorities and choice of enforcement strategies. They also include pernicious institutional selection and treatment effects related to hiring, training, and rewarding officers, difficulties matching geographic with "professional" boundaries, and problems in self-regulation and accountability. But the goal isn't just to avoid the specific injustices of criminal patrol; it is to avoid these types of problems by producing justice-enhancing police agencies and roles. We want separations of power not just to disperse it and create friction in exercising political power but also to create and preserve distinct political powers (cf. Pettit 1997, 178).

8.2. Distinguishing Agency Priorities

The rise of criminal patrol was not entirely welcome. Vollmer complained bitterly about those who think that police can effectively enforce vice laws while also carrying out their other duties and without becoming hopelessly corrupt themselves (1928, 326). But how should the policing functions be specialized? It strikes me as unlikely that principles of justice will demand unique, highly specific institutional forms given the endless complexity in possible institutional forms and their background contexts. Still, the principles I've defended point in the direction of separating the law enforcement and order maintenance functions of police agencies.

In addition to the corrupting influence of policing vice, Vollmer warned of some major traffic enforcement problems. First, (to put the point in contemporary terms) errors of traffic policing are likely to reduce perceived legitimacy because people will be frustrated or angry with the police. This reduces cooperation and support. Second, managing traffic draws resources away from other policing goals. These problems amplify one another: less, and less effective, policing of the "real" problems.

Vollmer pointed to specialized federal law enforcement as a precedent. They demonstrate hyper-specialization with respect to both the varieties of policing (with most being entirely law enforcement) and to statute. Because of such specialization, the Secret Service is unlikely to sacrifice their goal of protecting the president to devote more resources to making drug arrests.[2] Similarly, without an established order maintenance function, the DEA requires local law enforcement partners to really take advantage of the traffic stop filtering strategies. Yet, while the Capitol Police were created to provide security for Congress and patrol the grounds, that mission has grown to include criminal investigation and traffic enforcement.[3] Capitol police arrest report summaries reveal unfortunately ordinary policing tactics such as making traffic stops for broken taillights and searching vehicles on the basis of cannabis odor.

Though Vollmer complained about insufficient resources and attention for the crime prevention function, others influential in policing have observed that it is the order maintenance function that gets neglected. According to James Q. Wilson,

> If order were the central mission of the department, there might be a "family disturbance squad," a "drunk and derelict squad," a "riot control squad," and a "juvenile squad"; law enforcement matters would be left to a "felony squad." Instead, there is a detective division organized, in the larger departments, into units specializing in homicide, burglary, auto theft, narcotics, vice, robbery, and the like.

---

[2] To be clear, the Secret Service does engage in some drug enforcement, but that generally occurs in the context of multi-agency task forces rather than agents making a proactive Terry stop on their way to their next appointment.

[3] And, in a throwback to the very early days of policing, capturing nuisance animals like the rabid fox that went on a biting spree in April 2022 (Hedgpeth 2022).

The undifferentiated patrol division gets everything else. (Wilson 1978, 69)

By having a separate (well-funded) division focusing on the investigation of homicides, an agency prioritizes the most strongly authorized part of the criminal law.[4] By not having a separate division focusing on cyclists riding without a light, they de-prioritize an incredibly weakly authorized part of the traffic code. There is more specialization of the patrol function now, but I think the divisional approach has justice costs.

Separating the law enforcement and order maintenance functions of police agencies, and in turn further specializing the patrol agency, is one way to try to maintain these distinct goals. If traffic enforcement is conducted by an agency that primarily cares about traffic, it is less likely that other enforcement goals will crowd out the goal of managing traffic.[5] If routine patrols are conducted by an agency that takes its mission to be service, rather than fighting the bad guys, it is likely to spend more of its resources on providing service than fighting the bad guys, and to fight the bad guys differently. The police agency for the Southeastern Pennsylvania Transit Authority, for example, is primarily a patrol agency. As opioid overdoses rose on the transit infrastructure, they were motivated to experiment with a dedicated overdose response unit because it enabled them to more efficiently respond to problems that delay transit services. Their problem was not primarily *crime* (and even if it was, the city drastically reduced drug prosecution), and the agency took on a more explicit harm reduction focus (Ratcliffe and Wight 2022).

This separation would undoubtedly make certain police activities more cumbersome and difficult, but no one denies that there are many police strategies that are ruled out independently of their efficacy. If searching a stopped vehicle for drugs is a high-legitimacy-risk activity, making it harder to do (by separating traffic from drug enforcement)

---

[4] Notably, the Detroit Police Department of the mid-1950s had nearly twice as many people assigned to its vice squad as its homicide squad (Lvovsky 2021, 102).
[5] Misaligned financial incentives, like those created by asset forfeiture policies that let agencies keep some of what they seize, are unfortunately enough to overcome many institutional boundaries.

is a feature and not a bug. Of course, it is important for policing to be effective; the point is that some tradeoffs are just.

The history of policing features the blending of police functions, whether within agencies (e.g., criminal patrol) or across agencies (e.g., DEA and local police task forces). Why think that agency specialization will be more successful than the current divisional approach? Vollmer gives us one reason for thinking that the divisional specialization approach is inappropriate. Imagine that the traffic division is understaffed. The police chief, responsible for all the agency's divisions, pulls officers off their beats and into traffic enforcement, and requires the motor patrol officers to also focus on traffic violations (1928, 330). In this way, a single pool of resources combined with divisions with competing priorities can undermine the effects that the divisional structure might, in principle, have.

8.3. Shaping Role Priorities

By separating distinct kinds of policing according to goals and legitimacy-risk profiles, it is possible to influence the candidates who are drawn to work for an agency and to guide their behavior on the job. This can increase the likelihood of just policing and create opportunities for external control.

Because the service functions of policing are culturally and, in some ways, institutionally subordinated to its crime fighting function, non-crime fighting activity is often written off as social work. Police don't want to be "social workers with guns" (Moskos 2008, 84). Community policing in particular is often dismissed as social work (Gascón and Roussell 2019, 46; Herbert 2006, 97; Skogan and Harnett 1997, 12, 71, 80, 93). Officers are often, especially after time on the job, opposed to "harm reduction" activities that do not directly fight crime (Ratcliffe and Sorg 2017, 52; Moskos 2008, 203). Rivaling the absurdity of anti-panhandling stings, Seattle created a "power community policing" model that brought "community policing" officers together to engage in proactive crime fighting, including buy-bust tactics (Herbert 2006, 98). Even though *service* is an advertised police goal, agencies tend to hire those looking for adventure through crime fighting (Bratton and

Knobler 1998, 240). But even before agencies hire adventurers, the nature of the agency influences the composition of the applicant pool.

Beyond the problem of the service functions of policing being maligned by many officers, the selection effects associated with policing in general and aggressive crime fighting units in particular appear to cause problems of their own. Some units have obvious selection effects—if you don't want to be a soldier in the war on drugs you probably won't seek a place in the narcotics unit—and in some cases are invitation only (Moskos 2008, 137). Embodying a crime fighting conception of policing attracts crime fighters to the role.

Dual response teams like CAHOOTS or dedicated overdose patrols are promising experiments in altering conceptions of policing. They involve creating new roles or modifying old ones. Harm reduction fits uncomfortably with the law enforcement goals and much more easily with order maintenance goals. I think this explains some naloxone skepticism in policing, and to increase the harm reduction police activities, agencies need to emphasize the order maintenance and service functions of patrol rather than criminal patrol activities (Monaghan 2022b). One way to do that is to ensure that the agency prioritizes their service functions. This is just one possible example, but it usefully highlights two things: first, the conflict between the service and crime fighting functions, and second, the scale of catastrophe possible when public agencies lack the priorities and strategies to effectively respond to (dynamic) problems.

Agency structure also influences policing by creating paths for promotion and professional development. Patrol, foot patrol in particular, is instructive. The foot patrol model—at the center both of early policing and recent experiments with community policing—is liked by residents but not many officers. Many view it as punishment. It is low prestige and at the bottom of the agency hierarchy; officers typically begin their careers in patrol and cities with foot patrols, like Philadelphia and Newark, often staff them with officers fresh out of the academy. Meanwhile, officers in foot patrol experiments report wanting the experiment to end so they can engage in "real policing" (Ratcliffe and Sorg 2017). Some try to specialize in law enforcement while patrolling. No one, as Moskos has pointed out, is ever promoted to beat cop (2008, 108). It is important that agencies not be structured such that one of its service functions is carried out by people who are more interested in the crime fighting function.

Specialized patrol units with promotion opportunities can incentivize officers to take seriously the service function of patrol. Indeed, Lvovsky argues that many of the officers in the vice patrols of the mid-twentieth century were not enthusiastic about targeting homosexual men but saw the units as an opportunity for promotion (2021, 110). Breaking the promotion path out of patrol on the basis of crime fighting prowess might at least reduce the incentives that tend to deprioritize service goals. Obviously, the problem is not merely one of motivation or priorities. Specialization in policing allows for training to preserve and more accurately reflect agency priorities, and, presumably in turn, more effective policing.

Officers need to have certain attitudes to be excellent harm-reducing, order-maintaining, or foot-patrolling officers. But they also need to be encouraged to police in those ways by their department. Another potential reform rooted in more specialized agency boundaries, then, is to fix incentive effects by changing the kinds of performance metrics agencies use to evaluate police work. This is exceptionally difficult. It is much easier to measure arrests, summonses, and citations than to measure improvements to one's beat that result from non-enforcement activity. But this is, and for decades has been, a problem. Agencies tend to valorize danger, not service (Sierra-Arevelo 2016, 2019). As Wilson remarked decades ago, "it makes little sense for a department that takes seriously its order maintenance function to reward officers who perform it well by making them law enforcement specialists" (Wilson 1978, 292). Training and performance metrics are important, and the form of the agency will always influence these aspects of policing. Allowing patrol to be the proving grounds for crime fighters produces a tendency toward injustice and illegitimacy.

My claim is not that the patrol division is not specialized or that most police officers are uninterested in helping. The main claim here is that people respond to incentives and act with their self-conceived role in mind, and the form of the agency influences both. That, in turn, shapes the agency's activity. Police officers in the LAPD, for example, have the option to select into the units that police Los Angeles' skid row (Stuart 2016, 90). But we saw earlier that these selection effects don't make the policing in skid row necessarily just or legitimate. The LAPD in skid row make arrests based on their (misguided) belief that it is a way to help them (get into social service/rehabilitation programs and housing) rather than a way to punish them and prevent crime. Fortunately, specialization at least raises the possibility of enhanced control over the police. Enhanced control over the police can accommodate the increased legitimacy risks that come along with officers selecting into high-risk police units.

8.4. Democratic Oversight

There are several important connections between agency structure—geographic and statuary boundaries in particular—and the possibility of democratic oversight and authorization of policing worth attending to.

The specter of the police state encourages both decentralized political control over policing and the professional isolation of police departments. On the other hand, radical decentralization of policing poses problems of its own. Some think that governments can more effectively provide services with more centralization and conclude that police forces should also be centralized and consolidated (cf. Ostrom et al. 1973). Decentralization can also undermine the efficient and widespread adoption of best practices and allow bad police officers to be rehired by less exacting police departments.

These considerations and others suggest that the geographic boundaries of police agencies need to be drawn carefully. If the ideal is for communities to self-police just as they self-govern, then the boundaries of the relevant communities are normatively significant. Legitimacy-risk profiles become useful here: the geographic boundary of an agency will depend on the kind of policing it provides. Strongly authorized policing, where perspectival diversity does not track location, like the investigation of Federal Bureau of Investigation (FBI) index crimes, can be legitimately conducted by agencies with larger geographic boundaries. In principle, a state police department could conduct criminal investigation just as it conducts highway patrol. High diversity policing, like the order maintenance function of the patrol division, is less likely to be well provided by a statewide agency. Judgments about what counts as orderly and acceptable uses of public space are hyper-local. Just order maintenance policing requires institutional forms that can acquire local information and act upon it.

Similarly, the geographic boundaries of an officer's posting can improve the officer's discretion in a way that enhances *non-electoral* democratic authorization. Recall from Chapter 7 that democratic authorization can be secured outside of electoral mechanisms in part by making police power more responsive to the interests of the policed. In contrast to more formal community engagement procedures, long-term job assignments allow officers to gather more local knowledge, in turn enhancing the officer's ability to resolve disputes and exercise discretion responsively (Bittner 1967, 707).

Moreover, research on foot patrol finds that when officers come to know the residents they are policing, they are less likely to take a primarily punitive response to offenses. Researchers surveyed officers who were part of foot patrol experiments:

> They said that since they work the same beat every day they get to know a lot of the residents, which makes it difficult to be very enforcement oriented. They felt bad writing parking violations because they had befriended (at least in a work sense) many of the people. In writing summonses in their own beat, they thought it would detract from their relationship with the residents. (Ratcliffe and Sorg 2017, 56)

In other words, bringing officers more tightly into the community transforms discretionary police power from something that manifests in high burden or harsh ways to something lower burden and more lenient. Properly drawn geographic boundaries, those that track the democratic authorization legitimacy risk, can have ancillary risk-reduction effects.

Finally, there is the issue of compensating the risks of specialization with democratic oversight. By drawing new agency boundaries for more specialization, we also allow for more *electoral* authorization, and more familiar forms of democratic oversight and accountability. By isolating different kinds of policing within separate agencies, we make it easier to apply political pressure to them. Because the act of specializing police agencies transforms the selection effects, this is an important way to compensate for newly created risks. Take Immigration and Customs Enforcement (ICE) as an example. ICE engages in highly controversial policing. Many think that immigration restrictions are a violation of fundamental rights: freedom of association, contract, and movement. On the other hand, some think that increasing immigration will decrease wages and increase crime and undermine the integrity of a nation's culture. For this reason, the work that ICE does is weakly authorized (as well as proactive and high burden). But proponents of more immigration are highly unlikely to take a job with ICE. The specialized nature of the agency entails that only those who are comfortable engaging in this high-risk enforcement will apply there. In turn, this likely makes the agency less concerned with burden reduction, even harsher, and more proactive. Specialization clearly enhances this risk.

We could try to spread this enforcement goal out into other federal agencies. If no agency formally prioritizes immigration enforcement, the modal federal officer might de-prioritize it. Immigration laws at the border might become like bicycle light laws, but probably not. Alternatively, federal agencies might decide to focus on immigration at the exclusion of other things, and we might recreate the criminal patrol dynamic. There is a real trade-off here.

At the same time, the political campaigns to abolish or defund ICE are enabled by specializing federal law enforcement such that the extraordinarily high-legitimacy-risk policing is largely isolated. Sure, the political battle against ICE has, so far, been unsuccessful. But the task seems more easily achieved than a campaign to eliminate the entirety of federal law enforcement would be, and this is partly a result of the fact that some federal law enforcement is much more strongly authorized. The upshot is that specialization allows for better agency prioritization, while also allowing for people to select into agencies with highly controversial priories, and this is an inevitable cost of the other benefits of specialization that can be compensated for with more targeted democratic oversight. Similar reasoning applies to other distinctively high-risk policing at the local level.

8.5. Unwinding Consolidation

How should we unwind our police departments? In some cases, we should return to old specializations, and in other cases we should create new ones.

8.5.1. Returning to Old Specializations

One early police department stands out in terms of taking seriously the relationship between specialization, agency priorities, workplace culture, and selection/incentive effects. That is the agency that policed Manhattan's Central Park before being absorbed by the New York Police Department (NYPD) (Thacher 2015). After the park's construction, landscape architect Frederick Law Olmsted had intermittent control over the management of the park. One of the things he cared about was the nature of the park's policing. In particular, Olmsted did not want the city police to have jurisdiction. The reason is that the park needs a particular kind of order maintenance policing. Upper Manhattan was still semi-rural when the park was completed and residents used the land accordingly (felling trees, letting livestock graze, etc.). So it was important that, if the park were to remain usable for everyone, people not use the land in that way (or in other ways inconsistent with the purpose of the park), that they don't trample the grass and flowers, and so on.

The major focus of the park *keepers*—Olmsted used a term for watchmen that preceded the modern, narrow usage of "police"—needed to be preventing the kinds of accumulative harms that would ruin the park. Occasionally, there would be more "ordinary" crime in the park. According to Olmsted, the keepers could handle that just fine. But the city police are not up to the task of maintaining order in the park, and for the basic reasons we've just covered. When Olmsted lost control of the park management, the keepers began to look more and more like a regular police department. Olmsted complained:

> "[They] perform the same duties as the city police so far as there is occasion for them in the park, quite as faithfully in manner as the street

police," [Olmsted] wrote in an abandoned draft from 1872. "Beyond this—for the other class of duties—the keeping of the park—they are almost worthless. They hate them; they consider them beneath their notice as policemen." (Thacher 2015, 596)

He explained that the park police were becoming ineffective at their task because they began to adopt the workplace culture of city police departments:

> It is impossible to get men when denominated police men and dressed and paid and regarded by the public as policemen to trouble themselves with other duties than those of police men. (Thacher 2015, 600)

Olmsted lost his battle for control, and the primary policing of the park was taken over by the NYPD. But Olmsted noticed a deeply problematic mismatch between the police culture and agency prioritization of crime control and the requirements of just and effective order maintenance. The mismatch has only been exacerbated, David Thacher argues, as crime control has moved further to the center of policing and order maintenance has become a tool for crime control instead of a distinct police function (2015, 616). If the patrol division were staffed with a larger proportion of officers who wanted primarily to help in a quasi-social worker capacity, rather than to have an adventurous job where they got to wage a war on criminals, policing would almost certainly look very different.

By maintaining a distinct force of park keepers, we do what we can to ensure that the police exercise their power to actually "keep the park." New York City also had a separate transit agency that was ultimately absorbed into the NYPD. Like the park keepers, a transit police agency has a narrower focus than the NYPD. The narrow goal is to maintain order on transit infrastructure, not to enforce other parts of the criminal code. In making intentional separations of police power, then, we could do worse than returning to some of our old institutional structures that tend to preserve distinct agency priorities and benefit from purposeful specialization.

8.5.2. Creating New Specializations

I must emphasize that the point is not just to break out existing police functions, but to create new specializations as the need arises. The emergency medical technician and ambulance driver roles are new specializations that were once handled by the police. Although in certain cases we'll still want police officers handling these duties (if an officer can get you to the hospital more quickly than an ambulance, it would be odd to object unless there's some special countervailing reason), this is an obvious improvement.

People often point out that the difference between a mere shooting and a homicide is luck (how many rounds were fired, how accurately, where did they hit, how long until the victim makes it to the hospital, etc.). On the criminal investigation side of things, some have thus advocated for the creation of non-fatal shooting units in addition to homicide units. Denver, Colorado, and Philadelphia, Pennsylvania, are early experimenters. Instead of a narcotics enforcement unit, we should have more overdose response teams. Likewise, the CAHOOTS model shows that non-police teams working with the police can seriously improve how mental health calls for service are handled. But in some cases, the non-police teams need support from the police. In these cases, we still have the same powerful reasons to prefer someone with specialized knowledge and skills in responding to mental health calls, even if we also want their tactical position to be hardened and their power of interference strengthened. James Q. Wilson's idea of a family disturbance (or perhaps a more general "dispute resolution") unit strikes me as appealing. Many officers de-prioritize these calls for service. Very little about the current police agency structure is suited to producing high-quality domestic dispute resolution, and the stakes are enormous.

These institutional reforms are not guaranteed to succeed. Financial incentives, weak or low-quality democratic control over administrative agencies, and bad informal norms can undermine any institutional fix. There are also the practical limits on specialization. The patrol officer is likely to be stuck with residual problems and residual political powers to offer some kind of response.

8.6. A New Model of Police Professionalism

It is important to see how the arguments so far bear on the question of police professionalism. The related tension between the virtues of amateurism and professionalism, and more democratic control versus more professional isolation, have existed as for at least as long as the night watch. Despite professionalization, the police profession never became a profession like the paradigmatic professions of law and medicine. Scholars writing after the professional era deny that policing is genuinely a profession and note that the police culture has remained decidedly blue collar (Moskos 2008, 20; Kleinig 1996, 44; Bayley 1996, 66; Wilson 1978, 73). The status quo is unappealing. The police tend to resent politicians and others meddling in their affairs while also lacking the professional ethos and, more importantly, effective professional institutions that enable professional self-regulation. While we don't want professions to be *entirely* self-regulating, it is a necessary part of just policing.

8.6.1. Informational Asymmetries and Professional Accountability

The first thing to note is that policing requires specialized knowledge, and so informational asymmetries exist as in other professions, even if they're less severe than in medicine or law. Yet Wilson denies that the police are professionals on exactly these grounds:

> The patrolman is not a professional, and thus the opinion of a professional colleague cannot be sought to justify his actions (the way doctors may justify each other's actions as in accord with "approved medical practice"). (Wilson 1978, 73)

This epistemic point entails a point about accountability. Physicians can say with justification whether a course of treatment was an acceptable one even if it failed. Most others lack the requisite knowledge. We must, therefore, include that professional knowledge in our accountability mechanisms.

The necessity of professional discretion leads to this outcome. If good professional decisions could be arrived at by the brute application of a rule book, there would be no asymmetry. But because policing is not like that, we need professional self-governance for the same reason that discretion is unavoidable. In policing, as in medicine, that is compatible with, and requires, external accountability mechanisms, too. But given the informational asymmetries, the problem that Wilson identifies is with the lack of "approved policing practice," not something inherent to the task that makes policing nonprofessional.

If policing involves information asymmetries, then good policing requires that the police role move much further along the "occupation-profession" spectrum. Treating highly discretionary, complicated work as the sort of thing that requires *supervision* rather than *management* is a recipe for disaster (cf. Bayley 1996, 66). Models of police accountability, democratic or otherwise, are deficient insofar as they neglect the need for robust internal accountability mechanisms.

8.6.2. Approved Policing Practices

Many police controversies strike me as implicating "approved policing practices." This is an epistemic problem. If one problem is a lack of approved policing practice, more fine-grained institutional boundaries can encourage a new model of police professionalism by changing the epistemic and thus accountability "environments" of policing. More specialized opioid overdose response units, for example, are less likely to decline to administer naloxone for (the irrational) fear of absorbing fentanyl through the skin.

More specialized units are likely to produce more specialized bodies of knowledge and skill. But take Derek Chauvin's killing of George Floyd, perhaps the most high-profile police killing controversy. Chauvin kneeled on Floyd's neck and back for nine minutes and twenty-nine seconds, asphyxiating him. Police have known for decades that compression techniques, like sitting or kneeling on the torso for restraint, carry a high risk of death (Bratton and Knobler 1998, 247). Although Chauvin's union was supportive, many police administrators publicly criticized him. Yet compression techniques are still an apparently common tactic in some departments. More powerful professional norms surrounding approved practices would improve internal accountability and police performance.

So even if we say what the approved practices are, if they are unjust, accountability mechanisms will be, too. Judging by the frequency with which U.S. police use deadly SWAT raids, a considerable share of the profession seems to view them as an approved police practice in a range of cases. Because this is an approved practice, "accidents" are more likely to be accepted by practitioners as an acceptable cost of doing business. They won't apologize when they shoot your dog after raiding the wrong house.

8.6.3. Accountability Mechanisms

Contra Wilson, I think the problem is less with approved policing practices and more with professional accountability mechanisms. The standard accountability mechanism in policing relies on instruction and punishment from higher levels of the agency hierarchy, such as when a police administrator punishes a patrol officer for misconduct, or the Department of Justice uses a consent decree to control the police administrator. But the blending of police functions and the weak state of approved policing practices undermines those mechanisms rendered essential by the limits of external accountability and oversight. If officers don't take seriously the "social workers with guns" aspects of patrol work, they're unlikely to take a critical approach to other officers who don't perform those tasks well. The same is true for administrative expectations and performance metrics. Officers get no credit for defusing situations (Moskos 2008, 143). Specialization enables more specific, and hopefully more appropriate, metrics.

If good policing requires more internal accountability, and if officers criticizing other officers is a crucial part of just, legitimate, and effective policing, then police agencies should be structured to encourage that. Police accountability mechanisms are often criticized in connection with the so-called blue wall of silence, where police refuse to report misconduct or cooperate in internal investigations.

Now, this is not a special problem for the police. Academia, for example, is rife with professional misconduct though not exactly rife with whistleblowers. But it is a problem. We need horizontal accountability institutions like those built into the other professions, such as the morbidity and mortality conferences and ethics committee consults that are commonplace in medicine. Those internal accountability mechanisms stand in stark contrast to the fact that internal affairs divisions in police departments rarely find officer misconduct.

The mechanisms need to be created. Perhaps a division of each state police force, or a new federal agency, should, like the Department of Justice, devote attention to policing other agencies. The problem with internal affairs investigations is that they are internal. Likewise, though perhaps a bit paradoxically, creating oversight boards that adjudicate accusations of bad policing staffed *by police* could improve police accountability. They have the professional knowledge, but they would be in a role explicitly designed to provide accountability, very much unlike the police chief sweeping misconduct under the rug. Officers from other agencies could be convened to staff the professional oversight boards. Obviously, this requires a host of changes to drastically weaken police unions and the job security they provide. And of course, we want to ensure external accountability as well. Civilian oversight boards are important, though they can be surprisingly more lenient than those that include police officers (Rector 2021). The problem is not that the police cannot police themselves; it's that we don't have the right institutional structures in place.

Approved policing practices implicate external accountability mechanisms, too. We can only hold people to the scope of approved practice when there is ample training in what counts as approved practice. Specialization becomes important here because of the opportunity cost problem for training. Sympathetic responses to bad policing *and* arguments for defunding the police and transferring many of their duties to non-police alternatives both point to the fact that the police are asked to do too much. Moving rapidly from serving a warrant to a domestic dispute to a mental health crisis in the span of a single shift is difficult and calls on vastly different skill sets and bodies of specialized knowledge.

Much of the discussion in this chapter has been vague and speculative, in part because I think principles of just policing are compatible with a range of agency forms, and also because I think we are in an epistemically weak position with respect to predictions about how agency reforms will manifest. Nevertheless, the blending of police functions, and their high legitimacy-risk characteristics, seems to me responsible (alongside many contingent factors) for many of the injustices of contemporary U.S. policing. The London Metropolitan police hoped that they would be good enough at deterrence that they could abandon their efforts at detection. They were wrong and added a plainclothes detective unit to the agency ten years after dissolving the Bow Street Runners. The initial impulse to focus the police on deterrence, through the classic method of visible and audible patrol, seems to me the correct one even if they were wrong that deterrence could obviate detection and enforcement. I think they were also wrong to join the deterrence and detection functions into a generalist law enforcement agency once they recognized their initial mistake. Doing so objectionably collapses the space between deterrence and enforcement, in turn depressing the formation of more just policing.

Conclusion

Contemporary policing emerged from centuries of intellectual disagreements and political battles. Should the management of public space, the adjudication of small, interpersonal disputes, the proximate deterrence of and protection from unwanted behavior, and its detection after the fact, be provided privately or by the public? By amateur community members or professionals? Should political control be centralized or localized? And how do we resolve disputes about what counts as "unwanted behavior"? Perennial, unavoidable conflicts between people living in close proximity, and between rights and democratic decision-making, are both made more difficult and pressing by diversity and dynamism. These conflicts simultaneously require some system of social control and make justice and legitimacy difficult to identify and achieve.

Resolving these disagreements, or at least attempting an answer to the questions, is complicated by methodological issues. If we're asking about what justice requires of the state, there's an understandable urge to engage in a variety of idealizations, but then we risk idealizing away the very problems that require social control. The result is destined, then, to be sort of unsatisfying: just policing will look quite different from the normal visions of ideally just society we get from theorists and novelists. Beyond that, the answers are sensitive to the background conditions of policing. The informal model we rely on in thinking about social control plays a major role in the answers. I've argued that the model should include error-prone people and political procedures, deep disagreement, resource scarcity, and unintended consequences. Our problems emerge from the complex interactions of a variety of elements, often in unpredictable ways. Whether policing is just depends on how it interacts with coupled social systems.

This dependence poses a problem for the legalist orientation I've taken to underlie common, but more or less implicit, views about what

Just Policing. Jake Monaghan, Oxford University Press. © Oxford University Press 2023.
DOI: 10.1093/oso/9780197610725.003.0009

justice requires of policing. Standard models of political legitimacy take legislative authority to be primary, and the task of the executive to faithfully enforce its decisions. The executive is entitled to make some decisions about enforcement and implementation, but they should avoid legislative decisions. The "conduit model," as I called it earlier, takes full enforcement to be the ideal and produces a weaker, good faith enforcement requirement to apply in real conditions. But the enforcement dilemma requires us to choose between interpretive and priority discretion: vaguer rules require more interpretation, and more determinate rules require prioritizing some violations and de-prioritizing others. The criminal code functions mostly as a tool to empower, not direct, the police. Fortunately, components of the legalist orientation like the rule of law are compatible with police discretion.

Rather than law, the judicious, legitimacy-risk minimizing use of those tools, and legitimacy-risk-aware agency structures, are the sources of police justice and legitimacy. Risks to legitimate police power track, among other factors, the magnitude and distribution of burdens, the strength of authorization, and the initiation of police power. Practically, the patrol and enforcement functions of policing tend to correlate with different legitimacy risks, but they do not fully determine them. Whereas preventive patrol and homicide investigation are generally well authorized, reactive, and lenient, vice investigation and criminal patrol are very much not. Because full enforcement is impossible, police need a way to set priorities. Individual police officers should avoid activities that join high-risk features, and police agencies should use their administrative tools to de-prioritize high-risk policing.

Why should we accept a theory of just policing that focuses on reducing risks to justice and legitimacy? This might seem to put the cart before the horse. But police legitimacy is interesting in this context for two reasons. First, much of their power is pre-political, in the sense that it precedes and is claimed and organized by states. Anyone can provide the basic defensive force of policing, and we centralize it under political control only in certain circumstances. Second, by the time there is a professional police role, people are already making competing demands on their exercise of power. The theoretical task is limiting the power of the police and explaining how the powers that they've centralized or been granted must be wielded.

This explains my focus, throughout, on discretionary non-enforcement. Not only is it an unavoidable reality, many compelling principles of justice motivate non-enforcement. Police have reasons grounded in familiar political principles, including proportionality, neutrality, and responsiveness, to take a more restricted and strategic view of their proper role. Once we see discretion not as a necessary evil but a component of just and legitimate political administration, we are better positioned to structure agencies to better satisfy those principles.

Beyond the specific questions about policing, I think there are some general lessons for political philosophy here. One is that implementation details are essential to evaluating a system of rules. Methodological approaches that see rules either as not needing active enforcement, or as sufficiently determinate on the page such that they can be evaluated apart from their enforcement, are therefore deficient.

This means that justice cannot require the passive impartiality I think is implicit in the legalist impulse. Impartiality in that sense is perilously close to indifference. In the words of Rosa Brooks:

> For the most part, America's criminal justice system isn't deliberately cruel. It's just indifferent to the ways in which it breaks human beings. Few police officers want to contribute to mass incarceration or aid in the destruction of poor minority communities. But the absurdities and injustices are inherent in the system. Often, by the time the police get involved, the only available choices are bad ones. (Brooks 2021, 286)

Justice doesn't require—it prohibits—impartial (in the sense of indifferent) policing. It requires acting strategically, making the best of bad situations, understood according to a set of principles thin enough to accommodate our inevitable disagreements about how to live.

Naturally, everyone is dissatisfied with some aspect of policing, and many people are dissatisfied with basically all of it. There are two final points to end on, both motivated by the book's non-ideal approach. First, there is an inherent tradeoff between utopian theorizing and incremental reform. Second, realized forms of social control are valuable but inherently risky.

On the first point, it is crucial that reformers aim for more just basic structures rather than accepting our background problems as fixed and making improvements from there (Shelby 2016, 36). But the popular argument that focusing our attention on reform takes it away from finding fundamental solutions cuts both ways. We can't let a focus on grand reforms take all of our attention from making local improvements. Diversity of intellectual inquiry is valuable here because sometimes the background is as good as fixed in the near term. And the just (realized) basic structure is determined in part by the dynamic pathologies of our actual world. Rejecting, for example, reforms to use-of-force policies on the grounds that (1) it will only lend legitimacy to the police and (2) ideal justice requires a world without police is a good way to be stuck with unjust policing in the real world. The history of policing is deeply unjust, but it is difficult to look at historical accounts of policing without getting the sense that our problems are at least different and, in some ways, less severe. Police memoirs today don't boast about accepting bribes to overlook physical assault.[1]

On the second point, one of the major conclusions I've tried to motivate, alongside the particular claims about justice and legitimacy, is that social control is as risky as it is important. In imagining alternatives to today's police departments, or even in imagining more incremental reforms, it is important to keep in mind that "non-police" alternatives for social control, whether medical, religious, or otherwise ideological, can be coercive and unjust.[2] The metaphor of the state's "left and right hands" sharply distinguishes the supportive (i.e., medicine, housing, education) from the disciplinary (i.e., police, courts,

---

[1] On the other hand, here's a story from the memoir of early twentieth-century New York Police Department Captain Cornelius Willemse: "A few nights later I was standing outside the Haymarket, when a big, fine-looking young man walked up to me. 'Officer,' he declared, 'I'll give you $20 if you'll let me hit that hackman over there. He's a dirty thief.' 'He is, huh? Well, go ahead.' Twenty dollars was a lot of money in those days. Besides, the young man was sober and, knowing the night-hawk cab those days and the stunts they were pulling regularly on strangers, I figured he had plenty of cause for his anger" (1931, 77).

[2] A point recognized by some abolitionists who generalize their position to one that rejects "institutionalizing" responses to social problems (Purnell 2021), and one on full display in, for example, the collaborative efforts to control Los Angeles' skid row.

corrections) functions of the state.[3] We would be lucky if there were such a sharp distinction.

Relatedly, we should expect continuity between the police forces we have now and the reimagined public safety institutions of the future, just as there was continuity between the old night watches and the "new police" in London, Boston, New York, and elsewhere. This is simply a reflection of the slow, piecemeal nature of political change. We should expect not just some continuity of personnel or equipment but also some continuity of method. The new new police, whether separate mental health response teams, volunteer community foot patrols, violence interrupters, and so on, will have to rely on some methods of deterrence and detection that overlap with the police.

This point is worth emphasizing: sadly, there is probably no real world without people policing others. People seek social control. There are only worlds with more or less proportional, liberty- and diversity-respecting, responsive, and accountable policing. Some prefer the term "peace keeping" to "order maintenance" when describing the non-enforcement functions of the police, partly because the former is more neutral than the latter. But the term "order maintenance," with all of its baggage, is apt because we keep peace by enforcing some kind of order. There are bound to be disagreements over whether that order is a just one. All social control is fraught with injustice.

---

[3] See Zacka (2018, 23) for a brief discussion of Pierre Bourdieu's distinction.

References

Abizadeh, Arash. 2021. "Counter-Majoritarian Democracy: Persistent Minorities, Federalism, and the Power of Numbers." *American Political Science Review* 115 (3): 742–756.

Abrams, David S. 2013. "Putting the Trial Penalty on Trial Plea Bargaining after Lafler and Frye." *Duquesne Law Review* 51 (3): 777–786.

Abt, Thomas. 2019. *Bleeding out: The Devastating Consequences of Urban Violence—and a Bold New Plan for Peace in the Streets.* New York: Basic Books.

Adelson, Jeff. 2020. "A Crackdown on Claiborne Avenue Vendors Will Begin This Week in New Orleans, and Here's Why." *Nola.Com*, August 12, 2020. https://www.nola.com/news/coronavirus/article_72914176-dcf8-11ea-a1aa-7fdcd9742ea0.html.

Agan, Amanda, and Sonja Starr. 2018. "Ban the Box, Criminal Records, and Racial Discrimination: A Field Experiment." *The Quarterly Journal of Economics* 133 (1): 191–235.

Akinnibi, Fola. 2020. "NYC Pilot Tries Mental Health Responders in Place of Police." *Bloomberg CityLab*, November 13, 2020. https://www.bloomberg.com/news/articles/2020-11-13/nyc-pilot-sends-health-workers-in-place-of-police.

Alexander, Michelle. 2012. *The New Jim Crow*. New York: The New Press.

Allen, Bennett, and Alex Harocopos. 2016. "Non-Prescribed Buprenorphine in New York City: Motivations for Use, Practices of Diversion, and Experiences of Stigma." *Journal of Substance Abuse Treatment* 70 (November): 81–86.

Alschuler, Albert W., and Stephen J. Schulhofer. 1998. "Antiquated Procedures or Bedrock Rights: A Response to Professors Meares and Kahan the Right to a Fair Trial." *University of Chicago Legal Forum* (1): 215–244.

Anderson, Nels. 1967. *The Hobo: The Sociology of the Homeless Man.* Chicago: University of Chicago Press.

Apel, Robert. 2016. "On the Deterrent Effect of Stop, Question, and Frisk Stop, Question, and Frisk Practices." *Criminology and Public Policy* 15 (1): 57–66.

Arneson, Richard J. 2009. "The Supposed Right to a Democratic Say." In *Contemporary Debates in Political Philosophy*, edited by Thomas Christiano and John Philip Christman, 197–212. Malden, MA: Wiley-Blackwell.

Ba, Bocar A., Dean Knox, Jonathan Mummolo, and Roman Rivera. 2021. "The Role of Officer Race and Gender in Police-Civilian Interactions in Chicago." *Science* 371 (6530): 696–702.

Balko, Radley. 2013. *Rise of the Warrior Cop: The Militarization of America's Police Forces*. New York: Public Affairs.

Barkow, Rachel E. 2006. "Separation of Powers and the Criminal Law." *Stanford Law Review* 58: 66.

Barkow, Rachel E. 2019. *Prisoners of Politics: Breaking the Cycle of Mass Incarceration*. Cambridge, MA: Harvard University Press.

Barksdale, Anthony. 2020. "We Cannot Afford to Wait." *Violence Reduction Project* (blog). https://qualitypolicing.com/violencereduction/barksdale/.

Baumgartner, Frank R., Derek A. Epp, and Kelsey Shoub. 2018. *Suspect Citizens: What 20 Million Traffic Stops Tell Us About Policing and Race*. Cambridge: Cambridge University Press.

Bayley, David H. 1996. *Police for the Future*. Oxford: Oxford University Press.

Beall, Pat. 2018. "How Florida Spread Oxycodone across America." *Igniting an Epidemic* (blog). https://heroin.palmbeachpost.com/how-florida-spread-oxycodone-across-america/.

Beletsky, Leo, and Corey S. Davis. 2017. "Today's Fentanyl Crisis: Prohibition's Iron Law, Revisited." *International Journal of Drug Policy* 46 (August): 156–159.

Berg, Bruce L. 1999. *Policing in Modern Society*. Boston: Butterworth Heinemann.

Best, Joel. 1998. *Controlling Vice: Regulating Brothel Prostitution in St. Paul, 1865–1883*. Columbus: The Ohio State University Press.

Bittner, Egon. 1967. "The Police on Skid-Row: A Study of Peace Keeping." *American Sociological Review* 32 (5): 699–715.

Boettke, Peter J., Christopher J. Coyne, and Abigail R. Hall. 2012. "Keep off the Grass: The Economics of Prohibition and U.S. Drug Policy Symposium: A Step Forward: Creating a Just Drug Policy for the United States." *Oregon Law Review* 91 (4): 1069–1096.

Braga, Anthony A., Brandon S. Turchan, Andrew V. Papachristos, and David M. Hureau. 2019. "Hot Spots Policing and Crime Reduction: An Update of an Ongoing Systematic Review and Meta-Analysis." *Journal of Experimental Criminology* 15 (3): 289–311.

Bratton, William, and Peter Knobler. 2009. *The Turnaround: How America's Top Cop Reversed the Crime Epidemic*. New York: Random House.

Brayne, Sarah. 2014. "Surveillance and System Avoidance: Criminal Justice Contact and Institutional Attachment." *American Sociological Review* 79 (3): 367–391.

Breen, Thomas. 2020. "Cops Offer Addicts Clean Needles, Pipes." *New Haven Independent*, February 6. https://ctmirror.org/2020/02/09/new-haven-pol ice-offer-addicts-clean-needles-harm-reduction-kits/.

Brennan, Jason. 2014. *Why Not Capitalism?* Princeton, NJ: Princeton University Press.

Brennan, Jason. 2019. *When All Else Fails*. Princeton, NJ: Princeton University Press.

Brennan, Jason, and Hélène Landemore. 2021. *Debating Democracy: Do We Need More or Less?* Debating Ethics. New York: Oxford University Press.

Brooks, Rosa. 2021. *Tangled up in Blue: Policing the Nation's Capital*. New York: Penguin Press.

Brown, Michael K. 1988. *Working the Street: Police Discretion and the Dilemmas of Reform*. New York: Russell Sage Foundation.

Buchanan, Allen. 2002. "Political Legitimacy and Democracy." *Ethics* 112 (4): 689–719.

Bureau of Justice Statistics. 2015. "Bureau of Justice Statistics (BJS)—Mortality in Local Jails and State Prisons, 2000–2013—Statistical Tables." https://www.bjs.gov/index.cfm?ty=pbdetail&iid=5361.

Burki, Talha. 2020. "Prisons Are 'in No Way Equipped' to Deal with COVID-19." *The Lancet* 395 (10234): 1411–1412.

Butler, Paul. 2017. "The System Is Working the Way It Is Supposed to: The Limits of Criminal Justice Reform." *Georgetown Law Journal* 104 (6): 1419–1478.

Butler, Paul. 2018. *Chokehold: Policing Black Men*. New York: The New Press.

Cameron, Lisa, Jennifer Seager, and Manisha Shah. 2020. "Crimes Against Morality: Unintended Consequences of Criminalizing Sex Work." Working Paper 27846. Working Paper Series. National Bureau of Economic Research.

Chalfin, Aaron, Benjamin Hansen, Emily K. Weisburst, and Morgan C. Williams Jr. 2020. "Police Force Size and Civilian Race." w28202. National Bureau of Economic Research.

Chammah. 2020. "Your Local Jail May Be A House of Horrors." The Marshall Project. July 29. https://www.themarshallproject.org/2020/07/29/your-local-jail-may-be-a-house-of-horrors.

Cheng, Cheng, and Wei Long. 2018. "Improving Police Services: Evidence from the French Quarter Task Force." *Journal of Public Economics* 164 (August): 1–18.

Chicago Public Schools. 2021. "Safe Passage Program." Cps.Edu. 2021. https://www.cps.edu/services-and-supports/student-safety-and-security/safe-passage-program/.

Chin, Yoo-Mi, and Scott Cunningham. 2019. "Revisiting the Effect of Warrantless Domestic Violence Arrest Laws on Intimate Partner Homicides." *Journal of Public Economics* 179 (November): 104072.

Cho, Sungwoo, Felipe Gonçalves, and Emily Weisburst. 2022. *Do Police Make Too Many Arrests? The Effect of Enforcement Pullbacks on Crime*. IZA Discussion Paper No. 14907. https://ssrn.com/abstract=4114411

Christiano, Thomas. 1996. *The Rule of the Many: Fundamental Issues in Democratic Theory*. Boulder, CO: Westview.

Christiano, Thomas. 2004. "The Authority of Democracy." *Journal of Political Philosophy* 12 (3): 266–290.

Christiano, Thomas. 2010. *The Constitution of Equality: Democratic Authority and Its Limits*. New York: Oxford.

Coates, Ta-Nehisi. 2015. *Between the World and Me*. 1st ed. New York: Spiegel & Grau.

Cohen, Cathy J. 2010. *Democracy Remixed: Black Youth and the Future of American Politics*. Oxford: Oxford University Press.

Cohen, G. A. 2009. *Why Not Socialism?* Princeton, NJ: Princeton University Press.

Colquhoun, Patrick. 1806. *A Treatise on the Police of the Metropolis*. 7th ed. London: Bye and Law.

Cordner, Gary. 2014. "Community Policing." In *The Oxford Handbook of Police and Policing*, edited by Michael D. Reisig and Robert J. Kane, 148–171. New York: Oxford University Press.

Coyne, Christopher J., and Abigail R. Hall. 2018. *Tyranny Comes Home: The Domestic Fate of U.S. Militarism*. Stanford, CA: Stanford University Press.

Dau, Philipp M., Christophe Vandeviver, Maite Dewinter, Frank Witlox, and Tom Vander Beken. 2021. "Policing Directions: A Systematic Review on the Effectiveness of Police Presence." *European Journal on Criminal Policy and Research* (November).

Dulaney, W. Marvin. 1996. *Black Police in America*. Bloomington: Indiana University Press.

Duneier, Mitchell. 1999. *Sidewalk*. New York: Farrar, Straus and Giroux.

Dworin, Caroline H. 2008. "The Books and the Boos." *The New York Times*, October 18, sec. New York. https://www.nytimes.com/2008/10/19/nyregion/thecity/19vend.html.

Endicott, Timothy A. O. 1999. "The Impossibility of the Rule of Law." *Oxford Journal of Legal Studies* 19 (1): 1–18.

Epstein, Joseph, and Jonathan D. Popiolkowski. 2020. "Speed Limit Lowered to 30 after Deadly Delaware Park Accident." *The Buffalo News*. https://buffalonews.com/news/local/crime-and-courts/speed-limit-lowered-to-30-after-deadly-delaware-park-accident/article_91ab6857-0eb4-50c7-a715-90d232bb6c28.html.

Equal Justice Initiative. 2020. "Covid-19's Impact on People in Prison." Equal Justice Initiative. May 11. https://eji.org/news/covid-19s-impact-on-people-in-prison/.

Estlund, David. 2007. "On Following Orders in an Unjust War." *Journal of Political Philosophy* 15 (2): 213–234.

Estlund, David. 2009. *Democratic Authority: A Philosophical Framework*. Princeton, NJ: Princeton University Press.

Estlund, David. 2020. *Utopophobia: On the Limits (If Any) of Political Philosophy*. Princeton, NJ: Princeton University Press.

Eugene Police Department Crime Analysis Unit. 2020. "CAHOOTS Program Analysis." August 2020. https://www.eugene-or.gov/DocumentCenter/View/56717/CAHOOTS-Program-Analysis.

Evans, William N., Ethan M. J. Lieber, and Patrick Power. 2018. "How the Reformulation of OxyContin Ignited the Heroin Epidemic." *The Review of Economics and Statistics* 101 (1): 1–15.

Fagan, Jeffrey, and Tracey L. Meares. 2008. "Punishment, Deterrence and Social Control: The Paradox of Punishment in Minority Communities." *Ohio State Journal of Criminal Law*, 6 (1): 173–230.

Fagan, Jeffrey, Tom Tyler, and Tracey L. Meares. 2016. "Street Stops and Police Legitimacy in New York." In *Comparing the Democratic Governance of Police Intelligence: New Models of Participation and Expertise in the United States and Europe*, edited by Thierry Delpeuch and Jacqueline Ross, 203–231. Northampton, MA: Edward Elgar.

Feinberg, Joel. 1987. *The Moral Limits of the Criminal Law Volume 1: Harm to Others*. Oxford: Oxford University Press.

Ferzan, Kimberly Kessler. 2013. "Provocateurs." *Criminal Law and Philosophy* 7 (3): 597–622.

Fields, Gene. 2021. *Cops and Characters in The Big Easy: True Stories Involving Celebrities, Criminals and Everyday People*. New York: Bogart Books.

Fink, Sheri. 2013. *Five Days at Memorial: Life and Death in a Storm-Ravaged Hospital*. New York: Crown.

Fogelson, Robert M. 1977. *Big-City Police*. Cambridge, MA: Harvard University Press.

Forman, Jr, James. 2017. *Locking Up Our Own: Crime and Punishment in Black America*. New York: Farrar, Straus and Giroux.

Freiman, Christopher. 2017. *Unequivocal Justice*. New York: Routledge.

Friedman, David D. 1989. *The Machinery of Freedom: Guide to a Radical Capitalism*. Chicago: Open Court.

Frowe, Helen. 2016. *The Ethics of War and Peace*. New York: Routledge.

Fuller, Lon Luvois. 1969. *The Morality of Law*. New Haven, CT: Yale University Press.

Fuller, Thomas. 2021. "San Francisco's Shoplifting Surge." *The New York Times*, May 21, sec. U.S. https://www.nytimes.com/2021/05/21/us/san-francisco-shoplifting-epidemic.html.

Gabrielson, Ryan, and Topher Sanders. 2016. "Busted." ProPublica. July 7. https://www.propublica.org/article/common-roadside-drug-test-routinely-produces-false-positives?token=TuMy8gExpvZxdxiWRs7mTz21zSyVml5E.

Gallup. 2019. "In U.S., Medical Aid Top Reason Why Legal Marijuana Favored." Gallup.Com. June 12. https://news.gallup.com/poll/258149/medical-aid-top-reason-why-legal-marijuana-favored.aspx.

Garnett, Nicole Stelle. 2010. *Ordering the City: Land Use, Policing, and the Restoration of Urban America*. New Haven, CT: Yale University Press.

Gascón, Luis Daniel, and Aaron Roussell. 2019. *The Limits of Community Policing: Civilian Power and Police Accountability in Black and Brown Los Angeles*. New York: New York University Press.

Gaus, Gerald. 1996. *Justificatory Liberalism: An Essay on Epistemology and Political Theory*. Oxford: Oxford University Press.

Gaus, Gerald. 2018. "The Complexity of a Diverse Moral Order." *Georgetown Journal of Law & Public Policy* 16: 645–680.

Gaus, Gerald. 2019. *The Tyranny of the Ideal: Justice in a Diverse Society*. Princeton, NJ: Princeton University Press.

Gawande, Atul. 2010. *The Checklist Manifesto: How to Get Things Right*. New York: Henry Holt and Company.

Geller, Amanda, Jeffrey Fagan, Tom Tyler, and Bruce G. Link. 2014. "Aggressive Policing and the Mental Health of Young Urban Men." *American Journal of Public Health* 104 (12): 2321–2327.

Geller, Amanda, Irwin Garfinkel, Carey E. Cooper, and Ronald B. Mincy. 2009. "Parental Incarceration and Child Well-Being: Implications for Urban Families." *Social Science Quarterly* 90 (5): 1186–1202.

Gibbons-Neff, Thomas, and Eric Schmitt. 2020. "Pentagon Ordered National Guard Helicopters' Aggressive Response in D.C." *The New York Times*, June 6, sec. U.S. https://www.nytimes.com/2020/06/06/us/politics/protests-trump-helicopters-national-guard.html.

Goldstein, Herman. 1963. "Police Discretion: The Ideal versus the Real." *Public Administration Review* 23 (3): 140.

Goldstein, Herman. 1990. *Problem-Oriented Policing*. Philadelphia: Temple University Press.

Gonen, Yoav, and Eileen Grench. 2021. "Five Days Without Cops: Could Brooklyn Policing Experiment Be a 'Model for the Future'?" The City. January 3. https://www.thecity.nyc/2021/1/3/22211709/nypd-cops-brooklyn-brownsville-experiment-defund-police.

Gonzalez, Robert, and Sarah Komisarow. 2020. "Community Monitoring and Crime: Evidence From Chicago's Safe Passage Program." *Journal of Public Economics* 191 (November): 104–250.

Goodin, Robert E. 1988. *Reasons for Welfare: The Political Theory of the Welfare State*. Studies in Moral, Political, and Legal Philosophy. Princeton, NJ: Princeton University Press.

Goodnough, Abby, Josh Katz, and Margot Sanger-Katz. 2019. "Drug Overdose Deaths Drop in U.S. for First Time Since 1990." *The New York Times*, sec. The Upshot. https://www.nytimes.com/interactive/2019/07/17/upshot/drug-overdose-deaths-fall.html.

Greene, Jack, R. 2014. "Zero Tolerance and Policing." In *The Oxford Handbook of Police and Policing*, edited by Michael D. Reisig and Robert J. Kane, 172–196. New York: Oxford University Press.

Guerrero, Alexander A. 2010. "The Paradox of Voting and the Ethics of Political Representation: The Paradox of Voting and the Ethics of Political Representation." *Philosophy & Public Affairs* 38 (3): 272–306.

Guerrero, Alexander A. 2014. "Against Elections: The Lottocratic Alternative." *Philosophy & Public Affairs* 42 (2): 135–178.

Hadden, Sally E. 2001. *Slave Patrols: Law and Violence in Virginia and the Carolinas*. Cambridge, MA: Harvard University Press.

Harocopos, Alex, and Mike Hough. 2005. "Drug Dealing in Open-Air Markets." *Problem Oriented Policing Guides*, 31: 1–51. https://popcenter.asu.edu/content/drug-dealing-open-air-markets-0.

Harper, Jane. 2021. "Norfolk Police Tackled a Bicyclist for Riding without a Headlight. Bodycam Footage in a Lawsuit Shows It All." *The Virginia Pilot*, December 19. https://www.pilotonline.com/news/crime/vp-nw-bike-inj ury-lawsuit-20211219-a5ymjmwyrvanbnab73nxvly3ey-story.html.

Hart, Carl L. 2021. *Drug Use for Grown-Ups: Chasing Liberty in the Land of Fear*. New York: Penguin Press.

Hart, H. L. A. 1961. *The Concept of Law*. Clarendon Law Series. Oxford: Oxford University Press.

Hayek, F. A. 1945. "The Use of Knowledge in Society." *The American Economic Review* 35 (4): 519–530.

Hayek, F. A. 2011. *The Constitution of Liberty*. Edited by Ronald Hamowy. Chicago: University of Chicago Press.

Heath, Joseph. 2020. *The Machinery of Government: Public Administration and the Liberal State*. New York: Oxford University Press.

Hedgpeth, Dana. 2022. "Fox Caught on Capitol Grounds and Euthanized Tests Positive for Rabies." *Washington Post*, April 6. https://www.washingtonpost.com/dc-md-va/2022/04/06/capitol-fox-euthanized-kits-found/.

Herbert, Steven. 2006. *Citizens, Cops, and Power: Recognizing the Limits of Community*. Chicago: University of Chicago Press.

Hirschel, David, Eve Buzawa, April Pattavina, and Don Faggiani. 2007. "Domestic Violence and Mandatory Arrest Laws: To What Extent Do They Influence Police Arrest Decisions Criminology." *Journal of Criminal Law and Criminology* 98 (1): 255–298.

Huemer, Michael. 2013. *The Problem of Political Authority: An Examination of the Right to Coerce and the Duty to Obey*. New York: Palgrave MacMillan.

Huey, Laura. 2007. *Negotiating Demands: The Politics of Skid Row Policing in Edinburgh, San Francisco, and Vancouver*. Toronto: University of Toronto Press.

Hume, David. 1777. "Of the Original Contract." In *Essays Moral, Political, and Literary*, edited by Eugene Miller, 465–487. Indianapolis: Liberty Fund.

Hunt, Luke William. 2019. *The Retrieval of Liberalism in Policing*. New York: Oxford University Press.

Husak, Douglas. 2014. "Polygamy: A Novel Test for a Theory of Criminalization." In *Criminalization*, edited by R A Duff, Lindsay Farmer, S E Marshall, Massimo Renzo, and Victor Tadros, 213–231. Oxford: Oxford University Press.

Husak, Douglas N. 2008. *Overcriminalization: The Limits of the Criminal Law*. New York: Oxford University Press.

Iyengar, Radha. 2009. "Does the Certainty of Arrest Reduce Domestic Violence? Evidence from Mandatory and Recommended Arrest Laws." *Journal of Public Economics* 93 (1): 85–98.

Jones, Ben. 2021. "Police-Generated Killings: The Gap between Ethics and Law." *Political Research Quarterly* 75 (2): 366–378.

Kaba, Mariame. 2020. "Yes, We Mean Literally Abolish the Police." *The New York Times*, June 12, sec. Opinion. https://www.nytimes.com/2020/06/12/opinion/sunday/floyd-abolish-defund-police.html.

Kaba, Mariame, Tamara K. Nopper, and Naomi Murakawa. 2021. *We Do This 'til We Free Us: Abolitionist Organizing and Transforming Justice*. Abolitionist Papers. Chicago: Haymarket Books.

Kahan, Dan, and Tracey Meares. 1998. "The Coming Crisis of Criminal Procedure." *University of Chicago Legal Forum* 197: 1153–1184.

Kaste, Martin. 2019. "When Sheriffs Won't Enforce The Law." *WAMU*, February 21. https://wamu.org/story/19/02/21/when-sheriffs-wont-enforce-the-law/.

Kavka, Gregory S. 1995. "Why Even Morally Perfect People Would Need Government." *Social Philosophy and Policy* 12 (1): 1–18.

Kelling, George L, and Mark H. Moore. 1988. "Perspectives on Policing: The Evolving Strategy of Policing." *US Department of Justice, Office of Justice Programs, National Institute of Justice* 4. https://www.policefoundation.org/publication/perspectives-on-policing-the-evolving-strategy-of-policing/.

Kelling, George L., Anthony Pate, Amy Ferrara, Mary Utne, and Charles Brown. 1981. "The Newark Foot Patrol Experiment." *The Police Foundation*. https://www.policinginstitute.org/wp-content/uploads/2015/07/144273499-The-Newark-Foot-Patrol-Experiment.pdf

Kelling, George L., Tony Pate, Duane Dieckman, and Charles Brown E. 1974. "The Kansas City Preventive Patrol Experiment." *National Police Foundation*. https://www.policefoundation.org/publication/the-kansas-city-preventive-patrol-experiment/.

Kelling, George L., and James Q. Wilson. 1982. "Broken Windows: The Police and Neighborhood Safety." *The Atlantic Monthly* 249 (3): 29–38.

Kerouac, Jack. 1986. *On the Road*. A Penguin Book Fiction. New York: Penguin Books.

Kim, Andrew Chongseh. 2015. "Underestimating the Trial Penalty: An Empirical Analysis of the Federal Trial Penalty and Critique of the Abrams Study." *Mississippi Law Journal* 84 (5): 1195–1256.

Kleinfeld, Joshua, Laura I Appleman, Richard A Bierschbach, Kenworthey Bilz, Josh Bowers, John Braithwaite, Robert P Burns, et al. 2017. "White Paper of Democratic Criminal Justice." *North Western University Law Review* 111 (6): 14.

Kleinig, John. 1996. *The Ethics of Policing*. Cambridge: Cambridge University Press.

LaFave, Wayne R. 1965. *Arrest: The Decision to Take a Suspect into Custody.* Boston: Little, Brown, and Co.

Landemore, Hélène. 2020. *Open Democracy: Reinventing Popular Rule for the Twenty-First Century.* Princeton, NJ: Princeton University Press.

Lane, Roger. 1967. *Policing the City-Boston, 1822–1885.* Cambridge, MA: Harvard University Press.

Laudan, Larry. 2006. *Truth, Error, and Criminal Law: An Essay in Legal Epistemology.* Cambridge: Cambridge University Press.

Lazar, Seth. 2020. "War." In *The Stanford Encyclopedia of Philosophy*, edited by Edward N. Zalta, Spring. https://plato.stanford.edu/entries/war/.

LeGuin, Ursula K. 1974. *The Dispossessed: An Ambiguous Utopia.* New York: Harper & Row.

Levy, Jacob T. 2021. "The Separation of Powers and the Challenge to Constitutional Democracy." *Review of Constitutional Studies* 25 (1): 1–19.

Lin, Chi Hui, and Hellen Davidson. 2021. "China's Noisy 'Dancing Grannies' Silenced by Device That Disables Speakers." *The Guardian*, October 8. https://www.theguardian.com/world/2021/oct/08/chinas-noisy-dancing-grannies-silenced-by-device-that-disables-speakers?CMP=fb_gu&utm_medium=Social&utm_source=Facebook&fbclid=IwAR0XhaSU66mE3nCA6o_ff1ejASpMAMiECCb8M_tyOK5WUiud LBrehm02Cjk#Echobox=1633681697.

Lum, Cynthia, Christopher S. Koper, and Xiaoyun Wu. 2021. "Can We Really Defund the Police? A Nine-Agency Study of Police Response to Calls for Service." *Police Quarterly* 25 (3): 255–280.

Lvovsky, Anna. 2021. *Vice Patrol: Cops, Courts, and the Struggle over Urban Gay Life before Stonewall.* Chicago: University of Chicago Press.

MacNeil, Sara. 2019. "Sagging Pants Law Abolished in Shreveport." *Shreveport Times*, June 11. https://www.shreveporttimes.com/story/news/2019/06/11/sagging-pants-law-abolished-shreveport/1425135001/.

Mansbridge, Jane. 2003. "Rethinking Representation." *The American Political Science Review* 97 (4): 515–528.

Matier, Phil. 2021. "Tents Are Back in San Francisco's Tenderloin, and Scoring Drugs Is Easy—SFChronicle.Com." *San Francisco Chronicle*, January 24. https://www.sfchronicle.com/bayarea/philmatier/article/The-tents-are-back-in-San-Francisco-s-15891921.php.

McMahan, Jeff. 2009. *Killing in War.* New York: Oxford University Press.

McMillen, Daniel, Ignacio Sarmiento-Barbieri, and Ruchi Singh. 2019. "Do More Eyes on the Street Reduce Crime? Evidence from Chicago's Safe Passage Program." *Journal of Urban Economics* 110 (March): 1–25.

Meares, Tracey, and Dan Kahan. 1998. "Black, White and Gray: A Reply to Alschuler and Schulhofer." *University of Chicago Legal Forum* (1): 245–260.

Mello, Steven. 2019. "More COPS, Less Crime." *Journal of Public Economics* 172 (April): 174–200.

Mill, John Stuart. 1977. "Considerations on Representative Government." In *Essays on Politics and Society*, edited by J. M. Robson. Vol. 18–19. Collected Works of John Stuart Mill. Toronto: University of Toronto Press.

Mill, John Stuart. 1978. *On Liberty (1859)*. Edited by Elizabeth Rapaport. Indianapolis: Hackett.

Monaghan, Jake. 2017. "The Special Moral Obligations of Law Enforcement." *Journal of Political Philosophy* 25 (2): 218–237.

Monaghan, Jake. 2018. "On Enforcing Unjust Laws in a Just Society." *Philosophical Quarterly* 68 (273): 758–778.

Monaghan, Jake. 2020. "Boundary Policing." *Philosophy & Public Affairs* 49 (1): 26–50.

Monaghan, Jake. 2021. "Legitimate Policing and Professional Norms." In *The Ethics of Policing: An Interdisciplinary Approach*, edited by Ben Jones and Mendieto. New York: New York University Press.

Monaghan, Jake. 2022a. "Idealizations and Ideal Policing." *Philosophers' Imprint* 22 (9): 1–15.

Monaghan, Jake. 2022b. "Broken Windows, Naloxone, and Experiments in Policing." *Social Theory and Practice* 48 (2): 309–330.

Monkkonen, Eric H. 1981. *Police in Urban America, 1860–1920*. Cambridge, MA: Cambridge University Press.

Morabito, Melissa S., Jenna Savage, Lauren Sneider, and Kellie Wallace. 2018. "Police Response to People with Mental Illnesses in a Major U.S. City: The Boston Experience with the Co-Responder Model." *Victims & Offenders* 13 (8): 1093–1105.

Moskos, Peter. 2008. *Cop in the Hood: My Year Policing Baltimore's Eastern District*. Princeton, NJ: Princeton University Press.

Muir, William K. 1977. *Police: Streetcorner Politicians*. Chicago: University of Chicago Press.

Muldoon, Ryan. 2016. *Social Contract Theory for a Diverse World: Beyond Tolerance*. New York: Routledge.

Na, Chongmin, and Denise C. Gottfredson. 2013. "Police Officers in Schools: Effects on School Crime and the Processing of Offending Behaviors." *Justice Quarterly* 30 (4): 619–650.

Natapoff, Alexandra. 2012. "Misdemeanors." *Southern California Law Review* 85 (5): 1313–1376.

Natapoff, Alexandra. 2018. *Punishment Without Crime: How Our Massive Misdemeanor System Traps the Innocent and Makes America More Unequal*. New York: Basic Books.

Novisky, Meghan A., and Robert L. Peralta. 2015. "When Women Tell: Intimate Partner Violence and the Factors Related to Police Notification." *Violence Against Women* 21 (1): 65–86.

Nozick, Robert. 1974. *Anarchy, State, and Utopia*. New York: Basic Books.

O'Neill, Maggie, and Jane Pitcher. 2010. "Sex Work, Communities, and Public Policy in the UK." In *Sex Works Mattes: Exploring Money, Power, and*

Intimacy in the Sex Industry, edited by Melissa Hope Ditmore, Antonia Levy, and Alys Willman, 203–218. New York: Zed Books.

Ostrom, Elinor, Roger B. Parks, and Gordon P. Whitaker. 1973. "Do We Really Want to Consolidate Urban Police Forces? A Reappraisal of Some Old Assertions." *Public Administration Review* 33 (5): 423–432.

Perrow, Charles. 1984. *Normal Accidents: Living with High-Risk Technologies.* Princeton, NJ: Princeton University Press.

Pettit, Philip. 1997. *Republicanism: A Theory of Freedom and Government.* Oxford Political Theory. Oxford: Clarendon Press.

Pew Research Center. 2014. "America's New Drug Policy Landscape." April. https://www.pewresearch.org/politics/2014/04/02/section-1-perceptions-of-drug-abuse-views-of-drug-policies/.

Pierson, Emma, Camelia Simoiu, Jan Overgoor, Sam Corbett-Davies, Daniel Jenson, Amy Shoemaker, Vignesh Ramachandran, et al. 2020. "A Large-Scale Analysis of Racial Disparities in Police Stops across the United States." *Nature Human Behaviour,* 4 (7): 736–745.

Piza, Eric L., and Vijay F. Chillar. 2020. "The Effect of Police Layoffs on Crime: A Natural Experiment Involving New Jersey's Two Largest Cities." *Justice Evaluation Journal* 4 (2): 176–196.

Piza, Eric L., and Nathan T. Connealy. 2022. "The Effect of the Seattle Police-Free CHOP Zone on Crime: A Microsynthetic Control Evaluation." *Criminology & Public Policy,* January.

Plato. 1997. *Complete Works.* Edited by John M. Cooper. Indianapolis: Hackett.

Policing Project. 2015. "Statement on the Principles of Democratic Policing." The Policing Project. https://www.policingproject.org/statement-democratic-policing.

Pozo, Brandon del. 2022. *The Police and the State.* New York: Cambridge University Press.

Pozo, Brandon del, Lawrence S. Krasner, and Sarah F. George. 2020. "Decriminalization of Diverted Buprenorphine in Burlington, Vermont and Philadelphia: An Intervention to Reduce Opioid Overdose Deaths." *The Journal of Law, Medicine & Ethics* 48 (2): 373–375.

Purnell, Derecka. 2021. *Becoming Abolitionists: Police, Protests, and the Pursuit of Freedom.* Cranleigh, UK: Astra House.

Rajan, Mekha, and Kathy A. McCloskey. 2007. "Victims of Intimate Partner Violence: Arrest Rates Across Recent Studies." *Journal of Aggression, Maltreatment & Trauma* 15 (3–4): 27–52.

Rappaport, John. 2020. "Some Doubts about 'Democratizing' Criminal Justice." *The University of Chicago Law Review* 87 (3): 711–814.

Ratcliffe, Jerry H. 2021. "Policing and Public Health Calls for Service in Philadelphia." *Crime Science* 10 (1): 5.

Ratcliffe, Jerry H., and Evan T. Sorg. 2017. *Foot Patrol: Rethinking the Cornerstone of Policing.* New York: Springer.

Ratcliffe, Jerry, and Haley Wight. 2022. "Policing the Largest Drug Market on the Eastern Seaboard: Officer Perspectives on Enforcement and Community Safety." *Policing: An International Journal* 45 (5): 727–740.

Rawls, John. 1999. *A Theory of Justice*. Revised edition. Cambridge, MA: Belknap Press of Harvard University Press.

Raz, Joseph. 1979. *The Authority of Law: Essays on Law and Morality. The Authority of Law*. Oxford: Oxford University Press.

Rector, Kevin. 2021. "New Civilian Discipline Panels More Lenient on Accused LAPD Officers, Review Finds." *LA Times*, May 11. https://www.latimes.com/california/story/2021-05-11/new-civilian-discipline-panels-more-lenient-on-accused-lapd-officers-review-finds.

Remsberg, Charles. 1995. *Tactics for Criminal Patrol: Vehicle Stops, Drug Discovery and Officer Survival*. Glen Ellyn, IL: Calibre Press.

Resignato, Andrew J. 2000. "Violent Crime: A Function of Drug Use or Drug Enforcement?" *Applied Economics* 32 (6): 681–688.

Reynolds, Elaine A. 1998. *Before the Bobbies*. London: Palgrave Macmillan.

Richardson, Rashida, Jason M. Schultz, and Kate Crawford. 2019. "Dirty Data, Bad Predictions: How Civil Rights Violations Impact Police Data, Predictive Policing Systems, and Justice." *New York University Law Review Online* 94: 15–55.

Roberts, Jenny. 2012. "Why Misdemeanors Matter: Defining Effective Advocacy in the Lower Criminal Courts." *UC Davis Law Review* 45 (2): 277–372.

Rosenthal, Stuart S., and Amanda Ross. 2010. "Violent Crime, Entrepreneurship, and Cities." *Journal of Urban Economics*, Special Issue: Cities and Entrepreneurship, 67 (1): 135–149.

Rossi, Peter H. 1991. *Down and Out in America: The Origins of Homelessness*. Chicago: University of Chicago Press.

Salimbene, Nicholas. 2021. "The Genesis of Formal Police Agency Creation in U.S. Cities." *Police Practice and Research* 22 (1): 805–816.

Sanders, Teela. 2005. *Sex Work*. Devon, UK: Willan.

Saunders, Ben. 2010. "Democracy, Political Equality, and Majority Rule." *Ethics* 121 (1): 148–177.

Schmidtz, David. 2006. *The Elements of Justice*. Cambridge: Cambridge University Press.

Scott, James C. 1998. *Seeing Like a State: How Certain Schemes to Improve the Human Condition Have Failed*. New Haven, CT: Yale University Press.

Seo, Sarah A. 2019. *Policing the Open Road: How Cars Transformed American Freedom*. Cambridge, MA: Harvard University Press.

Sharkey, Patrick, Gerard Torrats-Espinosa, and Delaram Takyar. 2017. "Community and the Crime Decline: The Causal Effect of Local Nonprofits on Violent Crime." *American Sociological Review* 82 (6): 1214–1240.

Shelby, Tommie. 2016. *Dark Ghettos: Injustice, Dissent, and Reform*. Cambridge, MA: The Belknap Press of Harvard University Press.

Sherman, Lawrence. 1992. "Influence of Criminology on Criminal Law: Evaluating Arrests for Misdemeanor Domestic Violence." *Journal of Criminal Law & Criminology* 83 (1): 1–45.

Siemaszko, Corky. 2017. "Ohio Sheriff Says His Officers Won't Carry Narcan." *NBC News*, July 7. https://www.nbcnews.com/storyline/americas-heroin-epidemic/ohio-sheriff-says-his-overdosing-ohioans-my-guys-have-no-n780666.

Sierra-Arévalo, Michael. 2016. "American Policing and the Danger Imperative." SSRN Scholarly Paper ID 2864104. Rochester, NY: Social Science Research Network.

Sierra-Arévalo, Michael. 2019. "The Commemoration of Death, Organizational Memory, and Police Culture." *Criminology* 57 (4): 632–658.

Simmons, A. John. 1999. "Justification and Legitimacy." *Ethics* 109 (4): 739–771.

Skinner, B. F. 1948. *Walden Two*. Indianapolis: Hackett.

Sklansky, David A. 2008. *Democracy and the Police*. Stanford, CA: Stanford University Press.

Skogan, Wesley G., and Susan M. Hartnett. 1997. *Community Policing, Chicago Style*. New York: Oxford University Press.

Smith, Andrew F. 2014. "In Defense of Homelessness." *The Journal of Value Inquiry* 48 (1): 33–51.

Sousa, William H. 2010. "Paying Attention to Minor Offenses: Order Maintenance Policing in Practice." *Police Practice and Research* 11 (1): 45–59.

Stewart, Robert, and Christopher Uggen. 2019. "Criminal Records and College Admissions: A Modified Experimental Audit." *Criminology* 58 (1): 156–188.

Stringham, Edward Peter. 2015. *Private Governance: Creating Order in Economic and Social Life*. New York: Oxford University Press.

Stuart, Forrest. 2016. *Down, Out, and Under Arrest: Policing and Everyday Life in Skid Row*. Chicago: University of Chicago Press.

Surprenant, Chris W., and Jason Brennan. 2020. *Injustice for All: How Financial Incentives Corrupted and Can Fix the US Criminal Justice System*. New York: Routledge.

Tadros, Victor. 2020. "Democracy and War." *Stockholm Centre for the Ethics of War and Peace Ethical War Blog* (blog). February 27. http://stockholmcen tre.org/democracy-and-war/.

Táíwò, Olúfẹ́mi O. 2020. "Power over the Police." *Dissent Magazine* (blog). June 12. https://www.dissentmagazine.org/online_articles/power-over-the-police.

Taylor, Brian D., and Yu Hong Hwang. 2020. "Eighty-Five Percent Solution: Historical Look at Crowdsourcing Speed Limits and the Question of Safety." *Transportation Research Record* .

Thacher, David. 2001. "Conflicting Values in Community Policing." *Law & Society Review* 35 (4): 765.

Thacher, David. 2004. "Order Maintenance Reconsidered: Moving beyond Strong Causal Reasoning." *Journal of Criminal Law & Criminology* 94 (2): 381–414.

Thacher, David. 2015. "Olmsted's Police." *Law and History Review* 33 (3): 577–620.

Thacher, David. 2022. "Shrinking the Police Footprint." *Criminal Justice Ethics* 41 (1): 62–85.

Thacher, David E. 2014. "Order Maintenance Policing." In *The Oxford Handbook of Police and Policing*, edited by Michael D. Reisig and Robert J. Kane, 122–147. Oxford: Oxford University Press.

Thoreau, Henry David. 2002. *The Essays of Henry D. Thoreau*. Edited by Lewis Hyde. 1st ed. New York: North Point Press.

Thusi, I. India. 2022. *Policing Bodies: Law, Sex Work, and Desire in Johannesburg*. Stanford, CA: Stanford University Press.

Traub, James. 2004. *The Devil's Playground: A Century of Pleasure and Profit in Times Square*. New York: Random House.

Tyler, Tom R. 2004. "Enhancing Police Legitimacy." *The ANNALS of the American Academy of Political and Social Science* 593 (1): 84–99.

Uggen, Christopher, and Jeff Manza. 2002. "Democratic Contraction? Political Consequences of Felon Disenfranchisement in the United States." *American Sociological Review* 67 (6): 777–803.

Valentini, Laura. 2012a. "Ideal vs. Non-Ideal Theory: A Conceptual Map." *Philosophy Compass* 7 (9): 654–664.

Valentini, Laura. 2012b. "Justice, Disagreement and Democracy." *British Journal of Political Science* 43 (1): 177–199.

Venkatesh, Sudhir Alladi. 2006. *Off the Books: The Underground Economy of the Urban Poor*. Cambridge, MA: Harvard University Press.

Vitale, Alex S. 2017. *The End of Policing*. New York: Verso Books.

Vitoria, Francisco de. 1991. "On the Law of War." In *Vitoria: Political Writings*, edited by Anthony Pagden and Jeremy Lawrance, 293–328. Cambridge Texts in the History of Political Thought. Cambridge: Cambridge University Press.

Vollmer, August. 1928. "Vice and Traffic-Police Handicaps." *Southern California Law Review* 1 (4): 7.

Waldron, Jeremy. 2011. "The Rule of Law and the Importance of Procedure." *Nomos* 50: 3–31.

Wallace, Samuel E. 1965. *Skid Row as a Way of Life*. Bedminster, NJ: Bedminster Press.

Walzer, Michael. 2006. *Just and Unjust Wars: A Moral Argument with Historical Illustrations*. 4th ed. New York: Basic Books.

Weaver, Vesla M., and Amy E. Lerman. 2010. "Political Consequences of the Carceral State." *American Political Science Review* 104 (4): 817–833.

Weisburd, David, Stephen D. Mastrofski, Ann Marie Mcnally, Rosann Greenspan, and James J. Willis. 2006. "Reforming to Preserve: Compstat and Strategic Problem Solving in American Policing." *Criminology & Public Policy* 2 (3): 421–456.

Weisburd, David, Cody W. Telep, and Brian A. Lawton. 2014. "Could Innovations in Policing Have Contributed to the New York City Crime Drop Even in a Period of Declining Police Strength?: The Case of Stop, Question and Frisk as a Hot Spots Policing Strategy." *Justice Quarterly* 31 (1): 129–153.

Weisburst, Emily K. 2019. "Patrolling Public Schools: The Impact of Funding for School Police on Student Discipline and Long-Term Education Outcomes." *Journal of Policy Analysis and Management* 38 (2): 338–365.

Western, Bruce, and Christopher Wildeman. 2009. "The Black Family and Mass Incarceration." *The ANNALS of the American Academy of Political and Social Science* 621 (1): 221–242.

Williams, Hubert, and Patrick V. Murphy. 1990. "The Evolving Strategy of Police: A Minority View." *National Institute of Justice* 13 (1): 1–15.

Willis, James J., Stephen D. Mastrofski, and Tammy Rinehart Kochel. 2010. "The Co-Implementation of Compstat and Community Policing." *Journal of Criminal Justice* 38 (5): 969–980.

Wilson, James Q. 1978. *Varieties of Police Behavior: The Management of Law and Order in Eight Communities.* Cambridge, MA: Harvard University Press.

Woods, Baynard, and Brandon Soderberg. 2020. *I Got a Monster: The Rise and Fall of America's Most Corrupt Police Squad.* New York: St. Martin's.

Zacka, Bernardo. 2017. *When the State Meets the Street: Public Service and Moral Agency.* Cambridge, MA: The Belknap Press of Harvard University Press.

Zimring, Franklin E. 2017. *When Police Kill.* Cambridge, MA: Harvard University Press.

Index

For the benefit of digital users, indexed terms that span two pages (e.g., 52–53) may, on occasion, appear on only one of those pages.

legalism and, 47
overview of, 5
police abolitionism and, 7–9
professionalism and, 11–13
public safety reimagined as solution
to, 20–23
utopia and, 5–10
violence and, 8
proceduralism, 53–54, 53n.4, 56–57, 58,
74–75, 76–77, 78, 79–80
professionalism
accountability and, 195–99
agency structure and, 187–88, 195–99
approved policing practices
and, 196–97
foot patrols and, 197
history of policing and, 11–16, 84–85,
126, 178–80
informational asymmetries
and, 195–96
just policing and, 195
new model for, 195–99
police abolitionism and, 11–13
problem of policing and, 11–13
professional development and, 187–88
prohibition. See drug enforcement
Pronovost, Peter, 85n.4
proportionality principle
aggressive policing and, 103–4
behavior and violation distinction
and, 123–24
counterproductive enforcement
and, 115–24
defensive force and, 101–10, 123
definition of, 101
deterrence and, 114
discretion and, 102, 111–12
diverted buprenorphine possession
and, 121–24
drug enforcement and, 114, 121–24
exacerbating vice and, 116–18
excessively burdensome enforcement
and, 110–13
Golden Rule of policing and, 102–4
induced speeding and, 118–19
inefficient enforcement and, 113–15
just policing and, 90, 101, 105
legalism and, 102–3, 113

misdemeanor system and, 110–11
narrow and wide forms distinguished
of, 107–8
necessity principle and, 115
neutrality principle and, 143
officer decision-making and, 102–
3, 112–13
open container violations and, 119–21
other-defense and, 107–10
overview of, 101
philosophical usefulness of, 102
predictable disproportional policing
and, 110–15
public space conflicts and, 143
reasonable effectiveness principle and,
113–14, 115
self-defense and, 104–7
sex work enforcement and, 116–
17, 118
shoplifting and, 114–15
skid rows and, 102–4
systematically encouraged violations
and, 115–24
therapeutic policing and, 103–4
public space conflicts
accountability and, 133
complete streets analogy for, 137
containment in response to, 126–27,
136–44, 147–48
criminal justice system and, 42
disagreement and, 127–35, 145, 147–48
discretion and, 61, 72, 144
disorder and, 127–35, 144–48
dispersal in response to, 136,
140, 147–48
dynamism and, 145–48
fairness principle and, 141–44
history of policing and, 126
HOAs and, 145–46
homelessness and, 131–33, 138–39,
141, 142–43
just policing and, 24–25, 135, 146
legalism and, 139
neutrality principle and, 125–28, 133,
135, 136, 142–43, 144
no-go zones and, 143
political philosophy and, 126
proportionality principle and, 143